Setting Limits in the Classroom, Third Edition

Setting Limits

IN THE

Classroom

THIRD EDITION

*A Complete Guide
to Effective Classroom Management with
a School-Wide Discipline Plan*

Robert J. MacKenzie, Ed.D., and
Lisa E. Stanzione, M.A.

THREE RIVERS PRESS
NEW YORK

Library of Congress Cataloging-in-Publication Data
MacKenzie, Robert J.
Setting limits in the classroom: a complete guide to effective classroom
management with a school-wide discipline plan /
Robert J. Mackenzie and Lisa Stanzione.—3rd ed.
p. cm.
Includes index.
1. Classroom management. 2. School discipline. I. Stanzione, Lisa. II. Title.
LB3013.M27 2010
371.102'4—dc22   2009050910

ISBN 978-0-307-59172-2

Printed in the United States of America

Design by Jennifer Ann Daddio/Bookmark Design & Media Inc.
Charts and graphs by Andrew Barthelmes
Illustrations by Corie Lee Barloggi

12 14 16 18 20 19 17 15 13

Third Edition

To the many effective teachers
I've had the pleasure to observe and
work with over the years

Contents

Acknowledgments

Setting Limits in the Classroom began twenty-five years ago as a workshop for teachers. Then it became a book, and the book is now in its second revision. Literally, the book has grown as our program has grown. Our sincere appreciation goes to all who participated in these workshops over the years. Your experiences, and your willingness to share them, helped refine and improve the methods in this book.

Special thanks also go to those who have supported my workshops in major ways and to those who assisted with the writing of this book.

To Bob Trigg, former superintendent of the Elk Grove Unified School District, for funding and supporting our workshops for teachers for the first ten years.

To Dave Gordon, also former superintendent of the Elk Grove Unified School District, for funding and supporting our workshops for teachers during the subsequent eight years.

To the many effective teachers we've had the privilege to observe and work with over the years. You are the real masters of effective classroom management.

To Jamie Miller, Marjorie Lery, and all the other good folks at Prima Publishing for believing in my project the first time around.

To Emily Timberlake, editor, Three Rivers Press, for all your efforts to make this project happen.

To Dr. Jonathon Sandoval, professor of education, University of California, Davis, for your technical expertise with portions of the book.

To Scott MacKenzie for your assistance with the many charts and diagrams.

To Corie Barloggi, graphic artist, for all the wonderful artwork in the book.

To Cathy Pickett, former principal of Sheldon Elementary School; Lauran Hawker, current principal of Sheldon Elementary School; and the entire staff at Sheldon Elementary for making our program live to its fullest potential.

To the staff members of Franklin Elementary School in Elk Grove, California, for your support and inspiration.

To P. J. Foehr, principal of San Martin Gwynn Elementary School in Morgan Hill, California, for role-modeling the leadership needed to successfully launch a school-wide discipline program.

To Ginni Davis, assistant superintendent with Palo Alto Unified School District in Palo Alto, California, for being our adviser on administrative matters.

To Judy Wyluda, program director; Tad Schmitt, executive director; and all the good folks at Staff Development Resources and the California Elementary Education Association for promoting our workshops on a national level.

To all the parents and children we've seen over the years in our guidance work. Your successes have strengthened our beliefs in the process we've shared together.

Introduction

In many schools, the lessons of classroom management have become part of a "hidden curriculum." They're not discussed at curriculum meetings. They don't show up anywhere in the teacher's daily lesson plan, yet they require as much, if not more, of the teacher's time and energy as any other academic subject. We can't teach our academic subjects effectively until we can establish an effective environment for learning. Classroom management provides the foundation for all instruction.

We wouldn't consider teaching reading, math, science, or any other academic subject with outdated or ineffective methods, but when it comes to teaching our rules for acceptable behavior and the lessons of classroom management, our guidance practices are all over the map. When guidance practices vary from teacher to teacher, inconsistency is the rule. Students receive a series of mixed messages about rules and expectations and mixed lessons about acceptable behavior in the classroom. The inconsistency creates confusion and sets everyone up for conflict. The result—more instructional time spent with testing and disruption, less time for teaching and learning, and costly drains on administrative time and financial resources. The office becomes a dumping ground for inappropriate referrals.

To complicate things, most of the packaged guidance and discipline programs available to schools are outdated, simplistic, production-line approaches that ignore differences in children's temperaments and established principles of child development and learning theory. These approaches work fine with compliant students who permit us a wide margin for ineffectiveness. But who are the students who cause 90 percent of school discipline problems? They're not the compliant students. Teachers and administrators know them as the "frequent flyers" who repeatedly end up in the office. We call them "aggressive researchers" because they are always testing the limits to see how far they can go. Call them difficult, challenging, spirited, or strong-willed, they are the same 10 percent on every campus who cause 90 percent of the problems. You have to be at the top of your game when you work with this group. They permit no margin for ineffectiveness.

What sets our program apart from other approaches? The Setting Limits Program is a proven, research-based system of classroom management that works with the full range of students—compliant students, fence-sitters, the strong-willed 10 percent, and all those in between. The methods have been tested and used successfully by tens of thousands of teachers. They work. You should find them a refreshing alternative to the ineffective extremes of punishment and permissiveness that wear teachers down and get them nowhere.

Our bias is clear. Classroom management is simply too important to be neglected or handled ineffectively. The cost to teaching and learning, to our schools, and to our culture is too great. Guidance and discipline should be taught like any other subject with a sound curriculum, proven state-of-the-art methods, and consistency across grade levels and throughout the school.

As educational consultants and staff development trainers, we see thousands of students each year who are not stopping at the signals they confront in the classroom. They don't respect rules or authority, and many lack the basic social skills required to be successful students. Some are suspected of having emotional or learning problems, and a few do, but the vast majority are not suffering from any problem at all. They are simply exercising their willpower in the hope they can wear adults down and do what they want. Often, they're successful.

Their teachers have tried a variety of methods to stop the misbehavior. They've tried lecturing, threatening, reasoning, explaining, bribing, cajoling, writing names on the board, taking away recesses, and making students write apology letters. They've tried making them stand in the corner, sending them to the office, issuing citations, sending home daily behavior reports, and asking parents to spend a day in the classroom—all without success.

These teachers' discipline methods range from extreme permissiveness to harsh punishment and all points in between, but most share at least one thing in common. They're having trouble setting limits in their classrooms. They're doing the best they can with the tools they have, but the tools aren't working, and they don't know what else to do. They need to upgrade the tools in their toolboxes.

Setting Limits in the Classroom provides you with a complete program for effective classroom management as well as a school-wide discipline plan. You can say goodbye to all the ineffective methods that wear you down and get you nowhere. No more reasoning, explaining, lecturing, or threats. No more drawn-out consequences or exhaustive attempts at persuasion. And you can say goodbye to all the power struggles, too. Your students will know what you mean when you set clear, firm limits and support your words with effective consequences. Finally, all staff on your campus will have the tools they need to operate as a team working from the same plan.

In the chapters that follow, you'll learn an approach to classroom management that is clear, systematic, and developmentally appropriate for your students, one that has been tested and used successfully by thousands of teachers and parents. The methods work, and you can use them with the full range of primary and elementary school students, and of regular education and special education students.

An effective classroom is like a table supported by four important legs: effective structure, positive relationships, engaging instruction, and effective limit-setting practices. Not only do the legs support the table, they also support one another. All four are important. They provide balance for the table. When one or more of the first three legs are weak, you will have to rely more heavily on limit setting to support the weaker legs. This is not the goal of our program. Our goal is to help you build a strong and balanced table.

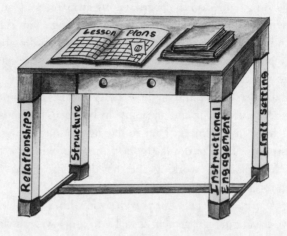

Chapters 1 through 4 of the book will help you develop the first three legs of your table. You'll learn how to structure your classroom for success, how to build positive relationships with your students, and how to use effective engagement strategies to hook students in to your lessons and keep them hooked throughout the lesson. The strategies should be fun for you and your students.

Chapters 5 through 8 will attempt to do what most books on classroom management leave out—that is, to help you recognize how students really learn rules and why the teaching-and-learning process breaks down. Our goal is to help you recognize the things that aren't working for you. Without this awareness, it will be difficult, if not impossible, to avoid repeating old mistakes, because most of these mistakes are made unconsciously. You'll discover your approach to limit setting, how children really learn your rules, the types of limits you're using, and the type of "classroom dance" you might be doing to get your students to cooperate.

With an understanding of what hasn't worked for you, you'll be ready to learn new skills. Chapters 9 through 18 form the core of the skills-training program. In these chapters, you'll learn how to give clear messages about your rules, stop power struggles before they begin, support your rules with instructive consequences, use parents and the office for backup support, manage crises and extreme behavior, and support students with ADD/ADHD and special needs who require more than effective classroom management to be successful in the classroom.

The final chapter is intended to provide relief for administrators and help them improve the efficiency and effectiveness of their school's discipline program. Whether your program requires a tune-up or a major overhaul, this chapter will help you put the parts back together so they work in an efficient and cost-effective manner. You'll learn how to develop a Setting Limits School-Wide Discipline Plan for your school. Everything you need is provided, even a sample plan.

This book is designed to be a curriculum material for staff development training. Suggestions for getting started are provided in appendix 3. A guide for beginning a teacher study group at your school, as well as teacher study group questions and discussion topics, is included in appendix 4.

Learning the methods in this book will be the easiest part of your skills training. Most are fairly straightforward. For many of you, the hardest part will be to resist the temptation to revert to old habits and do the things that haven't worked. Changing old habits is not easy, particularly when old habits become established on a school-wide basis.

Resistance to change is a normal and expected part of the change process. You may recognize intellectually that the management system you learn in this book will lead to the type of change you desire, but the changes they bring may not feel comfortable to you or your students in the beginning. You will likely encounter pressure and resistance to change, not only from your students but also from within yourself. Don't give up. The more you practice, the more comfortable you will feel, and the positive results will increase your confidence.

You should also expect to make mistakes and to have lapses when you begin practicing your new skills. That's okay. Mistakes are a normal part of learning. Your goal should be improvement, and you will improve the more you practice. If you have difficulty remembering what logical consequences to use in specific situations, make it easy on yourself. Refer to the Setting Limits Companion Guide in appendix 1 for assistance. Make a copy and keep it on your desk. If you encounter unexpected problems with any of the methods or procedures, refer back to the pertinent chapters for assistance. Take special note of the specific language used to carry out the techniques in the various examples.

Finally, many of the examples in this book reflect actual cases from counseling sessions and consulting work with teachers. In all cases, the names have been changed to protect the privacy of those involved.

The methods in this book have helped tens of thousands of teachers regain control of their classrooms and enjoy more satisfying and cooperative relationships with students. If you are willing to invest the time and energy needed to learn the skills, you too can share the rewards. Enjoy *Setting Limits in the Classroom.*

1

Creating Structure
That Works

Structure is the organizational foundation of the classroom. It sets the stage for cooperation and learning by clarifying your rules and expectations and by defining how you want your students to behave. In a well-structured classroom, most conflicts and behavior problems are prevented because children know what is expected. Rules, procedures, and daily routines are clear. There is less need for testing and less need for discipline.

Because structure is so basic, many teachers devote too little attention to it at the beginning of the year or overlook it entirely. They believe they can't afford to take valuable time away from academic instruction, or they assume children should already know what is expected or that they will pick it up along the way. The result is more time spent on testing and disruptions and less time on teaching and learning. Everybody loses. Teachers end up exhausted as they struggle to maintain order in their classrooms, and students lose valuable time for instruction.

This chapter will show you how to prevent the problems that accompany ineffective structure. You'll learn proven techniques for teaching classroom rules and procedures, defining basic student responsibilities, enlisting parent support and cooperation, and solving problems early,

before they get bigger. By the time you're done, you'll know how to create structure that will work for you throughout the year.

The Cost of Ineffective Structure

The lesson of structure begins the moment your students enter the classroom. There is no way to avoid it. Sooner or later—usually sooner—someone will do something he or she is not supposed to do, and all the students will watch for your reaction. What you do, or fail to do, will define a rule.

Imagine, for example, that you're a sixth-grade teacher, and it's the first day of school. One of your students arrives to class wearing a headset and rocking out to one of his favorite songs. You don't like it, but you decide to ignore it. "He'll probably put it away by the time I begin teaching," you say to yourself.

He might, but what is the rule you just taught? Of course, it's okay to arrive in class wearing a headset. What do you think this student and possibly others are likely to do in the future?

The issue is not whether the lesson of structure *should* be taught. It *will* be taught, one way or another. The real issue is who controls the lesson—the teacher or the students? When students control the lesson, the costs to learning, cooperation, and achievement are much greater. Consider the following.

It's the first week of school in Mr. Johnson's fourth-grade class. The bell just rang, and the kids have filed back into class. Mr. Johnson stands at the front of the classroom and waits for the kids to settle down.

His lesson has been carefully planned and organized. He scheduled ten minutes for instruction and thirty minutes for seatwork. He's ready to get started, but the kids are not. Two minutes have passed since the bell rang, and the noise level is high.

"Let's settle down a little," he says, directing his comments to several boys who are laughing and talking loudly. His words have little impact. The boys continue to laugh. Others are talking, too. Mr. Johnson waits patiently. Another minute passes.

"What's going on?" he thinks to himself. "I announced my rules the first day of class. They should know better." He tries again.

"Okay, class, I'm ready to start," he says in an annoyed tone. He waits a little more. Everyone settles down except two boys.

"Craig, Terry! Are you ready to join us?" Mr. Johnson asks. The boys exchange mischievous smiles, but they stop talking for the moment. Four minutes have passed. Finally, Mr. Johnson begins his lesson.

As he gives directions for the next assignment, Mr. Johnson notices that a number of students are not paying attention. "I don't want to explain this again," he says. His warning has little effect. He finishes his directions and passes out the worksheets. "You have twenty-five min-utes to complete the assignment," he announces.

"I don't understand," blurts one student. "Yeah, what are we supposed to do?" chimes in another. Several others look confused. There isn't time for individual instructions. Mr. Johnson is frustrated.

"If you guys had been paying attention, you would know what to do," he says. "Now, listen up." He repeats the directions for the benefit of those who had not listened, eating up another five minutes. Twenty minutes left.

Finally, everyone is working. As they do, Mr. Johnson roves around the room to help those with raised hands and to intervene with disruptions. As he helps one student, he notices Craig and Terry laughing and fooling around again.

"Excuse me, Brenda," says Mr. Johnson. He approaches Craig and Terry. "Guys, would you save it for recess, please?" They smile at each other again but stop for the moment.

Mr. Johnson returns to Brenda, but by this time other hands are in the air. One kid is blurting out in an attempt to get Mr. Johnson's attention. Other kids are disrupting. He deals with the disruptions first, then the blurter, then the raised hands, and so it goes for the rest of the lesson. Hands are still in the air as the bell rings. Many don't finish.

What happened? Mr. Johnson was prepared to teach his academic lesson but not the lesson of classroom management. His class lacks structure. As a result, he spent more than a third of his time dealing with blurting and disruptions.

What did his students learn? They learned the same lessons they had been learning all week. It's okay to enter the classroom noisily. Take your time to settle down. If you don't pay attention the first time, you will get a second set of directions. It's okay to blurt out. Worst of all, they learned that blurting out and disruptions are tolerated. Mr. Johnson is in for a long year. If he continues on this course, he's a good candidate for burnout.

Defining Basic Terms

Before we move forward with our task of helping you build better structure into your classroom, we need to discuss the "nuts and bolts" of the job. It's time to define some basic terms so you understand how these parts operate and fit together. Let's begin with structure.

> **Structure** is a broad and inclusive term that describes how the various parts of the classroom fit together. Rules, procedures, routines, desk configurations, equipment, people, activities, and time schedules are all components of structure. When we use the term *structure* in this book, we are referring primarily to **rules, procedures, and routines.**
>
> **Classroom management** is a very broad and inclusive term that refers to the full range of things teachers do to organize people, materials, space, and time for the purpose of teaching and learning. Classroom discipline, relationship building, community building, engagement strategies, and all the components of

structure are included within the general term *classroom management.*

Classroom rules come in four basic varieties: general rules, specific rules, rules in theory, and the rules we practice, that is to say, those we're willing to consistently enforce.

Classroom procedures inform students how things are supposed to be done in the classroom. It's the teacher's job to clearly communicate what they want done and how they want students to do it.

Classroom routines develop when students carry out classroom procedures automatically. Smooth, efficient routines are a defining characteristic of a well-structured classroom. Developing classroom routines is a central goal of any effective classroom management program.

Discipline is defined by *Merriam-Webster's Collegiate Dictionary* as training expected to produce a specific type or pattern of behavior. The key word in this definition is *training.* Does this sound like teaching and learning to you? Discipline in the classroom refers to the training methods that teachers use to gain cooperation from their students. Discipline is how we enforce our rules and procedures.

Limit setting refers to the methods we use to teach and enforce our rules and procedures in the classroom. The terms *limit setting* and *discipline* are used interchangeably throughout the book. Effective limit setting is an essential component of any effective classroom management plan.

Reinforcement refers to the things we do to increase a desirable behavior or decrease an undesirable behavior. Often, when we think of reinforcement, we think of **punishment** or the application of aversive or punitive consequences. Punishment is only one form of reinforcement, and it has limited training value.

Reinforcement errors occur when we encourage, support, or reward unacceptable behavior.

Reinforcement schedule refers to the frequency of reinforcement.

Logical consequences are another form of reinforcement that work effectively in classroom settings. Logical consequences are structured learning opportunities that are arranged by the teacher, experienced by the child, and logically related to the child's unacceptable behavior. Logical consequences stop misbehavior, but they're designed to teach, not hurt.

Plan Structure Before Students Arrive

If you wait until the first day of school to plan your classroom rules and procedures and get organized, then you've already missed the train because it has arrived and has left the station. This simple act of omission has put your students, not you, in charge of the lesson of structure.

When it comes to developing structure, your mantra should be "Be Prepared, Be Organized, Be Ready." Your plan should be in place well before your students arrive. Let's begin with classroom rules.

DEVELOPING CLASSROOM RULES

Classroom rules come in four basic varieties: general rules, specific rules, rules in theory, and the rules you actually practice. **General rules** specify the teacher's expectations for work habits and acceptable behavior in the classroom. Some typical examples: "Cooperate with your teacher and classmates," "Respect the rights and property of others," and "Carry out your student responsibilities."

Specific rules, as the term implies, provide more precise information for students about how they are expected to behave. Typical examples: "Raise your hand and wait to be recognized if you want to ask a question or make a comment" or "Use an indoor voice in the classroom."

Rules in theory can be general or specific but they really amount to nothing more than words that signal our hopes and expectations for how students should behave. As the name implies, rules in theory operate on the hypothetical level. How do they work? They are usually announced, but they may take the form of requests or directives.

Some teachers set themselves up for testing and conflict by confusing their rules in theory with the rules they actually practice. In reality, the two may be very different depending on what happens when our announced rules are tested or violated. Consider the following example.

Mr. Larson, a fifth-grade teacher, notices that some of his students have been bringing toys and trading cards to class and playing with them during instruction. He decides to put a stop to it.

"If you bring toys or cards to school, you need to keep them in your desk or backpack," he says. "If you have them out during class, I will take them away and return them to your parents at our next teacher-parent conference." Mr. Larson has established his rule in theory.

Later in the afternoon, Mr. Larson notices one of his students passing a troll doll to another girl in her table group.

"Mia, what did I say about playing with toys in class?" he asks. "Now put it away, please." He lets it pass with just a warning. The lesson isn't lost on others.

The next day, he catches Dale and Patrick playing with baseball cards. "Guys, do you want to lose them?" Mr. Larson asks. "If not, put them away." Again, he lets it pass with just a warning.

Before the week is over, there are several more incidents and several more warnings. In one case, Mr. Larson actually confiscates some cards but returns them after school with instructions not to bring them back.

What is the rule Mr. Larson actually practices? Of course, it's okay to play with toys in class. All you get is warnings. Why should anyone take Mr. Larson's rule very seriously? Rules in theory that are not supported with effective action are invitations for testing and noncompliance.

Rules in practice are defined by our actions or what students actually experience when all the talking is over. These rules represent our "bottom line," or our actual standards for acceptable behavior. The behavior we are willing to tolerate defines our actual classroom rules.

How do students know our rules in practice? They test, and then watch what we do. Our actions, or lack of them, will clarify what we really expect. When we support our announced rules with effective action, we earn credibility and students learn to take us seriously. Consider the following.

It's time for morning circle, a daily sharing activity in Mrs. Atkins's preschool class. The kids are all seated on the carpet near the blackboard. As the activity begins, Matthew, age four, presses his foot against the back of the girl in front of him and pulls on her sweater.

"Matthew, we don't put our hands or feet on others when we're in morning circle," says Mrs. Atkins. "We sit crisscross applesauce like this." She models the correct way to sit. Matthew cooperates for a few minutes, then decides to test. He gives Sara another nudge with his foot and tugs the back of her sweater.

"Matthew, you need to sit by yourself for the rest of circle time," says Mrs. Atkins matter-of-factly. She gets out a carpet strip for Matthew to sit on and places it about five feet away from the others.

Did Matthew's teacher practice the rule she announced? You bet. Her words said, "Stop," and that's what Matthew experienced when he decided to test. Her message was clear, and so was her rule. She may need to repeat this lesson many times with Matthew before he is convinced, but if she does, Matthew will surely learn the rule and take her words seriously. The rules we practice and are willing to support with consistent discipline are the rules kids respect and take seriously.

GUIDELINES FOR INTRODUCING RULES

- Keep your list of general rules brief.
- State your rules in positive or neutral language.
- State your rules in simple, clear terms.
- Post your rules in a visible area.
- Only state rules you're willing to enforce.

On the first day, you should be prepared to introduce your general rules or rules in theory. Keep them broad and inclusive, and avoid extensive lists that invite limit testing. Most teachers find that the following poster we use in the Setting Limits Program summarizes everything your students need to know about your general rules.

FIGURE 1.1: **Classroom Rules**

- Cooperate with your teacher and classmates.
- Respect the rights and property of others.
- Carry out your basic student responsibilities.

Sharing Expectations for Good Work Habits

One of the most important lessons children learn in the course of growing up is the lesson of good work habits, or how to be responsible for beginning a task, staying with it even when it's difficult, and completing it in a timely manner. Children who learn good work habits become successful students and successful people. Children who fail to master good work habits face increased risk of failure. For many students, good work habits can mean the difference between success and failure.

How do children learn good work habits? They acquire work habits the same way they acquire other skills—through a teaching-and-learning process. They need instruction, practice, corrective feedback, more practice, and repeated opportunities to experience the consequences of their efforts, both positive and negative. In an ideal world, the process should begin in the home then be reinforced in the classroom. Parents should be the first teachers of these important lessons. In the real world, however, many children receive little or no training in good work habits prior to arriving at school. The job, by necessity, falls on the teacher. The lesson must be taught. Teachers can help students develop good work habits by being clear about their expectations, by helping students plan out a study schedule, by acknowledging and rewarding compliance, and by holding students accountable when they do less than their part. The following guidelines should help you get started.

GUIDELINES FOR SHARING EXPECTATIONS FOR WORK HABITS

- State your expectations and describe procedures for completing assignments.

- State the consequences for compliance and noncompliance.
- Post a list of basic student responsibilities in a visible area.

FIGURE 1.2: **Basic Student Responsibilities**

- Keep track of your own books and assignments.
- Start your work on time and allow time to finish.
- Ask for help when you need it.
- Do your own work.
- Turn your work in on time.
- Accept responsibility for grades and other consequences.

ACCOUNTABILITY PROCEDURES

The lesson of responsibility is difficult to learn without accountability. Your students need to know from the beginning that they are expected to do their part and that there will be consequences, positive and negative, associated with their performance. The following accountability procedures will help your students learn responsibility and good work habits by holding them accountable for doing their part.

Makeup Sessions for Incomplete Work

There are ten minutes left until recess, and Jamie, a very capable nine-year-old, has fifteen problems remaining on her math worksheet. She's hoping to dawdle the time away and avoid finishing the assignment. Her suspicious teacher intervenes.

"Jamie, you have ten minutes to finish your math sheet. If it's not finished before recess, you'll have to take a clipboard and finish on the bench during recess."

"Rats!" Jamie says to herself. She hurries to finish before recess.

This accountability procedure has been a fixture in public school settings for generations. It works. The system is very simple. When capable students dawdle, avoid, procrastinate, or otherwise fail to complete assigned work during class time, they are required to make up that work during *their* time, in breaks or recess. In effect, the loss of their valued time becomes the logical consequence for not completing work in a timely manner. The procedure works great with capable but noncompliant students. The procedure is not recommended for students with ADD, learning disabilities, or other special needs who lack the skills or abilities to complete work in a timely manner.

Fun Friday

Fun Friday is a clever procedure used by elementary teachers to acknowledge and reward good work habits. Teachers set aside a block of time on Friday afternoons for preferred activities that students can do quietly at their seats. Teachers and students develop an "approved list" of educational activities that are placed in a cabinet or on a shelf in the classroom. Students become eligible for Fun Friday after they have completed all assigned work for the week. Students who are not eligible use the time to catch up on incomplete class work or homework. Consider the following example.

It's two o'clock on Friday afternoon, and Mr. Hodges, a third-grade teacher, makes an announcement to the class.

"It's time for Fun Friday. Everyone who has completed homework and class assignments for the week can select an activity from the approved list. I'll meet with those who haven't at the back table." All but three students head to the cabinet to select an educational game or other approved activity. Others decide to use the time to read or draw. The three remaining students take their incomplete work and join Mr. Hodges at the back table.

Friday Work Folders

Friday work folders are a simple and effective method for holding students accountable and helping parents stay up-to-date on their child's progress. The procedure is easy to carry out. Each Friday, the teacher sends home a packet of the work the student has completed and turned in that week. Attached to the packet is a note indicating whether all items were completed and which items remain incomplete. Parents review the packet, sign and date the entry on the back cover of the folder, make any comments they desire, and return the folder with their child on Monday. Teachers can help students remember to return Friday folders to school by offering group points or class points toward some reward.

Friday folders have many advantages. They keep parents informed and allow them to monitor the quality of their child's class work and homework. They provide an ongoing communication channel between school and home, and they serve as an early-detection system so parents and teachers can deal with student problems before they become more serious.

The Classroom Rental Center

The classroom rental center is a clever way to help students learn responsibility and organizational skills and to arrive to class prepared. When students are forgetful or unprepared, the rental center helps them experience the consequence of their forgetfulness or lack of preparation. Consider the following.

Brad is a bright and capable fifth grader who has a habit of arriving to class unprepared. As his teacher asks the class to take out their books in preparation for a writing assignment, she notices Brad doesn't have his book or notebook. He raises his hand.

"I forgot my book and notebook," he says.

"Step over to my rental center and select the items you need," says his teacher. "The rental cost will be erasing the whiteboards when recess begins." His teacher keeps a table with extra books, pens, pencils, writing paper, and other supplies next to her desk at the front of the classroom.

Sure, Brad's teacher could have given him the items he forgot, but what would that teach Brad about who is responsible for solving the problem? A trip to the rental center had the desired impact.

Ticket-In/Ticket-Out

Some students complete their homework but fail to turn it in on a regular basis. Ticket-in/ticket-out is an effective accountability procedure for helping students develop better and more responsible homework habits. The student's parents must be willing to participate in the procedure and do their part for the required period of time for the procedure to be effective. Training habits takes time. We recommend you use the procedure for a full academic semester. Here's how it works.

The student's job is to write down all of his or her homework assignments and show them to the teacher, who initials them for accuracy before the student is released for lunch recess. This task is the student's ticket out of the classroom. Each day, when the student arrives home, he or she reviews the assignments with his or her parents, then completes them.

The parents' job is to review the daily homework assignments for completion and make sure the student places them in his or her backpack. Before the child leaves the house the next day, he or she shows that the completed homework assignments are in the backpack. This is the child's ticket out the door.

The teacher's job is to ask for the student's completed homework assignment each morning when he or she enters the classroom. This is the student's ticket in. When parents hold their children accountable, good habits develop. When parents don't do their part, the procedure may break down, and you'll have to rely on other logical consequences, which you'll learn in chapter 11.

Teaching Classroom Procedures

The research evidence is clear. Teachers with the best-run classrooms spend most of the first two weeks teaching rules and procedures. They understand that the vast majority of classroom behavior problems can be resolved by improving procedures.

Classroom procedures are essential for providing students with the vital "how-to" information they need to carry out tasks and perform activities in an acceptable manner. When procedures are clear, students feel secure. They know what they're expected to do, and they know how to do it. There is less need for testing and more time for learning.

What's the alternative if we don't take time to teach our classroom procedures? Chaos, confusion, conflict, and disruption. There is less time for teaching and less time for learning. Achievement suffers. Teachers become frustrated and stressed and end up devoting excessive amounts of time to discipline to correct the behavior they didn't teach effectively in the beginning. Discipline, in the absence of effective structure, is simply damage control.

How do we teach procedures to our students? The process is similar to teaching academics. Lessons must be taught, practiced, reviewed, and practiced some more. Most students will master our lessons quickly. Some will need to experience the consequences of their acceptable or unacceptable performance repeatedly before they decide to cooperate and carry out the procedure correctly. A few students, and you know who they are, will require even more practice opportunities on their own time apart from the class and may require help from their parents. In short, your students will learn your procedures "the easy way" or "the hard way," but if you have the tools to teach the lesson however your students choose to learn it, you can't fail.

One of the best resource materials on the subject is Harry and Rosemary Wong's book, *The First Days of School*. The authors recommend a three-step procedure for teaching classroom procedures. Step one involves introducing, explaining, and demonstrating the procedure we want students to master. Step two involves practicing and rehearsing the procedure repeatedly so they get it right. Step three involves reinforcing their efforts, positive or negative, with consequences.

THE THREE-STEP MODEL FOR TEACHING PROCEDURES

Step One: Explain, model, and demonstrate the procedure.
Preschoolers and elementary-school age children need procedures to be taught in very concrete terms. Break the procedure down into steps, and teach it step by step. Telling them what to do is

important, but showing them how to do it increases the instructive value of the lesson. Posting lists of classroom procedures in visible areas can be very helpful for intermediate-level students.

Step Two: Practice the procedure, rehearse it, and practice some more. Students need repeated opportunities to practice the procedure, step by step, under your supervision. Provide corrective feedback at each step so students understand exactly how they are expected to carry out the procedure. The amount of practice your students will need depends upon their skill level, maturity, and temperaments. Remember, the goal is to practice the procedure until it becomes automatic and routine. We just practice until they get it right.

Step Three: Reinforce the procedure with consequences until it becomes automatic or routine. When students perform a procedure correctly, give them positive feedback in the form of "good job!" praise, pats, or smiles. Celebrate their successes. When students perform a procedure incorrectly, specify the correction needed and provide more opportunities for practice. You can practice some procedures on a whole-class basis, but a statute of limitations applies to this practice. Compliant students resent having to practice procedures they've already mastered. When only a few individuals need practice, it's better to use separate, strategic practice sessions. In chapter 12, you'll learn how to use Recess Academy to conduct these strategic practice sessions.

Now, let's see how the three-step model helps one teacher to teach a very basic and important procedure—entering the classroom. Consider the following.

It's the first day of school and Mr. Santin, a second-grade teacher, waits at the door to greet his new students. He asks his students to form a single line, then introduces his classroom entry procedure.

"In this class we always enter in a single line, walking, not running, with indoor voices, and we keep our hands and feet to ourselves. Keep an arm's-length distance from the student in front of you while you walk." He demonstrates what an arm's-length distance looks like. "Okay, let's go inside. When you arrive at your desks, take out your start-up activity."

Mr. Santin leads his kids inside. Things begin well, but the kids are excited and the line bunches up. Several kids start pushing. Several others dash for their desks when they make it through the door.

"Let's try it again," Mr. Santin announces, matter-of-factly. He asks everybody to go outside once again and form a line. "This time, keep one arm's length apart." He models how to establish an arm's-length distance from the next student in line. "Okay, let's walk slowly this time." He leads the excited kids in again.

"Much better!" announces Mr. Santin. He knows there will be many more opportunities to practice this procedure in the days and weeks to come. He also knows that a few students will likely need individual practice sessions, but he has the tools to get the lesson accomplished. The classroom entry procedure will not waste a lot of valuable instructional time in Mr. Santin's classroom. Effective teachers spend most of their time managing their classrooms with procedures, not discipline.

PRIORITIZING PROCEDURES

There are so many procedures to teach in a classroom, the kids can't learn them all at once. Where do you begin? Which procedures should be taught first? The solution is to prioritize the procedures you need to teach in order of their necessity and importance. Some procedures you'll have to teach right away. Others you can delay teaching until that activity arises in the natural course of the school day, week, month, or year. The following lists will help with your planning.

PROCEDURES TO TEACH DURING THE FIRST FEW DAYS AND WEEKS

- Entering the classroom
- Turning in papers
- Starting the day
- Homework procedures
- Asking questions
- What to do when you finish work early
- Coming to attention
- Keeping desks orderly
- Using an indoor voice
- Leaving your seat
- Cleanup procedures
- Using the bathroom
- Recess procedures

- Sharpening pencils
- Cafeteria procedures
- Asking for help
- Ending-the-day procedures
- Listening to directions
- Exiting the classroom
- Responding to questions

- Exiting the school grounds
- Silent signals
- Being a good listener
- Making up missed work
- Grading procedures
- Safety procedures
- Emergency procedures

PROCEDURES TO TEACH DURING THE FIRST FEW WEEKS AND MONTH

- What to do when the phone rings
- Fire drill procedures
- What to do when visitors arrive
- Emergency procedures
- What to do when there is a problem
- Being a good listener
- Organizing notebooks
- Organizing desk items
- Classroom rental center
- Checking out books
- Attending school assemblies

- Using the media center
- Using the library
- Using computers
- Fun Friday activities
- Bad-weather procedures
- What to do when the teacher is busy
- When the power goes out
- Substitute teacher procedures
- Field trip procedures
- Reporting bullying
- Reporting thefts
- Going to the library
- Lost-and-found procedures

Seating Arrangements and Desk Configurations

The overriding goals of an effective seating arrangement are to accomplish tasks, maximize learning and on-task time, and minimize disruptions and behavior problems. Many classroom management problems can be prevented by deciding in advance how and where to position students in the classroom.

Ask yourself the following questions before deciding on the best seating arrangement or desk configuration: What classroom tasks do I want to accomplish? What is the general maturity level of my students? Should close friends sit close together? How many students do I have with special needs such as learning disabilities, physical disabilities, ADD, and emotional and behavioral problems?

If you have an immature group, many students with special needs, or both, you may want to abandon desk groupings or pods in favor of conventional vertical rows. Most students with special needs function best when placed near the front of the class, near the board and teacher's desk; away from distractions such as the pencil sharpener, intercom, drinking fountain, hamster cage, and air-conditioning vent; and with their backs toward as many students as possible.

Desk groupings or pods are popular in many schools and work great for facilitating cooperative learning activities with compliant students. But not all kids are ready for this experience. You need to get to know your students first. Immature students are more likely to see desk groups as an opportunity to play around, seek negative attention, or disrupt. Desk groupings are absolutely the worst seating arrangement for students with ADD. This configuration surrounds them with distractions. What are the alternatives? ADD students do best in conventional vertical rows or unattached as "islands."

If you use islands, and we recommend that you do when they are needed, it's important to present this seating option as a "normal part" of your classroom seating plan. Students should not feel ostracized or stigmatized by the arrangement. When the option is presented in a positive manner to the whole class, most students who become islands are grateful for the opportunity. They do better, and they know it.

GUIDELINES FOR PLANNING SEATING OR DESK CONFIGURATIONS

- Assign students to their seats during the first day of school.
- Seat students facing the board and the teacher.
- Adjust your seating plan for easy access to all students and efficient movement through the classroom.
- Separate close friends and students prone to conflict.

- Strategically place students with special needs.
- Adjust your seating plan as students show more maturity.

Classroom Jobs or Chores

What a great concept! Here is an opportunity to enlist free help for literally dozens of jobs that need to be carried out in the classroom on a daily basis, and in most cases, the help is offered cheerfully, even proudly. Experienced teachers know that classroom chores are a wonderful tool for community building and for teaching responsibility and cooperation. The simple act of being a contributing member of the classroom helps students to feel needed, valued, and connected to their teacher, peers, and the classroom as a whole. When contributions are recognized and acknowledged publicly, students develop a sense of pride and belonging.

The list of potential classroom jobs is limited only by your imagination, but here is a list to help you get started.

POSSIBLE CLASSROOM JOBS

Line leader	Flag salute leader
Table group leader	Ball and equipment manager
Paper monitor	Blackboard monitor
Bookshelf monitor	Supplies manager
Office messenger	Lighting director
Classroom ambassador	Cleanup committee
Buddy helper	Conflict manager
Class meeting leader	Recycling manager

GUIDELINES FOR CLASSROOM JOBS

- Post list of classroom jobs in visible area.
- Rotate jobs weekly.
- Explain and model the job the first time it's assigned.
- Acknowledge effort and contributions publicly.

- Offer constructive feedback when needed.
- Provide formal recognition at the end of the week.

Enlisting Parent Support and Cooperation

The focus thus far has been on helping students get acquainted with the structure of the classroom. We've discussed effective methods for teaching rules and procedures, organizing seating and classroom chores, and supporting or enforcing rules and procedures with discipline or limit-setting procedures. The final step in creating effective structure is to enlist the support and cooperation of parents as partners in our classroom management system.

How do we enlist parent support? There is no one right way, but some guidelines can help you get off to a good start. First, be proactive. Contact parents early before small problems develop into big ones. Second, give them all the information they need to back you up and be supportive. It is not enough simply to expect their support. Provide them with the specific information and skills they need to be supportive.

What's the alternative if we don't make early contact, or fail to provide parents with the information or skills they need? How will they know what we expect or how to support us? The chances are they won't know, and will be ill-equipped to help when a problem has developed with their child. How are they likely to feel when our first point of contact is about a problem? Defensive? Angry? Embarrassed? Resentful? Sure. Is this any way to begin a cooperative working relationship?

Some teachers wait until their first set of teacher-parent conferences to share concerns they're having about a student's behavior. What parent likes to hear at their first conference with their child's teacher that their child has been misbehaving for the last eight to ten weeks? When we allow problems to develop into patterns, we don't inspire parent confidence in our classroom management skills. Teachers who wait too long to contact parents risk turning a potential supporter into an adversary.

The choices are clear: Either we share our rules and expectations early and start off on a positive note, or we keep parents in the dark and risk alienating them when the focus of our first contact is a discipline problem. Allies are always better than adversaries. Sending an introductory letter is an excellent way to get off to a good start.

One of the easiest ways to make a good impression is to send parents an introductory letter as early as possible (see Figure 1.3). This simple act sets a positive tone and conveys all the right messages to parents about your professionalism—"I'm prepared, I'm organized, and I'm ready." Your introductory letter should include:

- Your classroom rules
- Basic student responsibilities
- Homework expectations and procedures
- Grading policy
- Your discipline procedures
- Suggestions for how parents can support you at home

FIGURE 1.3

Introductory Letter for Parents

Teacher's name _____

Student's name _____

Dear Parents,

I'm pleased that your child will be a student in my classroom for this next school year, and I look forward to meeting you personally during our back-to-school night. I'm sure you're as committed as I am to seeing that your child gets off to a good start. For that reason, I am sending a copy of my classroom rules, my expectations for basic student responsibilities, my homework procedure, grading policy, and a description of my classroom management program.

I use the Setting Limits Classroom Management Program in my classroom. When concerns or problems arise, I make a complete effort to resolve the matter individually with the student. If we are unable to resolve the problem, then I may ask for your support or assistance. Together, we can usually resolve problems early and get students pointed in the right direction. When you visit our classroom, you'll see guidance posters on the walls with our classroom rules, basic student responsibilities, and guidance and discipline procedures. If you're curious about how our classroom procedures work, ask your child during the first several weeks for a more detailed description or call me.

Please support me by reviewing the attached lists of materials with your child. Attached you'll find a copy of our classroom rules, student responsibilities, homework and grading policy, and guidance and discipline procedures. Please provide a telephone number where you can be reached during school hours. Thank you for your support and cooperation. I look forward to a great year of learning.

Sincerely,

Parent phone number during school hours_____

Email address _____

Preparing Your Discipline Plan

An effective classroom discipline plan is the most important tool in your classroom management tool kit. These procedures define your "bottom line," the rules you really practice and the behavior you're willing to tolerate. Students don't miss this important lesson. Even in well-structured classrooms, some students are going to test your rules and procedures. When they do, you need to act decisively and support your rules with instructive consequences. Your credibility hangs in the balance. That's what the rest of this book will show you how to do.

Setting Limits in the Classroom will be your credibility preserver. In chapters 9–18, where you'll find the bulk of our skills-training program, you will learn the limit-setting tools you need to manage nearly every problem you encounter in the classroom, ranging from simple noncompliance with classroom rules and procedures to extreme acts of disruption, defiance, even crisis management. By the time you've finished this book, your classroom management tool kit should be complete. You'll be ready for day one and the rest of the year.

Launching Your Classroom Management Plan

If we've done our job, the mantra "Be Prepared, Be Organized, Be Ready" is probably ringing in your ears. If you've checked off the items on your readiness checklist, then you're about as ready as you can be. Let's launch.

ON THE FIRST DAY

- Greet students at the door and lead them to their assigned seats.
- Introduce your general rules or rules in theory. Keep them broad and inclusive, and avoid extensive lists.
- Post your general classroom rules in a visible area for students.
- Describe your classroom procedures in order of their importance and necessity. Procedures for entering and exiting the classroom, asking for help, using the bathroom, handling transitions such as shifting from whole-class to independent seatwork, and getting ready for recess and lunch should be at the top of your list.
- Review your expectations for basic student responsibilities.
- Place a poster of basic student responsibilities in a visible area in the classroom.
- Share your expectations for homework and describe homework procedures. Be clear about when assignments are given, when assignments are due, and what happens when work is not completed.

- Introduce your accountability procedures and explain how they work.
- Be prepared to introduce the discipline procedures you'll learn in chapters 11–15 early on the first day of class. You never know when this lesson is likely to take place. Be prepared to use your limit-setting tools the first time testing occurs. Others won't miss the lesson. How do you teach discipline procedures? You teach them the same way you teach any other procedure. Explain them, demonstrate them, and practice them. Share your classroom posters on logical consequences and time-out. Explain and demonstrate each procedure. Walk your students through some hypothetical situations so they can see how these procedures are carried out. Introduce the following procedures first:

  Makeup sessions for incomplete work
  Fun Friday
  Classroom rental center
  Logical consequences
  The Blurt Box (see chapters 11 and 12)
  Recess Academy
  Two-Stage Time-Out procedure
  Parents as backup support
  The office as backup support
  Logical consequences on the playground
  Logical consequences in the lunchroom

- Announce that you will send home a list of your classroom rules and discipline procedures and that you will review them with parents at the back-to-school night.

DURING THE FIRST TWO WEEKS

- Review your general classroom rules daily as well as any specific rules that have been tested or violated. Ask questions to be sure students understand what you expect.

- Review your list of basic student responsibilities daily.
- Review your accountability procedures daily.
- Set aside time each day to teach and practice classroom procedures. Add new procedures to work on each day and devote more time to procedures that students have difficulty mastering, such as sitting in morning circle, lining up for recess, or going to time-out. Present the lessons in a simple and concrete manner, particularly with preschool and elementary school students. Don't assume that your words will be enough to convey your message. Show them what you mean by modeling the behavior you expect them to use. Walk them through hypothetical situations to make sure they understand what you expect.
- Expect testing and be prepared to follow through. There is only so much you can teach with verbal instruction, practice, and review. Most of your students will be convinced you mean business when they see how much time and energy you're willing to devote to teaching your rules and procedures. They will accept your rules as stated and do their best to follow them. Some of your students, the hard-way learners, will have to experience the consequences of their poor choices many times before they will be convinced. These lessons won't be planned or scheduled. They might take place at any time during the day. When they do, you will need to follow through and support your rules with logical consequences.
- Adjust your seating or desk configuration as needed. Position your ADD/ADHD students in appropriate areas, separate friends who talk, and strategically position your most disruptive students to minimize opportunities for disruption.
- Use the Blurt Box and Recess Academy, discussed in chapters 11 and 12, with a high level of consistency to minimize disruption and help your hard-way learners to master your procedures.
- Make unsolicited phone calls to parents to share how pleased you are that their child is getting off to a good start.
- Review your rules, expectations, classroom procedures, discipline plan, homework, and grading policy with parents at back-to-school night.

- Make a list of parents who did not attend back-to-school night and follow up with a phone call. Ask if they received your introductory letter and if they have any questions about your classroom or how their child is doing. Try to limit your call to ten to fifteen minutes and cover the following:
  - Share a positive incident or observation that characterizes their child.
  - Ask whether they have any questions about the materials that you sent home during the first week.
  - Encourage them to review the information with their child.
  - Express your appreciation for their support.

DURING THE FIRST MONTH

- Continue teaching your rules and procedures as needed. Routines should be beginning to emerge.
- Expect testing and be prepared to follow through consistently with your discipline procedures. The heaviest testing usually occurs during the first four to six weeks of school. Your consistency will buy huge credibility points for later on.
- Use Recess Academy for your hard-way learners. Set aside time before or after school, during recess, breaks, or lunch for individual or small-group practice sessions for students who need additional help mastering important skills such as walking the corridor or sitting quietly during instruction. A brief lesson during the student's time can have a huge impact.
- Schedule parent conferences for students who test excessively or fail to comply with classroom rules and expectations during the first four weeks. You may need the parents' backup support. Ask parents to help their children practice needed skills at home (for example, not interrupting).

THROUGHOUT THE YEAR

- Review classroom rules and procedures as needed with individual students or groups of students who require additional practice.

- Continue to follow through and support your rules and procedures with logical consequences. Learning to follow rules and procedures and to respect authority is an ongoing process.
- Use Recess Academy as needed. Set aside time for students to practice the skills and lessons they haven't mastered. Arrange for practice sessions to occur during the student's time, such as recess, lunch, or before or after school, and not during class time.

Chapter Summary

Effective structure is an essential component of any effective classroom management program, but many teachers overlook the importance of structure in the beginning of the year. They assume that their students already know what is expected or that they will pick it up along the way—a costly assumption that sets up both teacher and students for a year of testing and conflict.

The lesson of structure will be taught one way or another. There is no way to avoid it. The real issue is, Who controls the lesson? When students control the lesson, the costs to cooperation and learning are much greater. Time that should be spent in instruction is spent instead handling testing, disruptions, and damage control.

The choices are clear. Either we begin early and invest the time required to teach our rules and procedures and enlist parent support, or we exhaust ourselves trying to accomplish these tasks as we go and risk alienating parents in the process. Prevention is always the better way to go. Creating structure early in the year leads to smoother sailing later on.

Developing Positive Relationships with Encouragement

Structure defines the path we want students to stay on, but structure alone may not motivate them to head in the intended direction. Cooperation is still a voluntary act. How can we inspire students to want to cooperate and follow our rules? By being positive and encouraging. Building positive relationships with students is the cheapest form of classroom management.

This chapter will show you how to do that. In this chapter, you'll learn how to build positive relationships and inspire children's cooperation through the power of encouragement and positive motivation. No shaming. No blaming. No humiliating children into cooperating. No bribes or special rewards for getting them to do what they should be doing anyway. The methods are quick, effective, easy to use, and fit neatly with the positive limit-setting practices you'll learn in this book. You'll find them a refreshing alternative to punishment and coercion.

Motivation and Instruction

Imagine you are a student with two different paths in front of you. One involves only work, and the teacher uses a lot of criticism, threats, and coercion to keep you on it. The other mixes work with pleasure, and the teacher uses a lot of encouragement and respectful guidance to keep you on it. Which path would you choose? Of course, the choice is clear.

This question illustrates a basic truth that applies to all of us, adults and children alike. The more positives we see in our path, the more likely we are to head in the intended direction. A path with positives is always more inviting.

When it comes to motivating children, most teachers head in one of two directions: They take a positive approach and use generous helpings of encouragement and rewards to inspire the behavior they want; or they take a negative approach and rely primarily on threats, punishment, and coercion to force children into cooperating. There isn't much in between.

The approach teachers use to motivate students has a lot to do with the type of limits they set. Teachers who are ineffective in their limit setting are accustomed to encountering resistance. They get angry and frustrated, and often they end up saying discouraging things to their students. They assume that the problem is their students' lack of cooperation, not the way cooperation is being requested. Discouraging messages and ineffective limits go hand in hand.

Teachers who are effective in their limit setting, on the other hand, expect cooperation but also recognize that children are most likely to cooperate when asked in a respectful manner. Encouraging messages inspire cooperation. Effective limit setting and encouraging messages also go hand in hand.

Encouraging and discouraging messages predictably lead in one of two directions: to cooperation or to resistance. If our goal is to inspire cooperation, then discouraging messages are one of the surest ways not to achieve our objective.

Negative Messages Inspire Resistance

It's nine o'clock in the morning, and Tyler, a fifth grader, is supposed to be writing in his journal but decides to distract his neighbors instead. He has already disrupted the class three times. Number four is about to happen. He chips a piece off the end of his eraser and flicks it at the girl sitting across from him. He gets the expected response.

"Cut it out, Tyler!" she complains, loud enough for the teacher to hear.

"What does it take to get through to you, Tyler?" says his exasperated teacher. "Can't you see others don't appreciate your clowning around? I expect your behavior from a first grader, but not a fifth grader. Why don't you act your age for a change?"

"Why don't you try to be an interesting teacher for a change?" says Tyler. He knows she's hooked. Things are about to escalate.

"Nobody talks to me like that!" his teacher explodes. "I've had enough of your disrespect. You may think that you can treat people like dirt, but you'll end up getting a taste of your own medicine." She hands Tyler two sheets of paper and directs him to the back table. "You can return to your desk after you write one hundred times 'I will not be disrespectful to my teacher.'"

"No way!" says Tyler defiantly. "You can't make me if I don't want to."

"You can't go out for any recesses until you do," she threatens.

"Big deal," says Tyler. "I could care less." He makes no move to begin the writing.

Tyler's teacher did not start off with the intention of provoking an angry power struggle with one of her students. Her goal was to stop Tyler's misbehavior and enlist his cooperation, but she was using one of the worst methods to achieve that goal.

Negative messages frequently have the opposite of their intended effect. They inspire resistance, not cooperation, and lead predictably to escalating misbehavior and power struggles. Discouraging messages are the fuel for hurtful classroom dances.

When Tyler disrupts class, his teacher becomes frustrated and angry and tries to shame him into cooperation by criticizing and humiliating him in front of his peers. The focus is on Tyler's maturity, not his misbehavior. Her message conveys no confidence in his ability to cooperate or behave acceptably. In effect, she's saying, "You're not capable, I have no confidence in you, and I don't expect you to cooperate." He doesn't.

Would you feel like cooperating with someone who said these things to you? Or would you feel more inclined to retaliate? Tyler responds as

many of us would—with resistance. He perceives her message as a personal attack. He digs in his heels and launches a counterattack.

Negative messages feel bad. They hurt and humiliate and are often perceived as personal attacks rather than as attempts to discourage unacceptable behavior. Their focus is misdirected, and that's why they backfire.

Let's not overlook another, more subtle message that accompanies our negative attempts to motivate. What we do is what we teach. Thus the methods we use themselves teach a lesson about communication and problem solving. By role-modeling hurtful, coercive methods, Tyler's teacher is teaching him that hurtful statements are an acceptable way to motivate others to cooperate. Without realizing it, she is teaching the very behavior she's trying to stop.

EXAMPLES OF NEGATIVE MOTIVATIONAL MESSAGES

Negative messages come in a variety of forms. Some are subtle and result from overinvolvement or helping too much. Others are explicit and direct, such as the messages Tyler's teacher used in the previous example. All discouraging messages convey little confidence in the child's ability to make good choices and behave acceptably. They tend to personalize misbehavior and carry an underlying message of shame and blame. Let's look at the underlying message in each of the following:

Can you cooperate just once in a while?

Underlying message: "I don't believe you can cooperate." The effect is to blame, diminish, single out, and humiliate.

Show me you have a brain and make a good choice for a change!

Underlying message: "You're not very bright, and I have little confidence in your ability to make good decisions." The effect is to diminish, shame, and humiliate.

Would it be asking too much to get a little respect?

Underlying message: "I don't expect you to treat me respectfully." The effect is to blame and diminish.

Is that the best you can do?

Underlying message: "You're not very competent. You don't live up to my expectations." The effect is to shame, blame, diminish, and humiliate.

I don't believe it! You actually did what you were asked for a change.

Underlying message: "I don't expect your cooperation." The effect is to shame, embarrass, diminish, and single out.

Try that again. I dare you.

Underlying message: "I don't expect your cooperation, so continue misbehaving so I can show you I'm the boss." The effect is to challenge, provoke, blame, diminish, and intimidate.

There's one jerk in every classroom.

Underlying message: "You're not worthwhile or acceptable." The effect is to reject, shame, blame, single out, and humiliate.

Now that's real bright!

Underlying message: "You make poor decisions. I have no confidence in your ability." The effect is to diminish, shame, blame, and humiliate.

I knew I couldn't count on you.

Underlying message: "You're not capable or trustworthy. I have no confidence in your ability." The effect is to shame, blame, diminish, and humiliate.

EXAMPLES OF NEGATIVE MOTIVATIONAL PRACTICES

- Rolling your eyes at the student.
- Using body language to show frustration, such as standing with hands on hips or arms crossed.
- Asking others what they think of a student's behavior (for example, "Raise your hand if you're tired of Jason disrupting the class and wasting our time").
- Making complaint calls to parents to report how bad a student's day went.
- Daily behavior charts that include misbehavior (for example, happy face/sad face with tally marks).
- Names on board with checks for random misbehavior with a hierarchy of consequences associated with each check.
- Names on the board indicating loss of privileges for misbehavior unrelated to the privilege lost (for example, "No Recess" followed by a list of names).

Positive Messages Inspire Cooperation

Jacob, a kindergartner, is waiting in line to go out to the playground when a classmate accidentally bumps him. Jacob gives him a push, and the boy falls down. The teacher intervenes.

"Jacob, we don't push in line," says the teacher matter-of-factly.

"Tommy bumped into me first," Jacob replies. "He was in my way."

"What are we supposed to do when others are in our way?" the teacher asks.

Jacob just stares at her blankly. "I don't know," he says.

"You're supposed to say 'Excuse me' and wait for them to move," says the teacher.

"Sometimes they won't move," says Jacob.

"You should ask an adult for help when that happens," says the teacher. "Now you have two good choices. What are you going to do next time?"

"I'll say 'Excuse me' and wait for them to move," replies Jacob. "If they don't, I'll ask you for help."

"Good!" says the teacher. "I'm sure you'll handle it fine. Now, what do you need to say to Tommy?"

"Sorry, Tommy," says Jacob.

"Thank you, Jacob," says the teacher with an appreciative smile.

Jacob's teacher uses encouragement effectively. Much of her success, however, is due to the way she starts off. She begins with a limit-setting message that is both firm and respectful. No one is blamed or singled out. In a few brief sentences, she creates a positive atmosphere for problem solving. Now her encouraging words can have the greatest impact.

The focus of her message is on choices and corrective action, not on Jacob's worth or capabilities. She provides the information and skills he needs to behave acceptably and then expresses her confidence in his ability to handle the situation better next time. Her message is positive and inspiring: "You're capable; I have confidence in you; I expect you to cooperate."

How would you feel if someone said that to you? Would you feel accepted and supported? Would you feel like cooperating? Jacob did, and so would most of us. Positive, encouraging messages meet our need for belonging, reaffirm our feelings of competence and self-worth, and instill confidence in our ability to handle challenging problems. Encouragement is a key ingredient for building positive relationships. The following guidelines will help you use this tool effectively.

GUIDELINES FOR USING ENCOURAGEMENT

Knowing *what* to encourage is the key to using encouragement effectively. The focus of our message should address our basic training goals: effort, better choices, acceptable actions, cooperation, independence, and improvement. All lead to greater responsibility. Let's look at ways to get the most from our encouraging messages.

Encouraging Effort and Risk Taking

According to the respected developmental theorist Erik Erikson, skill acquisition is the primary developmental task of early and middle childhood. Children want to be skillful and competent. They're naturally motivated to be that way. But for some students, learning in the classroom can be a scary experience because it involves risk taking, vulnerability, and the possibility of failure in the company of others.

What happens to students who repeatedly struggle and fail? They feel embarrassed, frustrated, discouraged, and less willing to take risks and attempt new tasks. Failure registers intensely in young learners. The more they fail, the more frustrated and discouraged they become. Over time, "trying" turns into "avoiding." The literature describes this pattern as "fear-of-failure-avoidance motivation." This is the internal experience that often accompanies repeated failure as students begin to turn off to the learning process. Preventing academic discouragement should be a major goal of every classroom.

How can teachers help students overcome frustration and discouragement and continue to take risks? By providing the encouragement students need to overcome emotional obstacles. Teachers are in a unique position to prevent the emotional and motivational consequences of failure by supporting struggling learners with encouragement. Encouragement, offered consistently, provides the safety young learners need to take risks.

A truly safe classroom encourages and invites students to take risks, to stretch themselves intellectually, to think critically, to attempt difficult tasks, and to make mistakes in the pursuit of learning. This form of safety requires a special relationship between a student and a teacher and brings out the best in both when it happens. Consider the following.

Mrs. Fickel's third graders finish silent reading and begin a discussion about the story. "Who are the main characters in the story?" asks Mrs. Fickel. She selects a Popsicle stick from a jar; it has Lance's name on it.

"Lance, who are the main characters in the story?" Lance looks hesitant and uncomfortable.

"I don't know," he says, hoping she'll let him off the hook. Not Mrs. Fickel.

"Let's find out what you do know," she says in an encouraging tone. "What are the names of some of the characters?"

"Mr. Kellers and Tommy," Lance replies with uncertainty.

"Good job, Lance!" says Mrs. Fickel. "Who else do you remember from the story?" She pauses and gives him a minute to think.

"Well, there's Tommy's sister, Juliana," Lance recalls. "And they have a dog, Spinner. I guess he's a character, too."

"Excellent job, Lance!" says Mrs. Fickel proudly. "You named all of the main characters, and you're right, Spinner is also an important character." Mrs. Fickel turns to the class.

"How many others thought a dog could be a character in a story?" she asks. Only a few hands shoot up. Lance can see he knew more than he thought.

"Thank you, Lance," says Mrs. Fickel before she moves on with her next round of questions. Lance looks proud and a little more confident. He needs more of these experiences, but he surely has the right teacher.

When Lance said "I don't know" to the original question, Mrs. Fickel could have easily moved on to another student, but what would have happened to Lance? He would have remained fearful and uncertain and would not be any closer to taking the risks he needs to take to stretch himself and learn to trust his own ability. Mrs. Fickel did not let him off the hook. Instead, she held firm and helped him over the hurdle by offering support and encouragement. He ventured into scary territory by taking a risk, and what happened? He grew a little in the process. Students like Lance need a lot of these experiences to develop to the fullest of their learning potential.

Encouraging Better Choices

Sometimes children misbehave because they are unaware that other, more effective choices are available for handling the situation. Teachers and other guidance providers are in an ideal position to help children explore their choices and make better ones. Consider the following.

Melissa, a fifth grader, is suspended from class for being disruptive. She arrives at the vice principal's office with a note from her teacher.

"What happened, Melissa?" asks the vice principal.

"I got really mad at Jenny," Melissa replies. "Jenny Mullins has been spreading rumors about me all week. She keeps telling everyone not to be my friend and telling lies about me. Jenny sits right behind me in class and whispers lies that she's going to tell others while we're supposed to be working. I turned around and told her to shut up. Then I called her a liar. I guess I was kinda loud. Mrs. Swain sent me here. I'm really tired of her doing this all the time."

"What do you think Jenny was trying to do?" asks the vice principal.

"Make me upset," Melissa replies.

"It sounds like she succeeded, too," observes the vice principal. "How could you handle this differently the next time it happens?"

"I could tell all of my friends what she's doing and tell them that she's lying."

"Do you think she would stop if you did?" asks the vice principal.

"Probably not," replies Melissa upon reflection. "It would just show her that she was getting to me."

"What else could you do?" inquires the vice principal.

"I could ignore her," says Melissa, "but that's really hard to do, especially when she bugs me in class."

"You're right," the vice principal replies. "Ignoring someone is hard to do when they sit directly behind you, but ignoring her is a good choice. She would probably stop if she saw it wasn't working. What else could you do?"

"I could ask Mrs. Swain to move me," suggests Melissa.

"That's a good choice," says the vice principal. "I'm sure that would help. Can you think of anything else?"

Melissa thinks for a moment. "Well, I guess I could ask Mrs. Swain to tell Jenny to leave me alone, but I don't want to look like a tattletale," says Melissa. "I could tell Mrs. Swain what's going on in case things get worse and Jenny won't leave me alone."

"I understand that you don't want to look like a tattletale, but Mrs. Swain may need to know what is happening," says the vice principal. "You've got some good choices to use next time. I'm confident you'll handle it just fine."

Melissa leaves the vice principal's office feeling supported and encouraged. She is aware of her options, and she is prepared to make a different choice the next time the situation arises.

Encouraging Acceptable Actions

Making an acceptable choice is an important first step, but getting kids to act on that choice is our larger training goal. Sometimes our encouraging words are most effective when we focus directly on actions.

For example, Cynthia, a sixth grader, knows she's not supposed to interrupt when her teacher talks to others, but she is eager to leave class for a student council meeting. She decides to interrupt anyway.

"May I go to the library, Mrs. Trefethen?" Cynthia asks excitedly. "My student council meeting is about to start." Mrs. Trefethen does not look pleased.

"Cynthia, what are you supposed to do when you want to talk to me while I'm in the middle of a conversation?" she asks.

"Wait for you to finish," replies Cynthia.

"Right," says Mrs. Trefethen. "Now go back to your desk and come back and try it again."

Cynthia returns to her desk and then approaches Mrs. Trefethen a second time. She's still talking. She waits patiently. When there's a pause in the conversation, she interjects her question. "May I go to the library for the student council meeting?"

"Sure, Cynthia," she replies, "and thank you for asking me the way you did." She gives Cynthia an appreciative smile. No feelings were hurt in this lesson. Mrs. Trefethen got her message across in a positive and respectful way.

Zach, a preschooler, received some instructive guidance when he used a commanding tone to get a classmate to pass some crayons.

"Give me the crayons, Jared," demands Zach. "You can't keep them all." The teacher hears him and intervenes.

"Zach, how are we supposed to ask?"

Zach remembers.

"Let's try it again," says his teacher.

"May I have the tray of crayons, please?" says Zach. Jared hands them over.

"Good job, Zach!" says the teacher. "That's the way we like to be asked."

No shaming. No blaming. No angry words or looks of disapproval. All Zach needed was a little encouragement and an opportunity to show he could behave acceptably.

Encouraging Cooperation

We don't need misbehavior to cue us to the need for encouragement. Anytime a child helps out, cooperates, or makes a contribution, we have an opportunity to use encouraging messages. Our encouragement increases the likelihood that children's cooperation will continue. Consider the following.

Trent, age four, notices his teacher walking toward the door with a tray full of snacks. Her hands are full. He opens the door and holds it open while she walks in.

"Thanks, Trent," says the teacher. "You're a great helper!" Trent beams with pride. The lesson isn't lost on others.

Mr. Gipson, a third-grade teacher, is called out of the classroom briefly when a parent arrives at his door. The kids have a great opportunity to clown around, but they don't. When he steps back into the room, everyone is working quietly at their seats. He appreciates their cooperation and lets them know.

"Thanks for handling things so well while I was called out," says Mr. Gipson. "You guys are great. I knew I could count on you."

A word or two of encouragement at the right time can have a big impact. The following are just a few of the many possibilities:

"I like the way you handled that."
"Your desk looks great today."
"Good job!"
"Your helping out makes a big difference."
"I knew I could count on you."
"Thanks, I appreciate your thoughtfulness."

Encouraging Independence

One of our larger guidance goals is to assist children to handle problems on their own. We do this by teaching effective problem-solving skills and by limiting our involvement so children have opportunities to practice those skills independently. Encouragement plays an important role in the process. It gives children the confidence to take risks and act independently. Consider the following.

Joey, a fifth grader, runs to tattle on a classmate. "Mrs. Lyman, Damien was copying from my paper."

"Did you ask him to stop or cover up your paper so he couldn't?" asks Mrs. Lyman.

"Well, no," replies Joey, expecting the teacher to handle it.

"Then that's what you need to do if it happens again," says Mrs. Lyman, with a smile. "I'm sure you'll handle it fine."

Randy and Carla, two kindergartners, quarrel over a scooter. "Give it to me," screams Carla, loud enough to attract her teacher's attention. It works. As the teacher approaches, both kids clutch the scooter tightly.

"I think you guys can work this out," says the teacher confidently. "Do you remember our plan for sharing?"

Randy does. He tunes back into the classroom and returns a few moments later with a timer. He sets it for five minutes. "I get to use it first," he announces.

"Okay," says Carla reluctantly, "but I get to use it next."

"You sure do," says the teacher. "Good job, guys! You handled it just fine. I knew you could."

Mrs. Morales, a fourth-grade teacher, passes out an assignment to the class. Less than a minute goes by before Tony comes up for his own personal set of instructions. "I don't understand what I'm supposed to do," he says.

"Did you read the directions carefully and think about what you're supposed to do?" Mrs. Morales asks.

"I think so," Tony replies, hoping she will do the thinking for him.

"Well, try it again," she says in an encouraging voice. "I'm confident you can figure it out on your own. If you still aren't sure after five minutes, I'll be happy to help."

"Rats!" Tony says to himself. "She didn't go for it." He heads back to his seat to figure it out on his own.

Five minutes later, Tony is busy with his assignment. He may not realize it, but he just received a lesson in independence. His teacher's encouragement and reluctance to rescue him made it possible.

Encouraging Improvement

Some skills, such as taking turns or learning not to interrupt, require repeated effort and practice before they can be mastered. The process is gradual. Adult impatience or expectations of immediate mastery can be very discouraging. Our energy is best directed toward encouraging improvement. The focus should be on effort, not outcome; process, not product.

Trey, a third grader, lives in a home where interrupting is okay. Whenever he has something to say, he just says it. His parents usually stop whatever they're doing and give him their undivided attention.

At school, things are different. Interrupting is not okay. When Trey interrupts, his teacher asks him to raise his hand and wait to be called. They've been practicing this skill for months, but progress has been slow. Trey's teacher feels frustrated.

"Maybe I should make him sit at the back table for five minutes each time he interrupts," Trey's teacher suggests to a colleague. "Maybe that will help him remember." The colleague has another suggestion.

"Try using encouragement first and see what happens," she suggests. "Each time he remembers to raise his hand, let him know how much you appreciate it. When he doesn't need prompting, thank him after he does it the right way."

The next morning, Trey wants to ask a question and remembers to raise his hand without prompts. "Thank you, Trey," says his teacher. "I really appreciate it when you raise your hand." He looks pleased.

Later in the day, Trey starts to blurt out an answer without being called on. "What are you supposed to do when you want to be called on, Trey?" asks his teacher. Trey remembers and raises his hand. "Thank you, Trey," she says with an appreciative smile. His teacher decides to continue the plan for a full month.

Several weeks later, the same colleague inquires about Trey's progress. "How's he doing?" she asks.

"Much better," replies Trey's teacher. "He remembers more than he forgets. In fact, he hasn't interrupted for several days." Encouragement is making a difference.

EXAMPLES OF POSITIVE MOTIVATIONAL PRACTICES

- Catching students being successful
- Positive referrals to the office for good behavior
- Congratulating students on task
- Awarding Happy Grams and notes of encouragement
- Using time with the principal as a reward
- Group points for cooperative behavior
- Teacher-Student Game (explained in chapter 4)
- Preferred Activity Time (explained in chapter 4)
- Making unsolicited complimentary phone calls home

Involving Parents in the Encouragement Process

One of the best ways to increase the motivational power of encouragement is to involve parents in the process. When parents and teachers combine their encouraging efforts, children feel even more inspired to make good choices and cooperate.

At the preschool and elementary levels, it's an effective practice to send home special commendations, awards, or certificates of merit acknowledging student effort, cooperation, or achievement. The commendations can be included with other materials in the student's Friday folder. The gesture is rewarding for everybody. Parents like to hear the good news and enjoy sharing that news with their child. The child feels good about having his or her efforts publicly acknowledged. Teachers gain a lot of cooperation and respect from parents and students by simply acknowledging what has taken place. This small investment yields big returns in cooperation.

Chapter Summary

In this chapter, we examined two contrasting approaches to motivating children and the teacher-student relationships that develop around each approach. We saw how negative and discouraging messages achieve the opposite of their intended effect. They inspire resistance, not cooperation, and fuel power struggles and classroom dances.

Positive and encouraging messages, on the other hand, are highly effective motivational tools. Encouraging messages meet children's needs for belonging, reaffirm feelings of competence and self-worth, and inspire children to tackle challenging tasks and problems on their own. Encouraging messages create safety in the classroom and positive relationships between teachers and students. Encouragement can make the difference between cooperation and resistance (see Table 2.1).

Knowing what to encourage is the key to using encouragement effectively. Our messages have their greatest impact when they focus on better efforts, better choices, acceptable actions, cooperation, independence, and improvement.

TABLE 2.1
Encouraging Versus Discouraging Messages

ENCOURAGING MESSAGES	DISCOURAGING MESSAGES
Inspire cooperation.	Inspire resistance, retaliation.
Motivate and empower.	Discourage and humiliate.
Convey respect, confidence, support.	Diminish, blame, reject.
Build positive relationships.	Create adversarial relationships.
Meet needs for belonging, confidence, self-worth.	Are perceived as a personal attack.
Focus on choices and behavior.	Focus on a child's worth and capabilities.

Engagement Strategies: Making Learning Enjoyable

Student engagement is an important leg of the four-legged table that supports an effective classroom. When students are engaged in our lessons, there's more time for learning and less time for goofing off. Research confirms what we all suspect: Increased levels of student engagement are consistently linked to positive achievement outcomes and academic success.

What's the alternative if we fail to engage students in our lessons? They become bored and disconnected from the learning experience, and some become off task and disruptive. Then we have to rely on limit setting to get the job done. Does this sound like damage control? You bet.

But keeping students engaged in our lessons is no easy task. Some students lack interest in the subject matter. Some lack skills. Some lack confidence. Some are so frustrated and discouraged that they've given up. Still others are turned off by the mundane and boring delivery of daily instruction.

This chapter will help you reignite the motivational spark in your students and keep them fully engaged throughout the learning process. The purpose of this chapter is not to teach you how to teach. You've already mastered that in your credential program. Our purpose is to give you effective strategies for increasing student engagement in your daily lessons. You'll learn a variety of proven, research-based strategies that are easy to use and enjoyable for both teachers and students. We didn't originate all of these strategies, and we attempted to credit the originators when possible.

The chapter is divided into three sections reflecting the three stages in the engagement process: (1) strategies for hooking your students into your lessons, (2) strategies for keeping them engaged throughout the lesson, and (3) strategies for making their learning relevant beyond the lesson. Let's look at how one fifth-grade teacher incorporates many of these strategies into her lesson about the solar system.

The students in Ms. Bridges's class recently completed an Earth science unit and are about to begin the next unit on the solar system. In the next unit, they'll discover that the solar system consists of planets and other bodies that orbit the sun in predictable paths. They'll learn that the path of a planet around the sun is due to the gravitational attraction between the sun and the planet. They'll discover what satellites are and be able to distinguish an asteroid from a comet. Before they complete the unit, Ms. Bridges will divide them into groups, assign each group a planet to research, and have them construct a model of the planet. Each group will give a report to the class based on its research.

Like most experienced teachers, Ms. Bridges knows that if she assigns her students the task of reading about the planets and reporting on what they've read, they will do the job, but with little enthusiasm or retention of the material. Ms. Bridges wants her students to connect with the unit on a deeper and more meaningful level. She wants them to be interested and excited about the projects they'll present to the class.

To "hook" the students into the lesson, Ms. Bridges begins with a KWL chart (see Figure 3.1). The chart is a visual representation of the process of learning and discovery. Students can see learning in progress because the process unfolds before their eyes. Ms. Bridges uses this strategy on a regular basis. Her students are very familiar with it.

Ms. Bridges begins the chart by asking her students to share any information they know about the solar system. Several students raise their hands to share. Jasmine says there are nine planets in our solar system. Ms. Bridges writes that in the K column. Marcus says that all the planets rotate around the sun. Ms. Bridges adds that to the K column.

Other students share what they know. Tony says there might be life on other planets. Andrew says that astronauts have been to Mars. Caitlin reports some planets have more than one moon. Ms. Bridges writes each comment in the K column without questioning or challenging them. She wants all of her students to feel safe to share what they think they know, right or wrong. The discovery process is part of the fun.

Next, Ms. Bridges asks the class what they want to learn about our solar system. Several hands shoot up. She can tell they're getting interested. She calls on Justin, who wants to know if there is life on other planets. Others seem curious, too.

She writes that in the W column of the KWL chart and continues to call on students to share what they want to know about the solar system. They ask a number of excellent questions: How do the planets stay in the air and not fall? What is a comet? What is a shooting star? How does the sun work? Can people live on other planets? Ms. Bridges records each of their questions in the W column.

Next, Ms. Bridges leads her students through a Picture Walk of the first chapter on the solar system. She asks them to look at each picture and read each caption as a whole-group activity. Then Ms. Bridges asks questions about the pictures that build upon her students' prior knowledge. This strategy only takes a few minutes. When the students finish the Picture Walk, they add additional thoughts and questions to the KWL chart. Now they are ready to begin reading the chapter.

Ms. Bridges knows from experience that asking her students to read aloud in a read-around format will lose the focus and attention of some students who are not reading. So she decides to introduce the chapter by reading the introduction aloud to the class and follows up by asking some comprehension questions to determine their level of understanding. They're ready to start.

She directs the class to read the first section silently and use Post-it notes to jot down key concepts and ideas they think are important and place them in the appropriate area in the text. The students are ready for the next strategy.

Ms. Bridges divides her students into groups of four and asks them to compile their information and create a set of important concepts and ideas everyone can agree on.

When this task is complete, Ms. Bridges announces, "Numbered Heads Together." The students are familiar with this strategy. They know what to do. She assigns a number to each student (1–4) in the group. She asks the groups to determine which concept they believe is the most important one in the section and to find it in their books. She gives them three minutes to complete the task then randomly calls the number 2 and asks all students who have been assigned number 2 to stand. They take turns, share their concepts, and read the important information aloud from the text.

"Is there any new information we should add to the KWL chart?" asks Ms. Bridges. The students quickly review the chart, add the new information they've learned, and write further questions about what they want to learn.

To sustain their interest throughout the unit, Ms. Bridges uses a variety of strategies in addition to the KWL chart, and varies those strategies on a daily basis. For example, she might start one lesson by having the kids do a *quick write,* a task where they are given five minutes to write down everything they've learned about the sun. No talking is allowed. They must write the entire time.

When the five minutes are over, Ms. Bridges directs her students' attention back to the KWL chart so they can add the new information. One student raises her hand and reports that the sun is not made of fire. It's mostly made up of the gases hydrogen and helium. Ms. Bridges thanks the student for sharing and asks the class to signal a thumbs-up if they've discovered the same information. Ms. Bridges writes the new information under the L column on the chart, and calls on a few more students to share what they've learned.

Halfway through the unit, Ms. Bridges plans a summary and review lesson by playing a game with her students. She sets up a Jeopardy board in front of the class with questions on cards in various pockets on the board. Students can earn more points for more difficult questions. She divides the class into two teams, then flips a coin to see who will go first. Laura is the first contestant. She chooses a pocket from the chart worth 200 points. Ms. Bridges pulls the card and reads the question aloud to the class.

"What planet is considered to be the smallest planet in our solar system?" asks Ms. Bridges. Laura has ten seconds to answer, or she can request consultation with her team for half the points. All students are silent as Laura decides what to do. They know that if they help Laura in any way, their team will lose their turn. Laura knows the answer.

"Pluto," she says. Her team cheers. Ms. Bridges gives 200 points to Laura's team, then turns to the other team.

Their first contestant is Jason, who has a learning disability. He worries what his teammates might think if he makes a mistake. Jason chooses a 500-point pocket. His teammates know he probably doesn't know the answer, but they remain quiet. Ms. Bridges reads the question to herself and decides to make this pocket a "consult and prove answer." Jason must consult with his team and find the answer in the textbook within one minute. Ms. Bridges reads the question on the card.

"What is the difference between a comet and an asteroid?" she asks. "Find the answer in the book to provide the evidence." The team gets to work. The other team also performs the task. They know that if Jason's team doesn't get the correct answer, their team has only ten seconds to answer. Both teams have to be ready.

The timer goes off. Jason's team is ready. Jason gives the explanation and indicates the appropriate page in the text. Ms. Bridges pauses playfully to build some excitement, then announces, "You got it!" Jason's team cheers. Jason beams with accomplishment. The game continues for twenty minutes. When the lesson is over, the students are reluctant to stop. Ms. Bridges promises them they can play Jeopardy again at the end of the unit.

Let's fast-forward four weeks. It's the end of the science unit, and Ms. Bridges fulfills her earlier promise. This time she broadens the game to include questions from the previous unit on planet Earth. She organizes the Jeopardy questions to connect concepts across both units so her students can generalize the concepts they've learned from one lesson to the next. Also, the students make their final entries on the KWL chart. They review what is written in each of the columns and discuss any misconceptions they may have had. The final column is complete. Andrew raises his hand to share something he learned.

"Astronauts haven't been to Mars," says Andrew, "but scientists have sent cameras on the Mars Rover to take pictures."

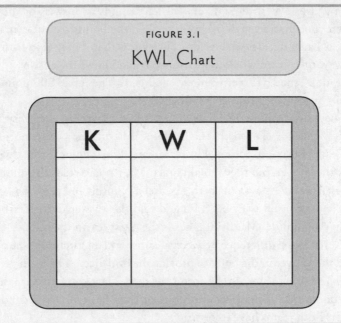

FIGURE 3.1

KWL Chart

K	W	L

Hooking Students into the Lesson

Engagement strategies that hook students into a lesson are important because they pique students' curiosity about a topic before we even begin to teach a lesson. They get students interested and focused. We can also determine any misconceptions students may have about the topic and if any accommodations need to be made to our lesson plans in order to match students' interest and level of knowledge. Here are a few strategies to get your students "hooked" on what you will be teaching.

Picture Walk

Description: Take a Picture Walk with your students before reading a story or beginning a new unit or chapter in the textbook. This strategy gets students interested in what they will learn and exposes them to the entire chapter or unit prior to reading it. Think of it as a preview of coming attractions.

Procedure: The Picture Walk is carried out as a whole-group activity.

- Ask your students to look at the pictures (they can read the bold titles if they want) and discuss what they see in the pictures.
- Ask questions to pique their curiosity.
- Ask students to make predictions about what they think is happening in the pictures.
- Challenge them to tell the story based only on the pictures.
- When working with intermediate-level students (grades four through six), encourage them to examine any charts, graphs, or timelines in expository text to pique their curiosity.
- For primary students (kindergarten through grade three), use big books for the Picture Walk. Point out the important details and ask probing questions to stimulate interest in the material.
- A popular variation of this strategy involves dividing students into pairs, then asking them to do a Picture Walk with their partners and report back to the group about what they predict is happening in the story.

Concept Carousel

Description: Concept Carousel is a great strategy for introducing material with lots of factual information that requires critical thinking. Examples include introducing expository texts in the areas of science, social studies, world geography, and literary genres.

Procedure: Write passages from the text on large sheets of chart paper and post them around the room. Divide your students into groups of four and ask them to walk from chart to chart discussing the topic, sharing their thoughts, and asking questions about the material. Ask students to write their thoughts and questions on the chart below each passage as they move from chart to chart. Use the following guidelines to structure the activity.

- To set up the Concept Carousel, the teacher should select passages, facts, and interesting ideas from the text and write them on the chart paper. Pictures work well with younger children.
- Assign one group to start at each chart.
- Give each group a different-colored marker pen to write their thoughts and ideas with. The different colors distinguish input from each group.
- Each group should spend between two and five minutes at each chart, depending on the age of the students and the complexity of the material.
- The teacher should circulate between the groups, listening, questioning, and pointing out interesting information as the groups rotate.
- Use a timer with an audible cue to indicate when the time begins and ends at each chart. When the time ends at each station, ask students to freeze before releasing them to the next chart with a signal.
- Continue this procedure until all groups have visited every chart.
- When they return to their original chart, ask them to discuss what others have written and share all the thoughts with the whole group.
- Some teachers find it helpful to pose questions or statements under each passage at the top of each chart in a sentence-completion format to help students get started. Consider the following:

  "A question we have about this is . . ."
  "This makes us think of . . ."
  "Some causes/effects of this might be . . ."
  "We see some problems/advantages with this because . . ."
  "When we read this, we feel . . ."
  "This sounds/looks like . . ."

- You can generate a never-ending list of questions. Use the questions in the curriculum as a guide.
- Concept Carousel is an effective way to help students study for upcoming tests and exams. Generate questions that will help them study for the material and write those on the charts. This procedure gives students an opportunity to share what they already know and refer back to their notes and the text to recall what they may have forgotten.

Keeping Students Engaged Throughout the Lesson

There are a variety of effective strategies to keep students engaged throughout the lesson, but one of the most powerful and effective strategies is also one we rarely think about, namely, the way we call on and respond to students during instruction. How we handle this has a huge impact on the students' level of engagement during the current and subsequent lessons. We can turn them on or turn them off by the way we respond to their answers. Because this process has such a powerful impact, we should consider it one of our most important engagement strategies.

Teaching to Mastery

Description: The name fully describes this strategy. Teaching to Mastery is just that—teaching students until they master the subject matter. Each of these techniques holds students accountable for their learning and shows them they're capable of answering the question.

Don't let a student off the hook if they say, "I don't know." You'll lose that student and many others if you do.

Procedure:

- When you call on a student to give an answer, hold that student accountable for giving the answer. When we quickly move on to another student or ask the student to choose someone to help him or her, we convey little confidence in that student's ability to answer the question.
- Restate the question or ask the student to restate the question and think for a while before selecting someone else.
- Ask the student to "prove" the answer and find it in the text.
- Ask the student to pair up with a partner and discuss the question; then call on that same student again.
- Give the student the page number to look up the information. Give them the necessary time, and then get back to that student for the answer.

Let's illustrate how one teacher uses the Teaching to Mastery strategy with her class of fifth graders. Mrs. Carroll reviews material for an upcoming math test with her class. She asks the class to reduce the fraction $\frac{15}{20}$ to its lowest terms. She pulls a Popsicle stick with Kevin's name on it.

"Kevin, what did you come up with?" she asks. Kevin shrugs his shoulders.

"I didn't do it," he replies. "I forgot how." Mrs. Carroll knows that Kevin has been able to figure these problems out during his independent work, so she probes a little more.

"Okay," she says, "let's go through the process together." She writes $\frac{15}{20}$ on the board and says, "Kevin, do you remember the first thing we need to do?" Kevin hesitates, and then responds.

"I think we have to see if both of the numbers can be divided by another number," he says.

"You're right, Kevin. That's exactly what we need to do. Where should we start?" Kevin hesitates again. Mrs. Carroll asks, "Can each of these be divided by 2?" Kevin thinks for a moment.

"No, but they can be divided by 5," he replies.

"Right again, Kevin," says Mrs. Carroll. "Now, do you remember how to do it?"

Kevin remembers and solves the problem.

If Kevin had not remembered, Mrs. Carroll would have continued scaffolding for Kevin by asking if the numbers could be divided by 3, then 4, then 5, and working through the problem until Kevin completed it. If Mrs. Carroll had given up on Kevin and called on another student, Kevin would have lost the opportunity to work through the problem. Instead she held him accountable for his learning and helped him build skills and confidence at the same time.

Think/Pair/Share

Description: The teacher begins the activity by giving students some time to *think* about a topic. One or two silent minutes are appropriate. Students may write notes about their thoughts during this time. Then the students *pair* with a partner and discuss their thoughts. The activity concludes by asking the students to *share* their thoughts with the class.

Procedure: This activity helps students to generate ideas, express their ideas to others, and summarize their ideas with the class. Here's how it works.

- Assign students to partners. Be sure to assign students with learning disabilities, English-language learners, and other special needs students to students who are sensitive, encouraging, and willing to take the lead in the discussion if necessary.
- The teacher poses a question, scenario, or problem.
- Students are asked to *think* about the question silently for a specified amount of time.
- When the teacher provides the signal, students *pair* with their partner and discuss their thoughts and ideas. The teacher structures the activity with a timer. Then the students are asked to switch so their partner can share.

- Partners can ask questions to clarify or explain, but they may not disagree with their partner's thoughts or ideas.
- Next, the teacher calls on several students to *share* the most interesting or important information discussed in their pair. It's fun to ask what their partner thought and shared, a practice that encourages good listening. Many teachers find that kids don't really listen to their partner because they are too excited about having their turn to share.
- A variation to this strategy is to join one pair with another to make a group of four and then ask the group to share with the class.

Let's look at how Mr. Davis uses Think/Pair/Share to get the most out of a lesson with his class of second graders.

Mr. Davis directs a language arts lesson on the importance of individual action and character. His students have learned about Abraham Lincoln, Marie Curie, Jackie Robinson, Sally Ride, Martin Luther King, Jr., and other individuals who have made a difference in the lives of others. Mr. Davis writes a question on the board, then reads it aloud to his students.

"What characteristics made Sally Ride a hero in our history?" he asks. Then he announces, "We'll be doing Think/Pair/Share."

He gives the class one minute to think about the question silently, and then he directs them to pair up and discuss their thoughts for two minutes. Mr. Davis sets the timer and circulates around the class. He listens to their thoughts and comments on their ideas. When the timer goes off, Mr. Davis randomly calls on students to share what they discussed with their partner. After each pair shares, Mr. Davis explores the experiences of other students.

"How many of you talked about that same trait with your partner?" he asks.

A number of hands shoot up. "Who talked about something different?" he asks, to solicit other points of view. Several hands are in the air, and he selects one of those students to add a different perspective.

Mr. Davis and his students enjoy this strategy. Students learn from one another and have opportunities to share their thoughts with others. Mr. Davis's students know from experience that they will have an opportunity to share, so they don't disrupt or compete for the floor.

Numbered Heads Together

Description: The purpose of this engagement strategy is to provide students with an opportunity to actively participate in the lesson while sharing and interacting with others.

Procedure:

- Divide students into groups of four.
- Assign each student a number (1–4).
- The teacher decides the appropriate amount of time, which varies from activity to activity, then uses a signal to get the activity started.
- The teacher poses a question to the class and allows students sufficient time to think.
- After the teacher gives the signal, students discuss the topic until the group comes to agreement or the time elapses.
- The teacher randomly chooses a number among 1–4, using Popsicle sticks for random selection.
- Selected students stand and wait for the teacher to ask the question. Students should chorally respond to objective questions and answer subjective questions individually or write their answer on their paper. What should the teacher do if there is disagreement among students? The teacher should further clarify the question or clarify the correct response. The sentence-completion format helps younger students get started with written responses.

SOME TOPICS FOR NUMBERED HEADS TOGETHER

- Math: facts, word problems, geometric figures.
- English language arts: vocabulary word meanings, word origins, grammar, discussing components of literature (setting, plot, theme,

characters, etc.), describing characters' traits, determining the main idea, listing important facts and/or details.
- Beginning reading: rhyming words, letter sounds, spelling words, clapping syllables.
- Expository text (science, social studies): map skills, generating hypotheses, chapter questions, history timelines, test review.

Quick Write

Description: The purpose of this activity is to help students express themselves in writing without worrying about grammar or writing mechanics. This strategy helps students capture their thoughts on paper and overcome the anxiety and stress some students experience when asked to produce written work. During the Quick Write, there are no right or wrong answers. The goal is to help students get their thoughts down on paper. This strategy has endless possibilities.

Procedure: The following is just a sampling of many possible applications:

- Ask students to write about a topic for two to three minutes before they begin a lesson.
- Ask students to write their predictions before beginning a new chapter in a book.
- Ask students to summarize what they remember from a previous story or chapter.
- Ask students to describe how they feel about a character, incident, or event in a story.
- Ask students to describe the characters, plot, or setting in a story.

Whiteboards for Whole-Class Response and Practice

Description: Whiteboards are an excellent way for students to quickly practice and display their responses, particularly when working with math problems, vocabulary development, and spelling patterns.

There are many other applications. Whiteboards provide teachers with a quick and effective method of determining students' mastery level.

Procedure: Each student is given a whiteboard, dry-erase marker, and something to erase the whiteboard with. (Small pieces of cloth work well.)

- The teacher poses a problem to the class, and everyone works it out on their whiteboards.
- The students "hide" their boards until the teacher gives the signal, to add a little game-show suspense.
- The teacher says, "Show me," and students show their work.
- The teacher receives instant feedback regarding who understands the lesson and who doesn't.

Thumbs Up/Thumbs Down

Description: Thumbs Up/Thumbs Down is an effective strategy for communicating the silent signals of agreement or disagreement, thereby minimizing blurting out or disrupting. The strategy can be used repeatedly throughout the day for whole-class, small-group, or individualized instructional activities.

- The teacher poses a yes-or no, agree-or-disagree question to the class and asks for thumbs up or thumbs down. For example: "Show me thumbs up when you're ready," or "Thumbs up if you agree, down if you disagree," or "Thumbs up when you know the answer." The class responds in unison.
- This simple procedure is a calm and organized way for students to express their agreement or disagreement with others, and it helps moderate potentially disruptive conflict.

Response Cards

Description: Response Cards can be used for whole-class response to multiple-choice questions or for true/false questions and answers.

The teacher can quickly determine the students' level of mastery. This strategy can be combined with Think/Pair/Share and Numbered Heads Together. Response Cards are an effective starting point for discussions when answers don't match.

Procedure: Give each student a set of three-by-five cards with A, B, C, and D written on them.

- The teacher poses a multiple-choice question to the class, either on the overhead or whiteboard, from the textbook or study guide.
- The teacher asks students to answer the question by choosing the card that matches the letter of the correct answer.
- Students "hide" their answers until the teacher gives the signal to reveal them.
- When the teacher says, "Show me," students show their answers.

Making Learning Relevant Beyond the Lesson

When a lesson or unit of study is complete, students have a lot to remember if they are going to be successful on the test or exam. Many students have difficulty studying for exams. They don't know what to study, get bogged down with insignificant details, and some don't study at all. How can you help students prepare for tests and exams and have fun at the same time? That's what the following strategies will show you how to do.

Team Games

Description: Team games can be played on a computer screen, whiteboard, or overhead projector. The games are the typical ones students recognize from television such as Jeopardy and Who Wants to Be a Millionaire? or they can be board games such as Trivial Pursuit and Concentration. Ask your students what games they like, and you can adapt the following strategies to fit almost any game.

Jeopardy: This game works well with factual information that can be divided into categories. When the lesson is about stories or narrative, organize the pockets on the Jeopardy board to correspond to the various elements of the story (for example, plot, setting, characters, theme).

Procedure:
- Questions and/or answers are written on cards that are inserted into pockets on the Jeopardy board.
- The answers or questions are organized by level of difficulty. The higher the difficulty level, the more points or "imaginary money" the student earns.
- The board is organized into point values and categories or topics.
- Students from each team take turns choosing a topic and value, then attempt to provide an appropriate question or answer.
- The teacher, or game facilitator, is in charge of the Jeopardy board. The teacher reads the question or answer (either format works) and determines if the student's response is accurate.
- For a variation to this game, students may consult with their team for twenty or thirty seconds for half the point value.
- It's fun to include "Daily Doubles" into the game, a variation where students have to act out or draw a Venn diagram about a particular question.

NOTE: For students with ADD/ADHD or learning disabilities, limited-proficiency English-language learners, or those with other learning issues, there is no "teacher rule" that states that the question on the card must be the question presented to the student. It's okay to present the student with an answer that must be "proven" by looking it up in the text, or to present the question as a team question. The goal is to hook kids into learning and to provide them with opportunities to be successful. When this happens, they'll be engaged and want to learn.

FIGURE 3.2

Topic	Topic	Topic	Topic	Topic
100	100	100	100	100
200	200	200	200	200
300	300	300	300	300
500	500	500	500	500

Who Wants to Be a Millionaire?

Procedure: This engagement strategy is a variation of the popular game show. Using fake money from a Monopoly game adds to the excitement and drama. Here's the format we recommend.

- Write questions on cards in order of progressive difficulty, with each question being worth higher points or money (similar to the real *Jeopardy!*).
- Divide the class into teams.
- Several formats work. The teacher can choose one student at a time to be "the contestant" and everyone else writes down their responses to each question, or students may play as a team. Either way, students who are not given the question should still write down their answer, or look the answer up in their books, notes, or other material.

- Questions may be provided in a multiple-choice format or as short-answer questions. The teacher decides. You get to write the rules.
- No one except the teacher should know the actual question on the question card. Use this to your advantage and help your struggling or at-risk students to be successful and enjoy the game.

Teachers can save time and expand the learning experience by involving students in creating the questions and the answers. Teach them how to use the bold titles in their textbooks and turn them into questions. Then search for the answers together in that section of the textbook. Even second graders can learn to ask and answer questions from their texts. It's always a nice surprise to include some of their questions on a classroom quiz or test.

Chapter Summary

Effective student engagement takes the teaching-and-learning process to the next higher level and is intrinsically rewarding for all. When students are engaged and turned on to learning, we don't need to rely as heavily on other forms of classroom management. Students want to get on board for the ride because the ride is fun. It feels like an adventure.

In this chapter, we examined a variety of practical, effective, and easy-to-use strategies for engaging students during the three phases of instruction. You learned strategies for hooking your students into the lesson, strategies for engaging your students throughout the lesson, and strategies for making learning relevant beyond the lesson. Mix and match the strategies if you like and add to your repertoire as you go. The engagement strategies in this chapter will help you find that spark of interest in your learners and keep it glowing throughout the year.

4

PAT: A Motivational Gift That Keeps on Giving

If there was a motivational tool that was easy to use, enjoyable for you and your students, and kept your students on task and cooperating throughout the full instructional day, would you use it? Of course. Most teachers would pay handsomely for such a tool. Well, here's the good news: The tool is available, and it's absolutely free! It's called PAT, or Preferred Activity Time, and you can use it with students at all grade levels. Before you begin thinking "I don't have any time to waste" or "I can't afford to give my students any *free* time," rest assured that PAT is designed to *save* you instructional time. The games and activities they earn for their cooperation are academic in nature and standards-based.

PAT is hardly a newcomer on the educational scene. The practice has been around a long time, and there are many variations to the basic model. One of the most thorough descriptions of PAT and its many variations is provided in Fredric Jones's excellent book *Positive Classroom Discipline*.

PAT is a group incentive system that uses the most valuable commodity in the instructional day—time—as the treasured resource. Students want it and will work hard for it, and you'll be happy to give it away when they do. PAT is win-win for everybody.

The genius of PAT is that accountability and team building are built-in components of the system. Your students, not you, are responsible for how they use their class time. They can earn bonus time for on-task behavior or incur penalties for off-task behavior. The choice is theirs. The more they cooperate, the more rewards they share and enjoy. Your job is simply to give PAT away as a group reward for on-task behavior, keep track of time earned or lost, and structure the PAT sessions. Consider the following.

It's Monday morning in December. The eight o'clock bell rings, and students begin to file into Mrs. Fahey's sixth-grade class. Her class is beginning to mature, but they did not begin the year this way. They take their seats and settle down. No time is wasted. Mrs. Fahey looks around the class and smiles. She gives everyone a warm "Thank you and good morning." Then she walks over to the blackboard and records "one minute" under the bonus column of her PAT chart. Mrs. Fahey's first act each day is to reward her students with a PAT bonus for entering the classroom appropriately, settling down, and getting ready for instruction.

In the top right corner of Mrs. Fahey's blackboard is a simple chart for recording PAT with one horizontal column and two vertical columns below that (see Figure 4.1). The horizontal column reads "Time in the bank" and reflects the ten-minute PAT gift Mrs. Fahey makes to her class at the beginning of each week. The two vertical columns below are labeled with a plus sign and a minus sign for recording bonus time and penalties.

After taking attendance and lunch count, Mrs. Fahey asks her class to take out their books and finish the writing exercise they started the previous day. While her students work at their desks, Mrs. Fahey roves around the classroom to check on their progress and assist anyone who needs help. As students finish the assignment, the classroom begins to get loud and distracting.

"How many think it's too loud in here?" asks Mrs. Fahey with her stopwatch in her hand. Several students raise their hands. The class quiets down. No penalty time is deducted. A short time later, Mrs. Fahey notices Ashley, one of her slower learners, trying hard to finish up on time.

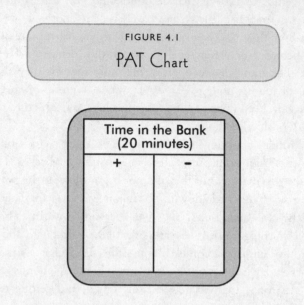

FIGURE 4.1

PAT Chart

"Good job, Ashley!" says Mrs. Fahey. "I really appreciate your hard work." She walks over to the blackboard and enters thirty seconds under the bonus column. As she does, she overhears several students whisper thanks to Ashley. She feels good about her contribution, and so does everyone else.

Later that morning, the class divides into cooperative work groups. Each group is supposed to pick a topic and prepare a presentation on some aspect of ancient Egypt. All the groups are focused and working well except for one. When Mrs. Fahey investigates, she sees Stefan poking and annoying several members of his work group.

"Take your book and your worksheet to the back table, Stefan," says Mrs. Fahey matter-of-factly. She sets her timer and sends Stefan for a ten-minute time-out. No PAT penalties or time deductions are given. Why not?

PAT is intended to support your limit-setting practices by rewarding on-task behavior and by discouraging off-task behavior. The system is not intended to replace your limit-setting practices. Disruption and attention-seeking behavior should be handled like any other classroom discipline problem, with the appropriate limit-setting procedure. In this case, it's a time-out.

After lunch recess, while the class works on their math worksheets, the principal announces over the intercom the results of a recent student body election. The announcement cuts nearly ten minutes from Mrs. Fahey's thirty-minute lesson plan. "They'll have to work very fast to finish up on time," she thinks. How do you get students to hurry rather than dawdle? She offers the class a hurry-up time bonus if they finish in the next ten minutes. They scramble to get it done.

"Thank you," she says when the activity is complete. She walks to the blackboard and adds two and a half minutes to the bonus column. "That's one lesson I won't have to teach over again," she says to herself.

Near the end of the day, while the class is supposed to be working at their seats on a science lesson, Mrs. Fahey notices Saul fumbling through his backpack at the back of the classroom. Mrs. Fahey holds up her stopwatch in the ready position.

"I was out of paper," Saul pleads, "and I still can't find a pencil." Mrs. Fahey looks at Saul patiently, clicks her stopwatch, and then directs a question to the class in a very matter-of-fact tone.

"Can anyone help Saul find a pencil?" About ten hands shoot up in the air. Saul collects the pencil, and Mrs. Fahey clicks off her stopwatch. She walks to the board and adds twenty-two seconds to the penalty column.

As the class lines up to leave at the end of the day, Mrs. Fahey passes out permission slips for an upcoming field trip and makes an announcement. "The sooner they're all returned, the more bonus time you'll earn."

On Fridays, Mrs. Fahey sets aside time for her class to enjoy the PAT they've earned. She adds the time bonuses to the ten-minute gift on Monday and deducts the penalties. Voilà! What's left is for the class to spend and use at that time or save and carry over into the following week for something even more fun.

During the first week, Mrs. Fahey and her students brainstorm a list of PAT activities, which can be enjoyed on an individual or whole-group basis. This year's list includes Jeopardy, Who Wants to be a Millionaire?,

Concentration, and Baseball, among others. Mrs. Fahey knows that not all students can handle the demands of team games and whole-class activities, so she also provides some individual activities as a backup. She maintains a PAT cabinet in her classroom loaded with magazines, comic books, books on sketching and cartooning, and board games such as Apples to Apples, Uno, chess, Monopoly, Boggle, checkers, Stratego, Battleship, and Scrabble. What the students choose to do is up to them, but each student must be involved in something.

Mrs. Fahey uses three simple guidelines to determine which activities make it on the "approved list for PAT" in her classroom. First, the activity must be fun and something her students really want. Second, the activity must be standards-based and involve thinking and learning. Third, the activity must be acceptable to both students and the teacher. Then they vote on them. Games and activities can be added or deleted as needed.

How PAT Is Supposed to Be Used

Before we describe how to use PAT, we should clarify what PAT is not. PAT is not time for the teacher to grade papers, time for students to "kick back," free time, recess, PE, art, computer time, or any other privilege that has simply been renamed. Most important, PAT is not a waste of instructional time. When the procedure is carried out correctly, it's exactly the opposite. PAT buys you time for instruction and learning.

So, what is PAT? PAT serves many purposes. It's an incentive system for rewarding students for cooperation, on-task behavior, good efforts, respect, and responsibility. It's a tool for teaching and rewarding smooth transitions, returning homework and permission slips, and getting your dawdlers and procrastinators to hurry up. Best of all, PAT is time for the students and teacher to have some fun together and build a sense of community in the classroom. Teachers get through their lessons. Students earn preferred time to enjoy themselves. What a great way to mix work and play in an academic way.

How PAT Works

PAT is simple to set up, easy to carry out, and can be easily adapted to any grade level. For kindergarten and first graders, we recommend the Teacher-Student Game as an effective version of PAT. Students earn tally marks or points, rather than time. We'll cover this variation of PAT in more detail later in the chapter. Let's begin by looking at how PAT works with grades two through six.

PAT begins with a gift that is offered without any strings attached. It's in the bank, free and clear. How much time should you give? This depends on the age and maturity level of your students. At the primary level (grades two and three), it's common to start off with a five-minute gift of PAT. At the intermediate level (grades four through six), it's common to start off with a ten-minute gift of PAT. Mature classes like Mrs. Fahey's do fine with one PAT a week. Less mature students often benefit from a more frequent reinforcement schedule, such as two times a week. Frequency varies from class to class depending upon maturity.

Once the gift of PAT has been made, the teacher's job is to catch students being responsible and on task and reward them with bonus points, or to observe them wasting time and being off task and give

time penalties. The combination of time bonuses plus time penalties adds power and effectiveness to this motivational system. Students control the penalties by their decisions to cooperate or not cooperate. The teacher just keeps track of time. Time bonuses are managed by the teacher, who has the enviable job of catching students being good and rewarding them for it. Generosity on the teacher's part works to everyone's advantage. Students are happy because they have more time for fun. Teachers are happy because lessons get completed and instructional time is used wisely.

AWARDING BONUSES

Bonuses come in several forms: unexpected bonuses, hurry-up bonuses, and automatic bonuses. Let's look at each. Unexpected bonuses are the most fun to give. Anytime you catch a student, a group of students, or the whole class being responsible, on task, or making a special effort to cooperate, you're in a position to reward them with an unexpected bonus. Even small awards of ten, fifteen, or twenty seconds, offered generously, can have a big impact. Everyone benefits. In our earlier example, Mrs. Fahey did this very effectively when she awarded the class thirty seconds of bonus time for Ashley's good efforts. The beauty of the system is that you can reward the class with time for any behavior you wish to encourage, whether whole-class, individual, or small group.

Hurry-up bonuses are awarded when you need your students to hustle and complete assigned work in a timely manner. Mrs. Fahey awarded her class a hurry-up bonus after her lesson was interrupted by an announcement from the office. She needed her kids to hustle. They did.

Either hurry-up or automatic bonuses are given for handling important transitions in the day, such as entering or exiting the class properly, shifting from large-group instruction to independent seatwork, or cooperating when resource staff come into the classroom. Since it's nearly impossible to determine how much time is saved by a smooth transition, teachers must select an amount of time to award and give that amount consistently. If you recall, Mrs. Fahey gave her students an automatic bonus of one minute for arriving promptly and being in their seats after the first morning bell. PAT bonuses are an excellent way to improve transitions during the day, the times when fooling around and off-task behavior are most likely to occur.

Let's look at how one teacher uses a hurry-up bonus to improve transitions. When Mrs. Ladd wants her second-grade students to hurry up or shift into a higher gear, she offers them a bonus by challenging them to beat the timer. This time she wants her students to move from their desks to the carpet to begin a phonics lesson, a transition that potentially could eat up a lot of time. They have to put away their math books, manipulatives, and folders, then move to the carpet. Mrs. Ladd decides to offer them a hurry-up bonus challenge.

"Please stop and listen," she announces. Her students are well trained. They follow her directions immediately. "I'm going to give you some instructions, then I'm going to set the timer for you to complete them. Show me a thumbs-up if you're listening and ready." All thumbs go up.

"Good job," says Mrs. Ladd. "I'm going to ask you to do three things. First, put away your math books." She writes "math books" on the board. "Next, quickly and quietly, put away all of your manipulatives." She writes "manipulatives" on the board. "Finally, silently walk to the carpet and sit down." She writes "carpet" on the board. Then she pauses.

"Raise your hand if you can tell the class all three of the directions you need to follow," says Mrs. Ladd. Most students raise their hands. Mrs. Ladd calls on Andrea.

"Andrea, please tell the class what we're going to do," says Mrs. Ladd. "If you don't remember, you can look at the board for a clue." Andrea repeats the instructions for the class.

"Good," exclaims Mrs. Ladd. "You have two minutes to put everything away and sit on the carpet. Go." The students work quickly and quietly. Mrs. Ladd offers several compliments to individuals and groups of students for their good efforts. As the last student sits down on the carpet, Mrs. Ladd stops her timer.

"Wow!" she says. "You guys are awesome! That only took you a minute and twenty seconds. You earned forty seconds of PAT. Because you worked extra hard and many of you helped one another to get the jobs done, I'm going to give you a full minute. Good job!" Mrs. Ladd records one minute on the positive side of the PAT chart. Then she turns to her class and says, "Everyone hold up your right hand. Give yourselves a pat on the back. We are really getting good with transitions." The students are proud of their accomplishment. They are ready for the next lesson.

RECORDING PENALTIES

Penalties serve an accountability function in the PAT group incentive system by holding students responsible for their off-task behavior. Penalties should be used judiciously. Teachers who award penalties in a blaming manner or assign excessive time penalties for minor off-task behaviors defeat the positive nature of PAT and risk turning it into an exercise in coercion. We recommend that you maintain a neutral tone and use a stopwatch or timer to record time penalties for off-task behavior to the second. The process is fair, accurate, and leads to positive learning, not resentment. Your students will perceive penalties for what they are, a logical consequence for their off-task or uncooperative behavior. When the class does incur penalties, you should always be on the lookout for bonus opportunities to offset the loss and keep the system positive.

Now let's consider another scenario to the earlier example in Mrs. Ladd's class. This time, when Mrs. Ladd offers her class the hurry-up bonus challenge, they dawdle past the allotted two minutes and take an additional seventeen seconds. What should she do? She should quietly walk to the board and record seventeen seconds on the penalty side of the PAT chart. She simply records the time. No shaming, blaming, criticizing, or sarcastic comments. The students know the drill. There is no need for any drama on the part of the teacher. When we threaten students with further loss of time, we risk damaging the positive nature of the incentive system. Avoid comments such as "At this rate, you're not going to have any time this week" or "If you don't get this completed in two minutes, I'm taking time from PAT."

PAT should be a positive experience for all. Maintain a positive tone throughout the process. When giving bonus time, be approving and generous. When recording penalties, do so without comment or negative tone.

During our workshops, we sometimes hear comments such as "PAT isn't working. The kids don't seem to care about losing time." When we follow up and observe how the teachers use PAT, we often notice that it is done punitively with negative undertones, threats, or admonishments.

A typical punitive interpretation of PAT is when the teacher starts off each week with a thirty-minute bonus, then tries to catch students being off task and deducts time increments each time this happens. PAT loses its positive motivational effect when used in this manner. It's not the PAT system that fails; it's the way it's carried out by the teacher.

PAT DURING SMALL-GROUP AND DIFFERENTIATED INSTRUCTION

PAT is particularly effective during small-group and differentiated in-struction. Let's see how Mrs. Woods does this with her fourth-grade class. Mrs. Woods divides her students into three groups and announces that she will work with each group for fifteen minutes, then rotate groups. She allocates forty-five minutes for the activity. She expects all other students to be working independently at their desks. She begins by reviewing the procedure with her students.

"While I'm working with the groups at the back, I will not be available to the rest of the class unless there's an emergency," she begins. "You can earn three minutes—that's one minute for each of the groups—by not interrupting me. If I need to interrupt my lesson because you're off task or goofing around, you will lose the amount of time it takes me to deal with the situation plus the one minute the group would earn by not interrupt-ing. You can also earn bonus time for cooperating, working hard, respect-ing my time, and for quick and quiet transitions. Are there any questions before we get started?" No one raises a hand. "I'll take questions between rotations. You may ask someone at your group for help if you need it. Group two, please bring your materials and meet me at the back table." The group quietly walks to the table to join Mrs. Woods.

As the lesson proceeds, Mrs. Woods notices how well the rest of the class works during her time with the group. "Miguel," she says, "will you please go put ten seconds on the positive side of our PAT chart? Everyone is working hard. Thank you, class."

During the transition between the groups, however, the class becomes noisy. Mrs. Woods holds up her timer and starts it, but doesn't say a word. Some students notice and begin telling others to quiet down. Within twelve seconds the class is quiet. Mrs. Woods walks to the board and enters twelve seconds on the penalty side of the PAT chart.

Then she announces the next rotation. "Group one, please quietly meet me at the back table." And so it goes for the final group. By the time the final rotation is finished, the class has earned three minutes for respecting Mrs. Woods's time, twenty seconds for cooperating and working hard, and an additional twenty seconds for smooth transitions. They lost twelve seconds because of the noisy transition between the first and second group. The class earned a total of three minutes and forty seconds. Mrs. Woods knows that the amount of instructional time saved is priceless.

The Teacher-Student Game

Younger students, in kindergarten through first grade, as well as less mature second graders, require a more frequent reinforcement schedule to get the benefits PAT has to offer. The Teacher-Student Game is an effective variation on the PAT theme that provides multiple PAT experiences a week, or even a couple of times each day. Many teachers report that a point system is a simpler and more effective method of awarding and recording cooperative behavior for younger students who have not mastered the concept of time. Here's how the procedure works.

When students cooperate during a lesson or do things you wish to encourage, reward them with points in the form of tally marks on the board. Rather than using a timer, teachers may want to count backward from 10 to 1 to see if students can complete a task within the allotted time. When students blurt out during instruction, leave their seats, dawdle, disrupt, or distract others, the teacher receives a point.

Be generous when giving points. They are only points, but students will work hard to earn them. The idea is to reward the positive behaviors you want students to demonstrate and use consequences and give yourself a point when students misbehave. Look for opportunities to acknowledge students who behave acceptably and award points to the group. You will probably find yourself saying something like "Wow, I really like how quickly you got ready. I'm going to give you two points for that," or "Thank you for raising a quiet hand; that's worth a point." Points are determined by the teacher and awarded by the teacher. Students are not allowed to ask for points.

If students earn more points than the teacher at the end of the lesson, which is the idea, they earn a short preferred activity. Games or activities that quickly review instructional concepts are powerful ways to accelerate learning. Popular activities are singing songs, learning parts of a dance, Hangman, Head-Shoulders-Knees-and-Toes, Simon Says, Tony Chestnut, and Around the World with letter cards. The possibilities are endless. Movement music activities are another favorite, and the Teacher-Student Game is the perfect time to use it. The kids can use a physical break after extended periods of sitting and concentrating. You'll enjoy it, too. Let's look at how one teacher introduces the game to her class.

"Boys and girls, we're going to play a game called the Teacher-Student Game," Ms. Gooding announces. "Whenever I see you being responsible, respectful, cooperating, or working hard, I'll give you points on the chart. Your points will be by the *S* for students. If you play around, talk to each other, forget to raise your hand, or distract your neighbors, I'll get points. It's not okay for anyone to take the learning away from anyone else. When that happens, I get points. Who can tell me some things that might happen that would cause me to get points?"

The children share their ideas, and Ms. Gooding adds a few more of her own ideas. "Is it okay to put your hands or feet on anyone in the group?" asks Ms. Gooding. The students give a silent signal for "no."

"That's right," says Ms. Gooding. "When that happens, I get a point and the one putting their hands or feet on others will have a time-out. Is it okay to call out the answer without raising your hand?" she asks. Again the students give the silent signal for "no."

"Right again," she says. "If that happens, I get a point and that student will get a time-out. Show me what you should do if you want to say something." The students raise their hands.

"Excellent!" says Ms. Gooding, as she puts two tally marks in the students' row. "Now, who can tell me the things that will earn you points?" Several hands go up to share.

"Wow, that's another point for you. You already know what to do. I think you're going to earn a lot of points," Ms. Gooding says proudly. She lets the students share the ideas they have about how to earn points. They are already on their way to a successful outcome.

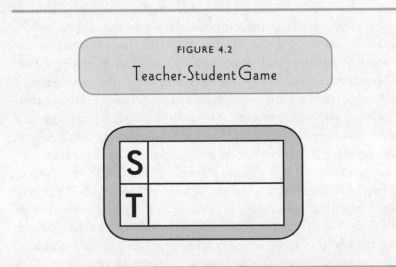

FIGURE 4.2

Teacher-Student Game

Introducing PAT to the Students

PAT should be introduced on the first day of school, or at least during the first week, but it's never too late to introduce it any time during the year. Mrs. Woods gives a good example of introducing PAT to her fifth graders.

It's the first day of school. Mrs. Woods has gone over the rules, procedures, and schedule with her class. Now it's time to share the fun part.

"How many of you have ever heard of Preferred Activity Time, or PAT?" she asks. Some hands go up. Mrs. Woods knows that some teachers interpret PAT as "free time," "extra time to get papers graded," or "extra recess." Mrs. Woods wants to clarify any misconceptions about the way PAT will be run in her class.

"I'm going to tell you how I do it in this classroom," she begins. "I'm sure you'll enjoy it. Our school days are so full of working on standards and getting through the curriculum that we rarely have time to play together or really get to know one another. I will know you as my students, and you will know me as your teacher, of course, but we won't really know much about each other beyond that. I want to know who you really are, what you really like, what your dreams and goals are. Also, I want to share about myself. PAT will provide us all with more time to play together and have fun together."

Then she explains how PAT works. "Each week, I'll give you ten minutes. You don't have to earn them. I'll just give them to you so we can have some fun. That doesn't sound like very much time, but you will have plenty of opportunities to add time to that ten minutes by cooperating, being respectful, working efficiently, and being on task. You can also lose time for being off task, unprepared, or uncooperative."

Next, she introduces the rewards. "I have lots of games that I'll be sharing with you that my previous students really enjoyed. Sometimes we'll do a special craft project like sculpting or an art project with watercolors or charcoal. Other times, we'll play board games in teams." She shows them the games in her cabinet.

"Most of the time we'll play games together that I'm sure you'll enjoy," she continues. "I have a Jeopardy board that my students really enjoyed last year. How many of you have seen the game show *Who Wants to Be a Millionaire?*" Hands go up.

"Well, I have a version of that game that I'll play with you, too," she says. "We'll play baseball in the classroom with questions that earn runs. We'll enjoy music and other activities together as well. It's time that we'll all look forward to." She asks her students if this sounds like something they think they'll enjoy. They say yes.

To get things started, Mrs. Woods announces, "Right now I'm going to break you into groups of four and provide your group with two pieces of paper. On the first sheet you'll write down all the off-task behaviors you can think of. We'll review those, and then we'll write down all of the on-task behaviors you can think of. Don't write anything until I tell you to."

Mrs. Woods has asked her class to prepare a list of off-task behaviors first, then the on-task behaviors. This is strategic. She wants the class to finish the activity with a clear understanding of on-task behaviors. Students tend to get silly when they prepare lists of off-task behaviors.

Next, she breaks the students into groups and provides each group with two pieces of paper. "Okay," she says, "choose someone in your group to be the recorder. You have ten seconds to do that. Go." She runs her timer for ten seconds. The recorders raise their hands.

"Everyone needs to participate by sharing his or her ideas," she adds. "You have two minutes to write down all the off-task behaviors you can think of. When the timer goes off, you need to stop talking, stop writing, and give me your full attention. Thumbs up if you're ready. Go."

The students write for two minutes. The room gets a little loud with laughter and silliness. Remember, they are writing about *off-task* behavior. When the timer goes off, Mrs. Woods asks each group to choose a reporter. She gives them ten seconds to do so. She directs each group to identify their three most off-task behaviors and put a star next to them.

"These are the behaviors the reporters will share with the class," says Mrs. Woods. She calls on the reporters one by one to share their top three behaviors and asks the other reporters if they had the same ideas. Mrs. Woods records the behaviors on a large piece of chart paper as the students report them. Mrs. Woods points to the list.

"These behaviors are what will cause you to lose PAT," she says.

Next, Mrs. Woods asks her students to spend two minutes writing down all of the on-task, cooperative, and respectful behaviors they can think of. When the timer goes off, the students share their ideas, and Mrs. Woods writes them on a separate chart.

"These are the behaviors that will help you earn PAT," she says. She expresses her confidence that the students will be able to earn a lot of PAT throughout the week. She immediately gives them the opportunity to earn some time.

"Let me show you how this works," she says. "I'm going to give you three minutes to quickly and quietly choose someone from your team to bring the two pages of ideas up to the front table and place them in this basket. Put everything else away, and show me that you're ready to learn. Don't do anything until I say 'Go.' Give me a thumbs-up if you're ready to show me how you can earn PAT." All thumbs go up.

Mrs. Woods gets her timer ready and gives the students the signal to begin. They complete the tasks quickly and quietly with one minute and fifteen seconds to spare.

"You're awesome!" she exclaims. "You saved a minute and fifteen seconds. I'm going to give you two minutes back this time. This is what I expect from you from now on."

The Teacher's Role

Teachers have three primary duties in the PAT incentive system: giving PAT, recording PAT, and structuring PAT for the enjoyment of all. The role of giver is fairly straightforward. The teacher makes an initial gift of PAT to the class at the beginning of the instructional day or week, depending on the age and maturity of the students. The initial gift represents a "good-faith investment" in cooperation.

The role of recorder requires strict attention to accuracy. It's essential that you keep an accurate record of time awarded for bonuses and time consumed by penalties lest you arouse protests, arguments, and complaints of unfairness. The credibility of the entire PAT system depends on it. When teachers are lax in this area, they invite testing, challenges, and bargaining for time. PAT is not *Let's Make a Deal*. It's based on behavior and responsible use of time.

What's the best way to record time accurately? Use a stopwatch or a timer. They don't lie. They're not arbitrary or biased. The practice is beyond reproach. When your students see you hold up your stopwatch or timer and hear it click, they know that they're losing time. There's no point in arguing or debating. The clock is running.

Once time is recorded, it should be entered on the PAT chart on the blackboard for all to see. A public record demonstrates your concern for fairness and accuracy and informs your students about where they stand at all times. Don't keep the total running on your timer or stopwatch. Enter the time on the board immediately after you stop the timer or stopwatch. Offer your students many opportunities throughout the day to earn time. The students need to see the payoff for their efforts. Remember, you are saving instructional time, not wasting it. The games and activities are academic in nature and therefore instructional. You can't lose.

The final duty of the teacher is to structure the actual PAT session for the enjoyment of all. How you structure your PAT sessions is limited only by your imagination and creativity. The key point to remember is to make it fun so your students will look forward to it and work hard for it. To get started, develop a list of individual or small-group activities. Then consult with your colleagues and develop a list of fun large-group learning activities that some or all of your students can share. You may want to take a tip from Mrs. Fahey and hold a brainstorming session with your students to develop a list of individual and whole-group activities for PAT. Students and the teacher should agree on the suitability of an activity before it makes it onto the approved list of PAT activities.

How often should your students receive PAT sessions? This depends on their age and maturity level. Younger students are very concrete learners, requiring more frequent reinforcement to learn the lessons PAT is designed to teach. Older students are less concrete and need less frequent reinforcement. For students (kindergarten through grade two), two PAT sessions daily—one at the end of the morning, the other at the end of the afternoon—is a common practice. Third and fourth graders usually do fine with one PAT daily. Fifth graders, sixth graders, and middle school and high school students usually do fine with one PAT weekly. These frequency levels are only guidelines. You may want to increase or decrease them based on the maturity of your students.

The Students' Role

All students confront the same set of choices. They can cooperate, use their time wisely, and watch their time bonuses accumulate, or they can dawdle, waste time, and watch their PAT disappear with penalties. The choice is theirs, but they cannot avoid being accountable for their actions because the time they earn or lose belongs to them as well as to the whole class. Everyone shares equally in the rewards and penalties. Students who goof off and waste time do not have an appreciative audience.

What You Should Expect

When you first introduce the PAT system to your class, you may encounter suspicion or reluctance among some of your students. "This sounds too good to be true," they say to themselves. "What's the catch?" Some will suspect PAT is just another cleverly packaged attempt to manipulate and control students to do more work. Some will scoff at it and reject it before they even try it. That's okay. Encourage them to give it a month and check it out. They'll change their thinking when they see how it works. Even selfish students who are willing to waste PAT at the group's expense will discover that more PAT is better than less PAT. Give them some time to let the lesson sink in.

Some students may try to set your PAT system up to fail. It's important to try to find out why. Don't make assumptions about a student's intentions. Talk with him or her and see if you can determine what's going on. Some students come from situations where they have failed to make good connections with others and don't do well in large-group activities. Some have emotional issues that prevent them from being a part of a group.

When you notice reluctance, address the issue individually with the student. Point out your observation and encourage them to join the activity if they choose. You might begin with a comment such as "I notice that each time I offer the class an opportunity to earn time, you seem to purposely try to make the class lose time. It's okay if you don't want to be a part of PAT; that means earning it or losing it as well as enjoying the benefits from it. You can choose not to be. But I won't allow anyone to take the opportunity away from those who want it."

If you know that the student has a developmental disorder that prevents him or her from being successful in large-group activities, offer them an individual activity and encourage them to take part in the group activities in small doses.

Some students want to exert control over the situation and set PAT up to fail. Don't allow it. Tell them they will not be any part of PAT, either earning, losing, or participating in the time, but that all of the classroom rules and consequences will still apply to them. Tell them that if they decide to be part of the process, they are welcome to join the class.

Students must agree to be part of the PAT process before they can share in the rewards. If Friday comes and they suddenly decide they want to play with the class during PAT, but have not chosen to be part of earning the time, they must wait until the following week. You can say something like "I'm pleased that you are choosing to be part of PAT. I think you'll enjoy it. However, that time will begin for you next week, when you are part of earning it. Today you have an assignment to work on during PAT."

As your class adapts to this new motivational system, you should begin to notice some curious things happening. First, your students will begin policing one another, reducing your need for limit setting. This translates into smoother transitions, more time for teaching, and less time spent with guidance and discipline. When students are off task or fooling around, you'll probably hear their classmates say, "Hey, knock it off. We're gonna lose PAT."

Second, you'll notice that your class works better as a group. Team building is a natural outcome of the PAT group incentive system. The system teaches students the benefits of cooperation and responsibility.

Once they realize that more cooperation and more responsibility mean more PAT, they'll be happy to cooperate, and they'll become better team players in the process.

Third, you'll notice that the tone and mood of your classroom is more positive. Sharing fun with your students on a regular basis provides a great foundation for strong, positive teacher-student relationships as well as positive student-student relationships. Your students will look forward to their PAT sessions, and so will you.

Chapter Summary

PAT is a group incentive system that holds students accountable for how they use their time. Time is the medium of exchange. It serves as an incentive, a reward, and a logical consequence for off-task behavior. But most important, PAT teaches students how to cooperate, be responsible, and use their time wisely.

PAT is win-win for everyone. Students want it and will work hard to get it when they can have fun with it. Teachers enjoy more time for teaching and learning, less time spent on limit setting, as well as smoother transitions, better cooperation, better relationships, and better achievement. PAT truly is a gift that keeps on giving.

How Students Learn Your Rules

Each day when it's time to line up for recess, Anthony pushes and shoves his way to the front of the line. Then when the bell rings, he sprints down the hallway, sometimes crashing into others, in an attempt to be first to arrive at the tetherball poles.

"I've told him over and over again that it's not okay to push in line or run down the hallway," complains his frustrated teacher, "but he does it day after day. I've explained how dangerous his behavior is. I've even asked his parents to talk to him. Nothing seems to help. I'm beginning to think he has some type of learning problem."

Anthony's teacher believes she is teaching a rule, but Anthony is not learning the rule she is trying to teach. This chapter will show you why. You'll discover how children learn your rules and why the teaching-and-learning process sometimes breaks down. By the time you finish this chapter, you'll be a step closer to teaching your rules in the clearest and most understandable way. Let's look at how Christi's teacher does it.

Christi, age four, pretends to cook breakfast in the miniature kitchen in her preschool room. Her friend Beth sits at a small table waiting to be served.

"Would you like some eggs?" asks Christi.

"Yes, please," replies Beth. Christi pretends to scoop the eggs onto a plastic plate, but the pan slips from her hand and falls into Beth's lap. Both girls laugh. Things start to get silly.

"You spilled eggs all over me!" says Beth, still laughing. She grabs her cup and pretends to pour juice over Christi's head. Both laugh. Things get even sillier. Christi picks up a plastic toaster and swings it over her head by the cord. She nearly hits Beth in the head.

"Put the toaster down, Christi," says her teacher matter-of-factly. "You can play with it the right way, or I'll have to put it away."

Christi hears the words, but she's very excited. She continues to swing the toaster. Her teacher reaches over and takes the toaster away. "You can play with it later this afternoon," she says, "if you play with it the right way."

Christi is learning her teacher's rules about using the play items in the classroom. The teacher may need to repeat this lesson before she masters the rule, but the teacher's methods will certainly lead to the desired outcome.

Christi's teacher is teaching her rules effectively. Her words say stop, and her actions convey the same message when she takes the toaster away. When our words are consistent with our actions, we don't need a lot of words or harsh consequences to get our message across. Our message is clear, and so is the rule behind it.

Why Teaching and Learning Break Down

Research by the Swiss psychologist Jean Piaget on children's intellectual development and Lawrence Kohlberg on children's moral development has provided a wealth of information about how children learn rules and form beliefs about behavior. Based on this research, we know that children's thinking and learning is qualitatively different from that of adults. Children think and learn concretely. For younger children, immediate sensory experience plays a greater role in shaping their reality than for adolescents or adults.

What does this mean to teachers in the classroom? It means that children's beliefs are largely determined by what they experience with their senses. What they see, hear, touch, and feel determines how they think things are. Their perceptions and beliefs about how the world works are based primarily on their concrete experiences.

Piaget's findings have important implications for how we go about teaching our rules to children. We do this in two basic ways: with our words and with our actions. Both teach a lesson, but only our actions are concrete. Actions, not words, define our rules.

How do most teachers teach their rules at the beginning of the year? They stand in front of the classroom and announce them, and many believe this should be enough. But words are abstract, not concrete. The teaching process is incomplete.

For example, if I announce, "We don't wear hats in the classroom," but each day several of my students wear them and nothing happens, what is the rule they learn from their concrete experience? Of course, it's really okay to wear hats in the classroom.

If, on the other hand, I take the hat away and return it at the end of the week each time one of my students wears it in the classroom, my students and I will probably share the same beliefs about my rule. They will know that I mean what I say.

When our words match our actions consistently, children learn to take our words seriously and to recognize the rules behind them. When our words do not match our actions, however, children learn to ignore our words and to base their beliefs on what they experience. In effect, we are teaching two rules: a rule in theory and a rule in practice.

This essential miscommunication is the source of most breakdowns in the teaching-and-learning process, and most teachers are not even aware that it's happening. They continue to teach their rules with words while their children learn by actions. This is what is happening to Anthony and his teacher in our opening example, and this is what is taking place in many classrooms throughout the country.

Although Piaget's and Kohlberg's research has been around since the 1970s, schools have been slow to incorporate these findings into guidance and discipline practices in the classroom. Many schools continue to use simplistic, outdated, and ineffective production-line discipline approaches that violate learning theory and well-established principles of child development. Writing students' names on the board under the frown or smile face, making students pull color behavior cards, making them write sentences or pick up trash, or asking parents to spend a day with their child in the classroom are just a few of the many examples of outdated and ineffective methods. We know what works. Isn't it time we started teaching our rules the way students really learn?

Why Limits Are Important

Can you imagine how much easier life would be if children were preprogrammed at birth with the limits and boundaries for healthy relationships? This is a wonderful fantasy, but not reality. Nobody is born with limits. We learn limits by growing up in families. They are taught to us first by our parents and the lessons are reinforced by other important people such as teachers in the course of our growing up.

When the limits children learn at home correspond to the limits that are accepted and practiced in our schools, children have a much easier time adjusting. When the limits children learn in their families are different from those accepted and practiced out in the world, the adjustment process is more complicated.

Limits don't complicate life or our interactions with others. In fact, the opposite is true. Limits simplify life. When children know how far they're allowed to go and how far others are allowed to go with them, they feel secure and comfortable in their relationships. Limits provide vital information children need to cooperate and get along.

Limits answer some very basic research questions children ask about how their world works. On the surface, limits operate like traffic signals by providing information in the form of green lights (do that) and red lights (stop that) for acceptable and unacceptable behavior. These signals answer the questions "What's okay?" and "What's not okay?"

Beneath the surface, however, limits answer a very different set of questions about the power and authority of the person sending the messages: "Who's in control?" "How far can I go?" "What happens when I go too far?" The answers to these questions define the balance of power and authority in teacher-student relationships and help children determine whether compliance with their teacher's rules is optional or really required.

Limit Testing: How Children Do Research

Children are natural researchers. They are astute observers of behavior. They know how to collect research data, and they know how to form conclusions based upon the data they collect.

How do children conduct their research? How do they clarify our rules and expectations and determine whether what we ask is really expected and required? They listen to what we say and watch what we do, but rarely do they come up and ask, "How much power and authority do you really have? How do I know you really mean what you say? And what are you going to do if I don't do what you ask?" My guess is that you probably haven't had this experience very often, if at all.

Most children don't ask these questions with their words, but they do think about them, and they do ask them with their behavior. They just go ahead and do whatever we asked them not to do, and then they wait to see what happens. This is limit-testing behavior, and this is how children do their research. It answers their basic questions more definitively than words. Much of what we consider to be misbehavior in the classroom is actually limit testing, or children's attempts to clarify what we really expect.

TEMPERAMENT AND LEARNING STYLES

Children are born with their own natural and unique style of interacting with the people, places, or things in their world. We call this unique style of interacting their "temperament." Much of what we know about children's temperament is based on the research of Alexander Thomas, Stella Chess, and their associates in the late 1950s.

These researchers identified nine traits that are present at birth and continue to influence an individual's development throughout his or her life. Approximately 65 percent of all children fit one of three basic temperament types or profiles: easy or flexible, difficult or feisty, and cautious or slow-to-warm-up. Approximately 40 percent of children fall into the category of easy or flexible, 15 percent as cautious or slow-to-warm-up, and 10 percent as difficult or feisty. The remaining 35 percent show a combination of the three basic temperament types. Although the research has been available since the 1950s, schools have been slow to incorporate these important findings into their guidance and discipline practices.

Reflect for a moment on the students in your classrooms over the years. Do you find that about 10 percent of your students cause 90 percent of the classroom discipline problems? Most teachers report this observation. These students fit the profile of "difficult or feisty." In the Setting Limits Program we refer to them as "strong-willed." They don't respond to discipline methods that seem to work with the majority of their classmates.

The remaining 90 percent of students in most classrooms fall into two distinct groups that generally correspond to the temperament research. The 40 percent of easy students and the 15 percent of cautious students make up the 55 percent percent majority we refer to as "compliant students." They don't do a lot of testing. Their underlying desire is to please and cooperate.

The 35 percent that show a combination of temperament traits we refer to as "fence-sitters." As the name implies, fence-sitters can go either way depending upon what the market will bear. We think of them as the swing vote because they can make or break your year. Winning over the fence-sitters is essential to the success of your classroom management.

TEMPERAMENT AND LIMIT TESTING

With a basic understanding of temperament types and learning styles, let's revisit the issue of limit testing. All children test limits to determine our rules and expectations. This is normal, but not all children test limits in the same way, and this fact often becomes a source of confusion for teachers and parents. Temperament has a lot to do with how children conduct their research.

Compliant children don't do a lot of testing because their underlying desire is to please and cooperate. Most are willing to accept our words as all the data they need and cooperate for the asking. They complete their research and do most of their learning the easy way. Consequences are seldom needed in the teaching-and-learning process. This is really good news for teachers. It means 55 percent of the students in our classrooms, the majority, are solidly in our corner. But their cooperation can be misleading if we try to generalize their learning experience to their classmates.

Compliant children respond cooperatively to nearly any discipline approach. Writing names on the board under the smile or frown face, having students pull color behavior cards, taking away recesses and favorite privileges, making them write sentences or apology letters all appear to work. The effectiveness of these techniques, however, has little to do with our discipline methods and a great deal to do with the students' temperaments. Compliant children give us a wide margin for ineffectiveness.

Fence-sitters are a powerful minority who can be swayed to cooperate or test depending upon what they observe going on around them. Fence-sitters are not big risk takers, but they are skillful researchers. They get most of their research accomplished by watching their strong-willed classmates. When strong-willed students consistently get away with violating rules or challenging authority, that's when the fence-sitters shift into gear and start testing more aggressively. If the fence-sitters observe their strong-willed classmates not getting away with violating rules or challenging authority, then fence-sitters will choose to cooperate.

Strong-willed students are the real "movers and shakers" in the classroom. We call them "aggressive researchers" because they frequently test limits and authority and require a lot of hard data in the form of consequences to be convinced to follow our rules and accept our authority. Announcing or explaining rules to strong-willed students is insufficient. The word *stop* is merely a theory or a hypothesis waiting to be tested, and they know how to find out what it really means. They continue to test and push us to the point of action to see what happens. Although they constitute only 10 percent of the school population, they are responsible for nearly 90 percent of school discipline problems.

Strong-willed students do most of their learning "the hard way." That is, they have to repeatedly experience the consequences of their

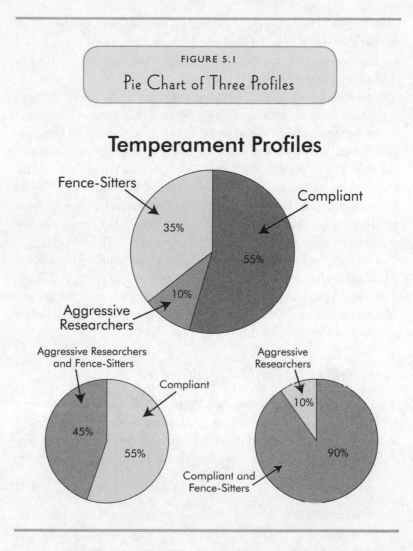

FIGURE 5.1

Pie Chart of Three Profiles

Temperament Profiles

choices or behavior before they are willing to accept our rules and authority. This is just a fact of life. It's how they learn. Each time they test they collect another important piece of research data that they put into the conclusion column that helps them form their beliefs about our rules and authority. They simply require a lot of data to be convinced.

Is persistent and aggressive research really normal behavior? The answer is yes. This is normal behavior for strong-willed children. This is what they do. It's our job to provide them with the data they need. Logical consequences are the best teaching tools for the job with this challenging group of hard-way learners.

Strong-willed children are the best measure of the effectiveness of any classroom management program because they leave us no margin for ineffectiveness. We have to be at the top of our game and use discipline methods that are well matched to their temperament and learning style. If not, we will pay a dear price. Not only will we lose their cooperation, we risk losing the cooperation of the fence-sitters. When this happens, we've lost the cooperation of 45 percent of our students. Holding the firm line with aggressive researchers is the key to winning over the fence-sitters.

Does a 55 percent success rate meet your definition of an effective classroom management program? Is this any way to teach one of the most important lessons in the classroom? Can you see why simplistic, one-size-fits-all, production-line classroom management approaches are a setup for failure?

SAME MESSAGE, DIFFERENT RESPONSE

When we take into account differences in children's temperaments and learning styles, we can begin to clear up some of the confusion about why children respond differently to the same guidance messages. Robert illustrates this point by sharing personal examples of raising strong-willed children.

> My oldest son, Scott, is compliant. He usually cooperates for the asking. My youngest son, Ian, is strong-willed. He requires hard data before he is convinced I mean business. My boys do their research differently, and I've learned to adjust my guidance messages accordingly.
>
> When my boys were preschoolers, I permitted them to watch a few minutes of TV in the morning if they were groomed, fed, and ready for school. They usually selected a program featuring their favorite action hero. Like most preschoolers, my boys liked to watch TV with the volume cranked up. When Scott did this, I simply said, "Scott, the

TV is too loud. Turn it down, please." This message was respectful but not very firm. How did Scott respond? He did what is in his nature to do. He got up from his seat and turned down the volume. He accepts my words as all the data he needs to make an acceptable choice and cooperate. I've learned to count on his cooperation.

If I use the same message with Ian, I know from experience what he's likely to do. He will just sit there and ignore me and wait for a clearer signal. The message Ian is hearing is "The TV is bothering Dad." This is not a problem for Ian. He can live with that. As Ian grew older and became more skillful, he would give me the words I wanted to hear and say, "I will" but continue to do what he wanted. This isn't really lying. What Ian really means is "I will when I have to, and I didn't hear that I have to."

Like many strong-willed kids, Ian is thinking, "Or what? What are you going to do if I don't?" He's looking for concrete, definitive information about what I really expect. So I've learned to provide him with all the data he needs to make an acceptable choice. I've learned to speak his language. When the TV is on too loud, I say, "Ian, turn the TV down, please, or I'll have to turn it off."

When Ian hears the word *off*, an interesting thing happens. He gets up, just like his compliant older brother, and turns the TV down. Why? Because he suddenly turned into a compliant person? No. He turns it down because he has the data he needs to make an acceptable choice. He knows from previous experience that I *will* turn it off. I had to turn the TV off about a dozen times before he collected enough data to be convinced.

Aggressive Researchers

My job as a child therapist brings me into frequent contact with the most aggressive researchers in schools. I see the kids who don't stop at the signals their teachers hold up in the classroom, the ones who push everything to the limit. Joey, a second grader, is a good example. He was referred to me after a series of suspensions for disruptive and uncooperative behavior in the classroom.

"Joey won't listen to anyone," commented his teacher. "He thinks

he can do whatever he wants. I've had numerous conferences with his parents, and they say he acts the same way at home. We're all at a loss for what to do."

When Joey arrived at my office with his parents, he plopped himself down in one of my comfortable blue swivel chairs and began sizing me up. Then he went right to work on me. We hadn't exchanged a word, but his research was under way.

What do you think Joey and many other children do when they first sit in my swivel chairs? You guessed it—they spin the chair around, and sometimes they put their feet in the chair, too. They know it's not okay. Their parents know it, and so do I, but the kids do it anyway. They look at me, then at their parents, and go ahead and see what happens. This is limit-testing behavior. When it happens, I know I am about to learn a great deal about how the family communicates about limits.

I don't need behavior rating scales, standardized tests, or lengthy clinical interviews to see what's going on. I just watch the child, the chair, and the parents for ten to fifteen minutes, and I usually have all the information I need to see what's going on.

Joey's parents responded to his chair spinning the way most permissive parents do. They ignored it. They pretended it wasn't happening and focused instead on telling me about all of the disruptive things Joey did at school. Joey continued spinning. Five minutes passed. Not one signal had been given.

Ten minutes into our session, I could see Joey's father was becoming annoyed. He made his first attempt at a signal. He said Joey's name softly and gave him a look of disapproval.

Joey did what most kids do when this happens. He acknowledged the gesture, stopped briefly, and then resumed his spinning as soon as his father looked away. Joey and his parents were reenacting a script, the same one they go through dozens of times each week whenever Joey misbehaves.

With his behavior, Joey was asking the same questions he asks at home and in the classroom: "What's okay?" "What's not okay?" "Who's in control?" "How far can I go?" "And what happens when I go too far?" He knew his parents weren't going to do anything about his behavior, so he was conducting his research to determine my power and authority and the rules that operated in my office. Between disapproving looks from his father, Joey continued to spin. I waited to see what would happen next.

A few more minutes passed, and then Joey's father did what many other parents do at this point. He reached over and stopped the chair with his hand. His signal elicited the same response as before. Joey acknowledged the gesture, waited for his father to remove his hand, and then continued spinning.

Joey's parents were doing their best to say stop, but Joey knew from experience that stopping was not really expected or required. All of the gestures were just steps in a well-rehearsed drama. The spinning continued. I could see why he wasn't responding to his teacher's signals in the classroom.

Fifteen minutes went by, and Joey still had not received a clear signal from his parents. Their anger was apparent. Finally his exasperated mother turned to me and said, "See what he does? This is the same thing we have to put up with at home!"

At this point, I intervened and helped Joey answer some of his research questions. In a matter-of-fact voice, I said, "Joey, I'd like you to use my blue chairs, but I have two rules you'll have to follow: Don't spin them, and don't put your feet in them. I'm confident you can follow my rules, but if you don't you'll have to sit in my orange chair for the rest of the session." I keep an old plastic orange chair in my office for these situations.

What do you think Joey did? Sure, he did the same thing most strong-willed children do. He tested. Not right away, but within a few minutes, he gave the chair another spin and looked for my reaction. He heard my words; now he wanted hard data. He wanted to see what I would do.

So I did what I always do when this happens. I pulled out the orange chair and said calmly, "This will be your chair for the rest of the session. You can try my blue chairs again next session." Then I stood next to him and waited for him to move with a look of expectation. Reluctantly, Joey moved into the orange chair, but he didn't do it in a respectful manner. He rolled his eyes, gave me a look of disgust, and murmured something under his breath I'm sure wasn't a compliment. The bait was skillfully presented and tempting, but I didn't bite. His final attempt to hook me into a power struggle didn't work.

What did Joey and I just work out? I just answered his research questions. He heard *stop*, and he experienced stopping. Now he knows what I expect and what will happen if he decides to test the next time he visits my office. Joey has the information he needs to make an acceptable choice.

You're probably wondering what happens when children refuse to get out of the blue chair. The interesting thing is that most don't test when they get the information they need to make an acceptable choice. I see more than a hundred chair spinners a year in my counseling work. Only a few continue to test when I bring out the orange chair.

What happens when they do? The process is still the same. The questions haven't changed. They are still asking, "Or what? What are you going to do about it?" So I try to give them the data they're looking for in the same matter-of-fact manner. I turn to their parents and say, "Your child doesn't want to get out of my chair. Do I have your permission to assist him into the orange chair?"

In more than twenty years, I've never had a parent say no. Most are so embarrassed about their child's behavior, they can't wait to get out of my office. Others are very curious to see whether I can actually get their child to cooperate.

Once I get their permission, I turn to the child and say, "Your parents say I can assist you into the orange chair, but I'd prefer that you move yourself. What would you like to do?" I take a few deep breaths, remind myself that I'm the adult in this situation, and wait patiently for fifteen or twenty seconds.

What do you think they do? A very few, maybe two or three each year, wait until I get up out of my chair before they are convinced I will act. Then they move into the other chair. The vast majority move on their own. Why? They move because they have all the information they need to make an acceptable decision. They believe I will act. Their questions are answered. Even aggressive researchers can make acceptable choices when provided with clear signals. Their cooperation demonstrates the power of a clear message.

What We Do Is What We Teach

When children like Joey misbehave at school, the focus is on their problem behavior, not the hidden forces that operate beneath the surface to shape that problem behavior. This is where my investigative work begins. I try to determine why the teaching-and-learning process breaks down. Is the problem teaching? Or learning? Or is something else going on? I try to answer these questions by examining the ways rules are taught both at home and in the classroom.

WHY PERMISSIVE RULES BACKFIRE

Permissive guidance methods often lead to breakdowns in the teaching-and-learning process because teachers confuse their words with actions and become frustrated when their message doesn't get across. Children learn a different rule than their teacher intends.

For example, Barry, a third grader, tilts back precariously in his chair while his teacher gives a lesson at the board. She notices and gives him a disapproving look. He straightens his chair briefly, but as soon as she looks away, he tilts back once again.

"He's not really hurting anything," his teacher says to herself. She decides to ignore it, and Barry continues to tilt. Ten minutes pass. Then he slips and nearly falls before catching himself.

"That doesn't look very safe to me," says his teacher. "I'm afraid you might hurt yourself. I'd feel more comfortable if you sat the right way."

"I'll be careful," says Barry.

"I know you will," she replies, "but accidents can happen even when you're careful, and I'd hate to see you get hurt. Please sit the right way, okay?" She waits for Barry to comply. He does, and she returns to her lesson, satisfied that her message got across.

It doesn't take long before Barry tests again. This time, he props his feet on the rails of his desk to stabilize his chair while tilting. When his teacher sees what's going on, she feels frustrated.

"I thought I asked you to sit the right way," she says with irritation. "What would the principal say if she walked into our classroom and saw you sitting like that?"

"But it's safe the way I'm doing it," argues Barry. He demonstrates how he can stabilize his chair by putting his feet on the sides of his desk.

"I'm still not comfortable with it," says the teacher. "I'm going to have to insist that you stop."

"Okay," says Barry reluctantly, "but I don't see what it's hurting." He stops tilting.

Do you think Barry and his teacher are finished with this issue? Barry's teacher sincerely believes she's saying *stop* when she points out the dangers of tilting back in the chair. She becomes frustrated and annoyed when he does not respond as expected. In actuality, she is communicating two messages, but she is aware of only one.

Her words say something that resembles *stop*, but what does Barry experience? He doesn't experience stopping. Instead he hears more talking. His teacher's action message is really saying, "Go ahead and do what you want. I don't like it, but I'm not going to do anything about it, at least not for a while."

Barry responds to the mixed message as many children do. He ignores the words and continues pushing with his behavior. He learns from what he experiences. What is Barry's interpretation of his teacher's rule? Sure, it's okay to tilt back in the chair as long as he can tolerate his teacher's attempts to persuade him not to.

PUNITIVE RULES INSPIRE REBELLION

Those who operate from a punitive model use both words and actions to teach their rules, but their methods often end up teaching a different lesson than they intended. This is what Mr. Silva experienced when he tried to handle a problem with one of his sixth graders.

Mr. Silva is writing instructions for an upcoming literature assignment when he hears a clicking sound coming from the middle of the room. He turns and sees several students looking at Mel, who slouches in his seat.

"Mel, what you're doing is not respectful," says Mr. Silva.

"It wasn't me," Mel replies.

"Don't lie to me!" says Mr. Silva. "Now sit up and pay attention. If I hear any more noises out of you, you'll spend your next recess on the bench."

"What a jerk," Mel murmurs under his breath.

"What was that, Mel?" inquires Mr. Silva angrily. "Would you like to say it a little louder for others to hear?"

"I didn't say anything," Mel replies.

"Oh, yes, you did," accuses Mr. Silva. "Whatever it was, I'm sure it was disrespectful. You just earned a recess on the bench. Your smart mouth got you in trouble again."

"Oh, ouch! That really hurts," says Mel sarcastically.

"You've just earned another recess on the bench," says Mr. Silva angrily. "Wanna try for three?" Mel clutches his chest in mock agony. "That's three!" says Mr. Silva. "How about all the recesses for the week?"

Mel is tempted to retaliate, but he believes Mr. Silva will follow through on his threat. Mel does not want to lose his recesses. He sits and glares his defiance.

Mr. Silva doesn't realize it, but he is teaching two rules about being disrespectful in the classroom. His words (rule in theory) say, "It's not okay," but what kind of behavior is he modeling? His actions (rule in practice) say just the opposite. He is teaching the same behavior he's trying to eliminate. Which lesson is Mel following?

Lessons at Home Affect Lessons at School

The home is the training ground for the real world. That's where children first learn the rules for acceptable behavior. They take those lessons with them into the classroom. Steven is a good example. When I first met him, he had been suspended from school four times for hitting, and it was October. The year had barely begun.

His fourth-grade teacher tried everything she knew to help Steven change. She explained the school's rules about hitting. She encouraged him to ask an adult for help whenever he got into a conflict, and she offered her assistance when Steven got into conflicts in the classroom. Nothing helped. She was frustrated and so were Steven's parents.

"Living with Steven is like being around a time bomb waiting to explode," said his mother. "He knows that hitting is not okay, but he does it anyway. He hits his younger brother, he hits other kids in the neighborhood, and he hits kids at school. We've talked to him over and over again, but it doesn't seem to sink in."

"What exactly do you say to him when he hits others?" I asked, curious about their verbal messages.

"Well, I get a little loud," confessed Steven's father. "It makes me angry to see Steven mistreating others, and I let him know I'm not going to tolerate it."

"What do you do to get that message across?" I asked.

"We paddle him when he needs it," Steven's father replied. "We don't believe in all this permissive stuff going on today. Kids need to know you mean business."

"How many times a week does Steven need that kind of reminder?" I asked.

"Two or three times, and sometimes more. He needs to know when he's gone too far," said his father.

"With that many reminders, why do you think Steven is having such a difficult time learning your rules?" I asked.

"We suspect he has some kind of a learning problem," Steven's mother replied. "We're considering having him tested."

As I got to know Steven, I could see he didn't need testing. The problem wasn't learning. It was teaching. Steven was a very capable learner. He was mastering all the lessons his parents were teaching about hurtful problem solving. He was good at yelling, threatening, and intimidating. He knew how to hit, and he was becoming skillful at blaming others when he got caught.

Steven understood his parents' words, but their spoken rules were not the ones they practiced. What did they practice? Hitting. Steven was learning a lesson in violent problem solving. At school he was simply following the lessons he had been taught.

Permissive training at home can also set kids up for problems at school. James is a good example. He was getting off to a rough start in kindergarten when I first met him. The note his teacher sent was revealing: "James pushes everything to the limit. When I ask him to join an activity, he ignores me and does what he wants. When I insist, he cries or throws a tantrum. He seems to think the classroom rules don't apply to him."

James's mother was equally frustrated. "He's the same way at home," she complained. "He refuses to get dressed in the morning. He won't come in when I call him, and getting him to bed is a nightmare by itself. I have to ask him over and over again. Most of the time, he just ignores me and does what he wants."

Like many children trained with permissiveness, James was accustomed to getting his own way, and he had developed a full repertoire of skills to make that happen. He was an expert at tuning out, ignoring, resisting, avoiding, arguing, debating, bargaining, challenging, and defying. If those tactics didn't work, James played his trump card. He threw a tantrum. His mother usually felt guilty and gave in.

James's intentions were not malicious. He did it because it worked. His experiences had taught him "Rules are for others, not me. I make my own rules, and I do what I want." James operated on these beliefs both at home and in the classroom.

It wasn't hard to understand why James had such an exaggerated perception of his own power and authority and why he was doing so much testing. At home the stop signals he confronted did not require stopping, and *no* really meant *yes* most of the time. When he misbehaved, he knew he would hear a lot of repeating, reminding, lecturing, and threatening, but none of those methods required stopping. His training had not prepared him for the real stop signs he was encountering in the classroom. James needs firm, consistent limits to help draw different conclusions from his research.

Teaching Rules Effectively

Teachers can't control the faulty lessons children learn at home, but they can help children move in a more acceptable direction by teaching their rules effectively in the classroom. Let's look at how one teacher does it.

Katy, a third grader, loves to play four square, but she doesn't like to follow the rules. Sometimes when her turn is over she refuses to leave the court.

"She's cheating again," several kids complain when Mrs. Martinez arrives on the scene. "She won't leave when her turn is over." Katy stands in the court with her hands on her hips, refusing to budge.

"You're going to have to play by the rules, Katy, or find a different game to play," says Mrs. Martinez matter-of-factly. "What would you like to do?"

"Okay," says Katy as she heads to the end of the line. The game resumes, but within minutes the kids complain again. Mrs. Martinez sees Katy standing in the court, refusing to leave.

"I won't do it again," says Katy when she sees Mrs. Martinez.

"That's a good choice," replies Mrs. Martinez, "but you're going to have to find a different game to play this morning. You can try four square again this afternoon." No shaming. No blaming. No harsh words or lectures. Katy hears the same message she experiences. She may need several more of these experiences before she masters the intended rule, but the methods will surely lead to the desired outcome.

Mr. Givens also is effective when he sees one of his fifth-grade students reading a magazine in class.

"Seth, magazines don't belong in class," says Mr. Givens matter-of-factly.

"I'm not disturbing anybody," says Seth, looking for a little bargaining room. Mr. Givens doesn't take the bait.

"You can put it away in your backpack," Mr. Givens replies, "or I will keep it in my desk until the end of the semester."

Now Seth has all the information he needs to make an acceptable decision. He knows what's expected and what will happen if he decides to test. Mr. Givens cannot fail to get his message across.

Chapter Summary

The research of Jean Piaget and Lawrence Kohlberg shows us that children learn concretely. Their beliefs and perceptions are based primarily on what they experience, not necessarily on what they are told. This fact has important implications for how we go about teaching our rules. We do it in two basic ways: with our words and with our actions. Both teach a lesson, but only our actions are concrete. Actions, not words, define our rules.

When our words match our actions consistently, children learn to trust our words and recognize the rules behind them. When our words do not match our actions, however, children learn to ignore our words and base their beliefs on what they experience. In reality, they are learning two sets of rules: our spoken rules (rules in theory) and our rules in practice.

This fundamental miscommunication about rules is why many well-intended guidance lessons break down. Most teachers are unaware it's even happening. They just continue to try to get their message across with their words while their students learn from what they experience.

Children are skillful at determining whether our spoken rules are also the rules we practice. They test. Limit testing is how children conduct their research, but children conduct their research differently based on their temperaments and learning styles. Compliant children do not need a lot of data to be convinced to follow our rules. Fence-sitters can go either way depending upon what they observe. Strong-willed children, on the other hand, are very aggressive researchers. They need a lot of data to be convinced that our spoken rules are actually the ones we practice.

We can help children complete their research and learn our rules by providing the signals they understand best: clear words and effective actions. These tools are the key to teaching our rules in the clearest and most understandable way.

How Teachers Teach Their Rules

Teaching rules in the classroom is an interaction between a teacher and a group of learners. In chapter 5, we examined the teaching-and-learning process from the learner's point of view and discovered that children learn rules differently based on their temperaments and learning styles. Compliant children learn rules the easy way. Strong-willed children learn rules the hard way. Fence-sitters do some of both. All three styles are natural and normal modes of learning.

Now it's time to examine the process from the teacher's perspective. When a teacher's limit-setting style is well matched to the learning styles of the full range of learners, we have what we call "a good match." We can safely predict a positive learning outcome. When a teacher's limit-setting style is poorly matched to the learning styles of students, we have a "bad match." We can predict a poor learning outcome.

How do you teach your rules? Are your methods well matched to the learning styles of your students? Are you getting the cooperation you expect from all of your students or just your compliant ones and some fence-sitters? This chapter will help you answer these questions. You'll discover how your discipline methods match up with the temperaments and learning styles of your students. By the time you're done, you'll know what tools you need to add to your discipline tool kit to get the best match with your students.

Seeing Ourselves in the Mirror

Years ago, when I first began giving workshops, I didn't ask the participants what discipline methods they already used, nor did I spend any time discussing different training models. I just assumed we were operating with a common understanding about what works best, and I jumped in during the first session and shared the methods I knew would be effective. As it turns out, this mistake led me to an important discovery.

After my first few workshops, I began receiving thank-you notes with appreciative comments that really concerned me. "Thanks for helping me become firm with my limits," one teacher said. "I don't nag all day like I used to. Now I only ask them two or three times, then I give them choices." Another teacher commented, "Limited choices work great. When my students dawdle, I give them a choice—you can finish on time or lose your recess for a week. They usually finish up."

I became particularly concerned when one fifth-grade teacher told me how much he liked logical consequences. "When my students are disrespectful to me, I make them stay in during recess and write me an apology letter. Then I make them read it to me in front of the class."

"Was this in one of my workshops?" I wondered. How is it possible that someone could so misinterpret the methods I was sharing? But the comments continued, and to my dismay, parents were doing the same thing in my parenting workshops.

Then it occurred to me what was happening. We all thought we shared a common understanding, but we were viewing our discipline methods from very different perspectives. Those who believed in punishment used them punitively, and those who believed in permissiveness used them permissively. Some did both. They all thought they were doing things in new and different ways, but they were simply repeating their old mistakes with new methods. I could see this was not a conscious process.

When I give workshops today, my first task is to hold up a mirror to help the participants become acquainted with their current guidance approach so they can recognize and avoid their old mistakes. I usually begin by demonstrating how a typical discipline problem can be handled in three different ways: permissively, punitively, or democratically. Then we examine the teaching-and-learning process that accompanies each approach. Most teachers find this helpful. They recognize their approach by examining the methods used by others.

Let's look at how three teachers handle a typical playground problem—rough play. Each uses a different guidance approach.

It's morning recess. A group of boys divides up into teams to play a karate commando game. The teams hide, sneak up on one another, and then hold mock battles. It's the last part that leads to problems. Several students have been hurt. The game has been banned from the playground, but some students try to play it anyway.

The mock battle is under way when Mrs. Fisher, the yard duty teacher, notices what's going on. She watches with concern. The boys see her, too, but the game continues with more flying kicks and punches that barely miss.

Finally, one boy is grazed by a kick. He holds his side and grimaces. Mrs. Fisher intervenes. "Guys, that game doesn't look safe," she says. "I'm afraid someone is going to get hurt. Kicks can cause serious injuries. That's why we don't allow that game."

"We are just pretending," says one student. "We'll be careful."

"I know you will, but what you're doing worries me. I really wish you would stop," she says. They do, as long as Mrs. Fisher is in the area, but as soon as she leaves, the battle resumes.

Next recess, Mr. Howard is on yard duty. When he sees the boys playing the karate game, he rushes to the scene. "Stop!" he shouts. "Are you guys playing the karate game again?"

"No, we were just fooling around," says one student.

"Don't lie to me, young man, or you'll find yourself in even more trouble," warns Mr. Howard. He points an accusing finger at the boy and gives him a stern, intimidating look. "Now tell me, who all was involved here?"

Mr. Howard spends the next ten minutes interrogating the group. He listens to their pleas of innocence or guilt and threatens further consequences if he discovers anyone lying. Finally, he is satisfied he has the culprits. He writes up five citations and sends the offenders to the office. "I hope this helps you remember the rules next time you decide to play that game," he adds.

The boys are angry and set on revenge. As they reach the edge of the playground, they get off some parting shots. "You're a great teacher, all right," shouts one student sarcastically. "A great jerk is more like it!" adds another. They all laugh.

"Keep it up guys!" shouts Mr. Howard. "The principal will hear about this, too. You are just adding to your punishment."

A few days later, it's Mrs. Taylor's turn to supervise recess. When she sees what appears to be the beginning of a mock karate battle, she approaches the group. "Guys, you'll have to choose another game to play," she says in a matter-of-fact tone. "That game is not allowed. If you play it again, you'll have to sit out the rest of the recess on the bench. Thanks for cooperating."

No lectures. No pleading. No threats or accusations. She simply gives them the information they need to make an acceptable choice. Sure, there was some grumbling. The boys weren't happy about it. A few were probably tempted to test, but nobody wanted to spend their recess on the bench. Cooperation was the best choice.

Each teacher in the previous examples was trying to teach a rule about acceptable playground behavior, but only one enjoyed much success. Mrs. Fisher used the permissive approach. Her methods were respectful but not very firm. The boys ignored her and did what they wanted. Mr. Howard used the punitive or autocratic approach. His methods were firm but not very respectful. The boys became angry and retaliated. Mrs. Taylor used the democratic approach. Her methods were firm and respectful. She gave the boys all the information they needed to make an acceptable choice. They cooperated.

Do you think the three teachers in the examples would show similar inconsistency if they were teaching a lesson in reading, spelling, or arithmetic? Not likely. Why, then, is there so much inconsistency when it comes to teaching our rules and standards for acceptable behavior?

Actually, the teachers in the examples are no further apart in their discipline methods than the rest of us. When it comes to teaching the lessons of guidance and discipline, inconsistency is the norm, not the exception. The varying methods simply reflect the range of practices used in our schools. We are all over the map. Some believe in permissiveness. Others take a punitive or autocratic view. Some are democratic, and still others flip-flop back and forth between the extremes of permissiveness and punishment.

Most of us teach our rules from one of four basic training models. Each model is premised on a different set of beliefs about how children learn, the teacher's role in the training process, and the proper distribution of power and responsibility between adults and children. Each model teaches a different set of lessons about cooperation, responsibility, and your expectations for acceptable behavior. Only one model is well matched to the full range of temperaments and learning styles teachers encounter in the classroom. Let's take a closer look at each of these models.

THE PERMISSIVE APPROACH

(Respectful but Not Firm)

Permissiveness emerged prominently in the 1960s and '70s as a reaction against the rigidity and autocratic nature of the punitive approach. Many parents and teachers were looking for a new and more democratic approach to raising children based on principles of freedom, equality, and mutual respect.

Putting these principles in place, however, was not as easy as it sounded. This was uncharted territory for those of us who grew up with the punitive model. How do you do it? Was it a simple matter of relaxing our rules and expectations and giving children more freedom and control? That's what many tried. They experimented with open classrooms, relaxed structure, more freedom and control for students, and relaxed standards for acceptable classroom behavior. But the experiment often backfired because a vital ingredient was left out—limits.

Freedom without limits is not democracy. It's anarchy, and children trained with anarchy do not learn respect for rules or authority or how to handle their freedom responsibly. They think primarily of themselves and develop an exaggerated sense of their own power and control. The examples of a failed experiment are all around us.

Let's look at how one teacher uses the permissive approach to handle another typical classroom problem—disruption.

Mrs. Weaver, a sixth-grade teacher, passes out worksheets for the next assignment and tells the class they have twenty minutes to finish up before lunch. The students began working quietly at their seats.

After a few minutes, Mrs. Weaver hears Nate talking to a girl in his table group. He talks softly at first, so Mrs. Weaver ignores it, but his talking continues and the volume increases. She decides to intervene.

"Nate, don't you think it's getting a little loud in here?" she says. "Others are trying to work."

He settles down for a while, but within a few minutes, he talks to someone else, softly at first, then louder.

"Nate, you have fifteen minutes to finish up before lunch," reminds Mrs. Weaver. "You need to do a little less talking and little more working, okay?"

Five minutes go by before Nate disrupts again. This time he laughs and jokes with another boy. Mrs. Weaver feels annoyed. She walks over and looks at him impatiently. "How many times do I have to ask you?" she asks.

"I wasn't too loud," argues Nate.

"Well, you sounded too loud to me," replies Mrs. Weaver. "Besides, what you're doing isn't respectful to me or your classmates, and I don't appreciate it. If you don't stop talking, I'm going to move you from your table group. I'm not going to ask you again."

Nate returns to his work briefly, but within a few minutes, he talks again. Mrs. Weaver intervenes.

"I've had enough of this, Nate!" says a frustrated Mrs. Weaver. "Move your desk away from your group." She points to an area about six feet away.

"But, Mrs. Weaver, that's not fair!" protests Nate. "I was asking Tim for some help. I wasn't bothering anybody."

"You were distracting him from his work," counters Mrs. Weaver. "What are you supposed to do when you need help?"

"Raise my hand," says Nate.

"Right!" replies Mrs. Weaver. "I hope you remember it. This time, it's a warning. If I hear any more talking, I will move you. I really mean it." Nate settles down once again.

What did Nate experience? It wasn't a compelling request to cooperate, at least not for long. Instead he experienced a lot of words and very little action. Based on his experience, he has little cause to regard Mrs. Weaver's rule about disrupting very seriously.

Permissive teachers use only half the tools in their limit-setting tool kit. They rely heavily on their words, but they're reluctant to follow through with effective action. Permissive teachers are constantly shifting gears and trying different verbal tactics to convince and persuade their students to cooperate. They do a lot of repeating, reminding, warning, offering second chances, pleading, cajoling, bargaining, bribing, arguing, debating, reasoning, assuring, and trying other forms of verbal persuasion.

Consequences, if they are used at all, are typically late and ineffective. By the time everything is said and done, teachers usually end up compromising away their rules and authority or giving in altogether. Often, children end up getting their own way. Permissiveness is humiliating to teachers. It's the fast lane to burnout.

EXAMPLES OF PERMISSIVE DISCIPLINE PRACTICES

- Ignoring or overlooking blurting, disruption, or other misbehavior.
- Saying "Shh . . ." when students blurt out or talk disruptively.
- Allowing students to blurt out and speak without raising a quiet hand.
- Giving warnings and second chances for misbehavior.
- Asking students to pull color behavior cards for misbehavior.
- Allowing students to make the classroom rules.
- Arguing and debating with students about your classroom rules.
- Raising your voice to be heard over a loud classroom noise level.
- Offering bribes and special rewards for cooperation.
- Repeatedly giving reasons and explanations without consequences.
- Allowing students to choose their own seating and desk configurations.
- Pleading and begging for cooperation.

- Giving off-campus suspensions when parents cannot stay home.
- Bargaining and negotiating for cooperation.
- Allowing students to treat you disrespectfully.
- Allowing students to treat one another disrespectfully.

As a discipline approach, permissiveness is much worse than punishment for both children and adults. It doesn't accomplish any of our basic training goals. It doesn't stop misbehavior. It doesn't teach responsibility, and it doesn't teach our intended lessons about following rules or accepting authority. Permissiveness does not provide children with the information they need to make acceptable choices about their behavior.

What do children learn from permissiveness? They learn that cooperation is optional, not required. They also learn to ignore our rules and push us to the point of action to clarify what we really expect. Permissiveness is an invitation for limit testing. Which groups of students are most likely to test? You guessed it. The strong-willed students and the fence-sitters won't miss this invitation. Students trained with permissiveness become skillful at ignoring, tuning out, resisting, avoiding, arguing, debating, bargaining, challenging, and defying. They don't do it maliciously. They simply do it because it works. Their experiences have taught them that "rules are for others, not for me. I make my own rules, and I do what I want."

Children trained with permissiveness learn they can wear adults down and get their own way. This is the primary reward for their limit testing. But there's another reward that's just as appealing—the live entertainment children get from watching their teacher. Permissive teachers unwittingly provide students with some very entertaining floor shows.

How do you think Nate felt in our earlier example, each time his teacher tried to deal with his disruption? Was he in control? Clearly. Did he enjoy the show? Definitely. Did his friends enjoy the show? You bet. Mrs. Weaver doesn't realize it, but she provided a lively floor show for the entire class.

Permissive discipline is a "reinforcement error" because it actually encourages and rewards unacceptable behavior. Let's take a closer look at what happened between Nate and his teacher by examining a diagram of their interaction. We'll place Mrs. Weaver's behavior on the left side of the diagram and Nate's behavior on the right. Visual diagrams often reveal, better than words, the various steps in an interaction sequence (see Figure 6.1).

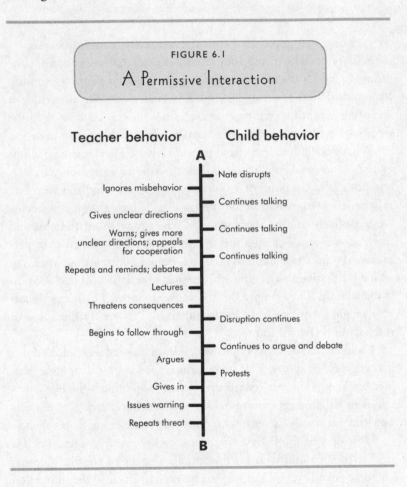

FIGURE 6.1

A Permissive Interaction

Teacher behavior   Child behavior

                        A

                            Nate disrupts

Ignores misbehavior
                            Continues talking

Gives unclear directions
                            Continues talking
Warns; gives more
unclear directions; appeals
for cooperation
                            Continues talking

Repeats and reminds; debates

Lectures

Threatens consequences
                            Disruption continues

Begins to follow through
                            Continues to argue and debate

Argues
                            Protests

Gives in

Issues warning

Repeats threat

                        B

The first thing you probably notice is the length of this diagram. Permissive teachers use a lot of different tactics. Mrs. Weaver is no exception. She begins at point A by attempting to ignore the misbehavior, a strategy that seldom works. Nate continues talking. When his volume increases, she attempts to give him a signal. She asks him whether the noise level is too high and points out that others are working quietly.

Did you hear a clear message that Nate should stop talking? Neither did Nate. He resumes talking a short time later. So Mrs. Weaver tries a different tactic. She points out how little time he has to complete his assignment and asks him to do a little less talking.

What is "a little less talking"? Does that mean some is okay? How much? And how will Nate know? Of course, he has to test, and that's exactly what he does. He continues talking.

So Mrs. Weaver switches gears again. She tries repeating and reminding. Does this work? No. Nate tries to talk her into an argument. It works.

She takes the bait and argues with him about the volume of his talking, but now the argument is a source of disruption. She lectures him briefly about respect and threatens to move him away from his table group if he disrupts again. Is Nate persuaded by the lecture or threat? Not a chance. He thinks she's bluffing, so he calls her on it. He continues testing.

With her credibility on the line, Mrs. Weaver finally decides to act. She tells Nate to move. It looks as though she might actually follow through, too, but Nate skillfully hooks her into another round of arguments and debates. She listens, tries to be fair, then decides to let the incident pass with just a warning. The encounter ends at point B with Mrs. Weaver repeating her threat to move Nate if he continues talking.

Why didn't Nate cooperate? The reason is simple: He didn't have to. Cooperation was optional, not required. Mrs. Weaver was unwilling to support her words with effective action (consequences). She relied instead on persuasion to get her message across.

Can you imagine what things would be like if our traffic laws were enforced this way? Visualize yourself driving home. The traffic is light, and each time you approach an intersection, you run the stoplight. Eventually a cop sees you and pulls you over.

"You ran three stoplights," he says. "That's against the law." Then he launches into a lecture. "Our laws are there for your safety and protection. If everyone disregarded stoplights we would have a lot of serious accidents. I would appreciate it if you would please try to follow the law in the future." After the lecture, he gets back in his car and drives off, and that's all that ever happens. Would this stop you from running stoplights in the future? Do you think this approach would serve as a deterrent to others?

Permissive teachers are a lot like the cop in my example. They give lots of warnings, reminders, second chances, and persuasive reasons why kids should stop at their stop signals. They may threaten to write tickets, and sometimes they actually do, but most of the time kids talk their way out of it, and teachers let things pass with a warning. Without tickets (consequences) to hold them accountable, kids have little cause to regard their teachers' rules seriously.

Essentially, permissiveness is a discipline approach based on yellow lights. Do you stop at yellow lights every time when you can safely make it through the intersection? Not likely. Why don't you stop? Most adults don't stop for the same reason kids don't stop. Stopping is optional, not required.

What signals do adults take seriously? Red lights. Why? Because we associate red lights with consequences that affect us in meaningful ways—tickets, fines, higher insurance rates, accidents, and possibly injuries. Children respond much the same way. Permissive teachers don't get the responses they want because they are holding up the wrong signals.

Why are permissive teachers reluctant to use consequences to enforce their rules? Most have the best intentions. They don't mean to be vague or inconsistent. They're trying to be respectful, but they don't know how to be firm and respectful at the same time. Permissive teachers believe that teaching rules the easy way should be sufficient. They believe students will stop misbehaving when they realize that stopping is the right thing to do. The teacher's job, therefore, is to convince students to accept this belief.

This reasoning holds up for the 55 percent of students in our classrooms who are compliant. Compliant students are eager to please. Most will cooperate just because it's the right thing to do. What about the strong-willed students and the fence-sitters? Often, the only reason they cooperate is because they have to.

Do you recall our earlier example about the boys in the karate game? Why did they finally stop playing a dangerous game? Was it because stopping was the right thing to do? No, they stopped because they had to. They didn't want to experience the consequence that accompanied the choice to continue. They finally got a clear message about what was expected.

When our words are supported by effective action, children receive a clear signal about our rules and expectations. They understand that our spoken rules are the rules we practice and they learn to take our words seriously. When our words are not supported by effective action, however, children learn to ignore our rules and continue to do what they want. The message they receive comes across like this: "I don't like what you're doing, but I'm not going to make you stop, at least not for a while."

How do kids know when they really are expected to stop? Often, they don't. The only way they will know is by testing. That's what permissiveness encourages them to do (see Table 6.1). Permissiveness violates learning theory and fails to provide many students with the data they need to cooperate.

What kind of relationships do you think develop around a permissive discipline approach? Do you think Mrs. Weaver in the earlier example has much credibility in the eyes of her students? Do you think they respect her? Do you think they feel secure knowing that she is the adult in charge in the classroom?

THE PUNITIVE APPROACH

(Firm but Not Respectful)

The punitive or autocratic approach has been a stable fixture in American schools for a long time. It was the dominant training system prior to the 1960s and remains one of the most widely used discipline models. Its trademark has been its predictability. Children respond to coercion and punishment the same way today that they did fifty or more years ago. Compliant children cooperate. Strong-willed children rebel. Fence-sitters can go either way.

The punitive approach seems to work with compliant students who need guidance the least and backfires with strong-willed students who need guidance the most. The punitive approach is a very poor match for strong-willed students. It makes them angry and resentful and inspires retaliation and power struggles.

Teachers who rely on the punitive or autocratic approach often find themselves in the roles of detective, judge, jailer, and probation officer. Their job is to investigate children's misdeeds, determine guilt, assign

TABLE 6.1

The Permissive Approach

Teacher's beliefs	• Children will cooperate when they understand that cooperation is the right thing to do. • My job is to serve my children and keep them happy. • Consequences that upset my children cannot be effective.
Power and control	• All for children.
Problem-solving process	• Problem solving by persuasion. • Win-lose (children win). • Teachers do most of the problem solving.
What children learn	• "Rules are for others, not me. I do as I wish." • Teachers serve children. • Teachers are responsible for solving children's problems. • Dependency, disrespect, self-centeredness.
How children respond	• Testing limits. • Challenging and defying rules and authority. • Ignoring and tuning out words. • Wearing teachers down with words.

blame, impose penalties, and carry out sentences. Teachers direct and control the problem-solving process, which is often adversarial. Penalties tend to be drawn out and severe. Let's look at how one teacher uses this approach to handle a problem with disruption.

Mr. Stover, fourth-grade teacher, is writing instructions on the blackboard when he hears giggling at the back of the room. Several students look at Jason, who does his best to appear innocent. Mr. Stover isn't convinced.

"Okay, guys, what's going on?" asks Mr. Stover in an annoyed tone. "What's so funny?"

"He made us laugh," says one student, pointing to Jason. Jason shrugs his shoulders. Mr. Stover gives him a stern, disapproving look and then returns to his work on the blackboard.

A few minutes pass, then more giggles, only louder this time. When Mr. Stover turns, he sees Jason making mocking hand gestures to the amusement of his classmates. "That's enough, Jason!" says Mr. Stover angrily.

"I wasn't doing anything," replies Jason, believing he hadn't been observed.

"Don't lie to me," says Mr. Stover. "I saw what you were doing, and I don't appreciate it. I expect that kind of behavior from a first grader but not from you. Keep it up and you're going to find yourself in big trouble." He gives Jason another stern, intimidating look.

A few minutes pass, and then Jason makes an even bolder move. When Mr. Stover's back is turned, Jason stands up and shakes his finger in a mock punitive gesture. The giggles turn into laughter. Mr. Stover intervenes again.

"What does it take to get through to you, Jason?" asks Mr. Stover. "Do you enjoy making a fool of yourself?"

"Do you enjoy being such a boring teacher?" counters Jason.

"That's enough!" shouts Mr. Stover, his face flushed with anger. "You've gone too far. Take your chair out in the hallway and write one hundred times 'I will not be disrespectful to my teacher.' "

Jason spends the next twenty minutes in the hallway. Then the bell rings for recess, and he tries to join his classmates. Mr. Stover intercepts him.

"Not so fast, Jason," says Mr. Stover. "Where are the sentences?"

"I didn't write them," says Jason defiantly, "and you can't make me."
"You won't go out to recess until you do," says Mr. Stover.

"Oh yeah? See if I care," says Jason. He would rather sit out the recess than give Mr. Stover the satisfaction of thinking he won.

Sure, Mr. Stover did get his message across, eventually, but what did he really accomplish? Did Jason leave the encounter with increased respect for Mr. Stover's rules or authority? Did Jason receive an instructive lesson in cooperation or responsibility? No. Jason learned what he experienced—a lesson in hurtful communication and problem solving.

What types of relationship is Mr. Stover likely to develop around his punitive discipline methods? Will his students view him as a teacher or a bully? Do you think they respect him? Look up to him as a role model? Does fear and intimidation provide a lasting basis for positive relationships?

As a training model, the punitive approach has many limitations and only partially accomplishes our basic training goals. It usually stops unwanted behavior in an immediate situation, but it doesn't teach acceptable lessons in communication or problem solving. The cooperation that it achieves comes at the expense of the teacher-student relationship. Students cooperate out of fear, not respect. Many feel resentful. Some seek revenge. Let's take a closer look at the methods Mr. Stover used by examining a diagram of the interaction (see Figure 6.2).

At point A, Mr. Stover notices the disruption and intervenes with some quick detective work. His tone is angry and adversarial. The focus is on right and wrong, guilt and blame, good guys and bad guys. The kids pick up on the dynamics quickly. They deny their guilt and attempt to place the blame on each other. The game of cops and robbers is under way, but so far the robbers are winning. Mr. Stover's detective work leads nowhere. So he tries intimidation.

Now the students know he is hooked. Their disruption continues, but Mr. Stover gets his evidence. He catches Jason in the act. When Jason denies his guilt, Mr. Stover accuses him of lying and confronts him with the evidence.

At this point, Mr. Stover's anger and frustration take over. He has completely personalized the conflict, and he is determined to make Jason pay for his crimes. The issue of disruption is now secondary to the

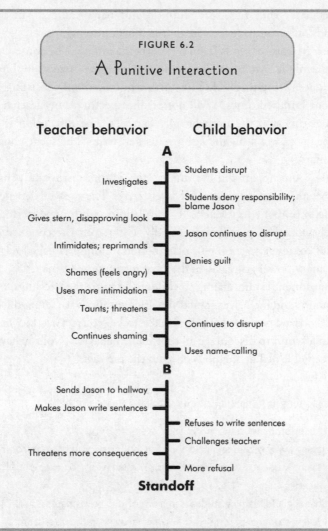

FIGURE 6.2

A Punitive Interaction

Teacher behavior   **Child behavior**

A

Students disrupt

Investigates

Students deny responsibility;
blame Jason

Gives stern, disapproving look

Jason continues to disrupt

Intimidates; reprimands

Denies guilt

Shames (feels angry)

Uses more intimidation

Taunts; threatens

Continues to disrupt

Continues shaming

Uses name-calling

B

Sends Jason to hallway

Makes Jason write sentences

Refuses to write sentences

Challenges teacher

Threatens more consequences

More refusal

Standoff

hurtful and escalating power struggle that dominates the interaction. Mr. Stover begins by shaming and blaming Jason in front of the class; then he adds a challenge. He tells Jason to "keep it up" and threatens further consequences if he does.

Isn't this like waving a red cape in front of an angry bull? What would you predict? Right, the strategy backfires. Jason feels humiliated and retaliates with further disruption and name-calling. Mr. Stover responds on the same level. The drama moves into high gear.

Next Mr. Stover sends Jason out of the classroom. The consequence, by itself, might have been effective in stopping the disruption, but Mr. Stover doesn't stop there. He adds further humiliation by insisting Jason write one hundred times "I will not be disrespectful to my teacher."

Does this stop the misbehavior? Partially. The disruption is over, but not the power struggle. Jason refuses to write. The scene ends in a standoff.

Sure, punishment did eventually stop Jason's disruptive behavior, but does this prove punishment is effective? The answer depends on your definition of effectiveness. If your definition is limited to stopping the behavior, then punishment usually works. But the cooperation it achieves comes at a very high price: injured feelings, damaged relationships, angry power struggles, and loss of instructional time.

Punishment is humiliating to children. It hurts their feelings, makes them angry, and incites resistance or fearful withdrawal. Often, the hurtful methods are perceived as a personal attack ("you're a bad kid") rather than an attempt to discourage an acceptable behavior ("your behavior is not acceptable"). The methods obscure the message.

EXAMPLES OF PUNITIVE DISCIPLINE PRACTICES

- Making students stand in a corner.
- Taking away recess and field trips for misbehavior in the classroom.
- Making students write sentences for misbehavior (for example, "I will not . . .").
- Shaming and blaming students in front of their classmates.
- Making students pick up trash for misbehavior in the classroom.
- Sending home negative daily behavior reports.
- Sending students to time-out for several hours.
- Giving detentions without emphasizing corrective skill training.
- Taking away privileges for weeks or months at a time.
- Asking parents to remove privileges at home for misbehavior at school.
- Asking parents to sit with their child throughout a school day.

- Writing students' names on the board under the frown face.
- Taking away privileges in the spring for misbehavior in the fall.
- Making students write confession letters.
- Using sarcastic or demeaning language with students.
- Shaming disrespectful students to show them how it feels.

Imagine how people would respond if our traffic laws were enforced in punitive ways. Visualize yourself driving home. You approach a traffic signal, and the light turns red. There isn't another car in sight, so you take a chance and run the light. As soon as you do, you see a flashing red light in the rearview mirror. The cop pulls you over.

"Are you blind or just stupid?" he asks as he approaches your car. "Couldn't you see the light was red?" He orders you to get out of your car and writes you a citation. But before he hands it to you, he insults you again and hits you twice with his nightstick.

Would you respond by looking at the officer with appreciation and say, "Thanks, I needed that. I understand your point, and I'll be sure to stop next time"? Probably not. Most likely, you would feel angry and resentful. You understand the rule the officer is trying to enforce, but you don't feel good about the way the message was communicated. If you are strong-willed or a fence-sitter, you might even consider ways to get back.

When it comes to being humiliated, children respond much as adults do. Compliant children usually cooperate out of fear, not respect. Strong-willed children become angry and resentful. They rebel, seek revenge, or become sneaky and find ways to fly below our radar. Fence-sitters can go either way.

When students treat one another with threats, intimidation, humiliation, and other hurtful tactics, don't we call this bullying? If it's not okay for students to behave this way, then why is it okay for teachers?

If punishment has so many limitations, then why do so many teachers continue to use it? Most teachers who use punitive discipline methods were raised that way themselves. They have no other tools in their discipline tool kit. The methods feel natural to them, and they don't question their effectiveness. They believe the lessons have to hurt if students are going to learn from them. When power struggles develop, punitive teachers assume the problem is with the student, not their own methods.

THE MIXED APPROACH

(Neither Firm nor Respectful)

As the name implies, the mixed approach is a combination of the punitive and permissive training models. The mixed approach is characterized by inconsistency. Teachers do a lot of flip-flopping back and forth between punishment and permissiveness in search of a better way to get their message across, one that is both firm and respectful. The goal is elusive because they lack the methods to achieve it. So they continue to flip-flop.

There are several variations of the mixed approach. Some teachers start off permissively with lots of repeating, reminding, warnings, and offering second chances, then they become frustrated and try punitive tactics—threatening, shaming, blaming, and imposing harsh and drawn-out consequences. Others start off punitively with stern commands, investigation, shaming, blaming, and threats and then give in and take a permissive posture when they encounter resistance.

Still others remain loyal to one approach for longer periods of time.

TABLE 6.2

The Autocratic or Punitive Approach

Teacher's beliefs	• If it doesn't hurt, children won't learn. • Children won't respect my rules unless they fear my methods. • It's my job to control my children. • It's my job to solve my children's problems.
Power and control	• All for teachers.
Problem-solving process	• Problem solving by force. • Win-lose (teachers win). • Teachers do all the problem solving and make all the decisions. • Teachers direct and control the problem.
What children learn	• Teachers are responsible for solving children's probems. • Hurtful methods of communication and problem solving. • Dependency, disrespect, self-centeredness.
How children respond	• Anger, stubbornness. • Revenge, rebellion. • Withdrawal, fearful submission.

They try permissiveness until they can't stand being ignored or taken advantage of any longer, then they flip-flop and try punishment until they can't stand how tyrannical they sound. Then they flip-flop back to permissiveness. The cycle of flip-flops just takes longer to repeat itself.

How do kids respond to the mixed approach? The mixed approach brings out the worst in both children and adults. Let's see what happens when one teacher uses this approach with a group of disruptive sixth graders.

Miss Carey, a first-year teacher, is teaching a geography lesson when a paper airplane whizzes past her shoulder. She turns and sees a group of boys laughing and taking particular pleasure in her annoyance.

"Come on, guys," she says. "There's a lesson going on here. Would you like to join us?" The laughter stops for the moment, and Miss Carey proceeds with her lesson.

Within minutes, she hears more laughter and sees Andrew sitting at his desk with his jacket zipped up over his head. She waits for him to stop, but he just sits there and pretends to follow along. His buddies can barely control themselves.

"Andrew!" exclaims Miss Carey, loud enough to get his attention. He unzips his jacket enough to create a hole to peep through.

"Can I help you?" he asks. His friends continue to laugh.

"You sure can," replied Miss Carey. "You can take your jacket off your head and sit the way you're supposed to. I don't appreciate your clowning around. I really wish you would show a little respect."

"Okay," says Andrew with a smirk. He sits up rigidly in his seat, chest out, eyes forward, as though he were standing at attention. "Is that better?" he asks.

"You know what I mean," she replies. "I don't want to have to tell you again."

Andrew relaxes his shoulders slightly and then shoots a quick grin at his buddies. Miss Carey returns to her lesson. Her patience is wearing thin.

A few minutes later, Miss Carey is startled by a loud thud. Andrew is lying on the floor next to his desk. Everyone is looking at him.

"I can't believe it!" he exclaims with feigned surprise. "I fell out of my seat! And I was trying so hard to sit the right way, too." He grins at his friends, who can barely control their laughter.

"I've had it!" explodes Miss Carey. "If you insist on acting like a jerk, then do it outside my classroom." She hands him a referral to the office and points to the door. "Take as long as you want, but don't come back until you can figure out how to cooperate. You'll get F grades on everything you miss while you're gone."

Does Andrew sound like an aggressive researcher with a supportive cast of fence-sitters? Is Miss Carey putting on an entertaining floor show for the classroom? You bet.

Clearly, Andrew pushed things to the limit, but did his behavior cause Miss Carey to explode, or did she set herself up by allowing things to go too far? Let's answer these questions by examining a diagram of their interaction (see Figure 6.3).

What happens the first time Andrew and his buddies disrupt? Do

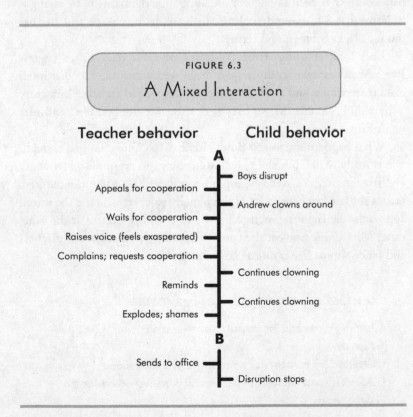

FIGURE 6.3
A Mixed Interaction

Teacher behavior	Child behavior
	A
	Boys disrupt
Appeals for cooperation	
	Andrew clowns around
Waits for cooperation	
Raises voice (feels exasperated)	
Complains; requests cooperation	
	Continues clowning
Reminds	
	Continues clowning
Explodes; shames	
	B
Sends to office	
	Disruption stops

they receive a clear message to stop? No. Miss Carey appeals for their cooperation. She points out that there is a lesson in progress and invites them to join in. Does this mean they have a choice? If it does, the choice is clear. They continue testing.

What happens the second time Andrew disrupts? Does Miss Carey give him a clear signal to stop and tell him what will happen if he doesn't? No. She tells him she doesn't appreciate his behavior and says she wishes he would show a little more respect. What does that mean? How little is too little? Andrew gets right to work trying to find out. He continues to disrupt and to be disrespectful.

What happens the third time Andrew disrupts? Does he finally get the information he's looking for? No. Miss Carey tells him that she doesn't want to have to tell him again. Tell him what? She probably believes she has been saying *stop* all along, but she hasn't been saying it in terms that Andrew understands. She is trying to be respectful, but her message lacks firmness and clarity.

Let's look at things from Andrew's perspective. He's an aggressive researcher who really enjoys negative attention. He disrupted class three times, and each time nothing happened to make him stop. Why should he take Miss Carey seriously? He doesn't. He continues disrupting.

What happens the fourth time? Finally Miss Carey has had enough. She is ready to act, but she has allowed things to go too far. Her anger and frustration take over. She explodes and ends up using the punitive tactics she tried so hard to avoid. Like many teachers who use the mixed approach, she lacks the methods to be firm and respectful at the same time. Miss Carey has lost the cooperation of her aggressive researchers and fence-sitters. She is on the fast track to burnout.

EXAMPLES OF MIXED DISCIPLINE PRACTICES

- Ignoring disruption for several days, then taking away recess the next day.
- Overlooking misbehavior when you're in a good mood.
- Allowing some students to disrupt and punishing others for the same behavior.

- Threatening to use consequences, then failing to follow through.
- Allowing students to enter the classroom noisily, then becoming angry.
- Using different consequences for the same misbehavior.
- Asking students to be quiet, then yelling at them when they're too loud.
- Allowing late homework assignments from some students but not others.
- Ignoring disruptive talking from favored students.
- Combining incompatible classroom management systems.
- Sending home negative daily behavior reports without using consequences to stop the misbehavior in the classroom.
- Requiring some students to raise their hands to speak, then responding to others who blurt out.
- Asking parents to take away privileges at home for misbehavior in the classroom.
- Tolerating disruption in the classroom until it becomes intolerable, then sending students to the office.
- Telling students your classroom procedures but tolerating whatever behavior occurs.
- Ignoring, warning, giving second chances, then punishing.
- Punishing some students for being disrespectful but tolerating it from others.

THE DEMOCRATIC APPROACH

(Firm and Respectful)

Fortunately, there is an alternative to the ineffective extremes of punishment and permissiveness. I didn't invent it, but I did have the good fortune to observe it, describe it, connect it to its theoretical foundations, and eventually teach it to hundreds of thousands of parents and teachers. When I was a graduate student in educational psychology at the University of California at Davis, one of my professors asked me to assist him in a research study on teacher effectiveness. The purpose of this 1978 study was to examine teacher behaviors that contribute to time on task with students. Research shows that on-task time correlates more powerfully with achievement than does any other variable.

My job in the study was to observe effective teachers in their classrooms and record the specific things they said and did that led to on-task time. This was an eye-opener because most of these teachers did not have easy classrooms. They had students with ADD, learning disabilities, and behavioral problems and had more than a few comedians and attention seekers.

The effective teachers I observed did not give in to misbehavior. They didn't lecture, cajole, bargain, or negotiate. They didn't use threats, intimidation, or long, drawn-out consequences. They didn't compromise their standards.

Instead they maintained a respectful attitude, held their ground firmly, stated their rules and expectations clearly, and followed through with instructive consequences when students chose not to cooperate. These teachers were solidly in control of themselves and their classrooms. They made classroom management look easy.

What impressed me most was the fact that their guidance methods worked with the full range of students: compliant students who cooperate for the asking, strong-willed students who require generous helpings of consequences, and fence-sitters who can go either way, even students with special needs. It didn't matter. These teachers had the tools to get the job done. They were prepared to teach their rules the easy way or the hard way, whatever the situation required, and they got results. They got the most cooperation, the most respect, the most on-task time, and the best achievement from their students. I didn't realize it at the time, but I was getting a crash course in effective limit setting from some real pros.

A few years later, after the study had been published and was collecting dust on some library bookshelf, I had an opportunity to pilot a teacher workshop series on effective classroom management for a large northern California school district. "Great!" I thought. "I'll use the outcome data from the 1978 UC Davis study. We know what works. If I can teach it, others can use it."

The pilot was a success. Teachers found the approach easy to learn and use, and they got results that were just what the teachers in the study achieved. The workshop became a training program that eventually became a book, but the real credit belongs to the many effective teachers I observed who understood how to create optimal learning environments for children by balancing firmness with respect. I call it the *democratic approach* because it provides freedom and choice within clearly defined limits. It's a blueprint for effective teaching and learning and healthy development.

The democratic approach is a win-win model that accomplishes all of our basic training goals. It stops misbehavior. It teaches responsibility. And it conveys, in the clearest way, the lessons we want to teach about our rules and standards for acceptable behavior. The methods are well matched to the full range of students and solidly grounded in research and well-established principles of child development.

The democratic approach succeeds where others fall short because it focuses on what effective guidance and discipline is all about—teaching and learning. The teacher's job is to guide the learning process by providing clear limits, acceptable choices, and instructive consequences that hold children accountable for their actions. No threats or detective work. No lecturing or cajoling. No flip-flopping back and forth. And no power struggles. The methods don't hurt. Children are simply provided with the information they need to make acceptable choices about their behavior and then allowed to experience the consequences of those choices. The teacher is prepared to teach the discipline lesson the easy way or the hard way, however students choose to learn it.

EXAMPLES OF DEMOCRATIC DISCIPLINE PRACTICES

- Separating students who talk during instruction.
- Removing toys or items from students who play with them during instruction.
- When dawdlers fail to complete work during class time, require them to make up incomplete assignments during their recess time.
- When students abuse privileges, suspend those privileges temporarily.
- When students make messes, require them to clean up the mess.
- When students fail to master a required skill such as raising a quiet hand to speak, require them to practice that skill during their recess time.

- When students misuse classroom equipment such as computers or scissors, separate them from the item temporarily.
- When students tilt back in their chair, remove their chair temporarily.
- When students chew gum during instruction, have them practice not chewing gum in the classroom during their recess time.

Does the term *democratic* mean that all guidance decisions are put to a vote and decided by consensus? No. The term is used to illustrate how boundaries are arranged and how power and control are distributed in the classroom. In democratic classrooms, the teacher is still the adult in charge. Children are provided with freedom and choices within well-defined limits and allowed to make decisions about their own behavior. How much freedom and choice are they allowed? Children are given only as much freedom and choices as they can handle responsibly. Let's look at how one teacher uses the democratic approach to handle a problem with class disruption.

Josh and Aaron, second graders, sit across from each other in the same table group. They are supposed to be working on a handwriting assignment, but they fool around instead. First Josh tosses an eraser at Aaron and hits him in the chest. Aaron flicks it back. Then Josh throws a wad of paper and hits Aaron. When Aaron throws it back, he hits Carly instead. She complains to the teacher.

"Mr. Jordan, Aaron threw something at me."

"Josh threw it at me first," says Aaron.

"No, I didn't," says Josh. "You threw an eraser at me!"

Mr. Jordan intervenes. "Josh and Aaron, you both should be working quietly on your handwriting assignment. Would you like to work quietly at your desks or by yourselves at the back tables?" Mr. Jordan keeps two tables in the back corners of the room for cooldowns, time-outs, or for when students need to be separated from their table groups. He looks at each for an answer.

Aaron is convinced. He decides to settle down. Not Josh. He enjoyed the brief soap opera his disruption created, and he's hungry for more. When Mr. Jordan walks away, Josh fires off several more paper wads at

Aaron. One hits Aaron in the head. The other sails over Aaron's shoulder and catches Mr. Jordan's attention.

"Pick up your assignment, Josh," says Mr. Jordan matter-of-factly. "You'll have to finish at the back table." Josh heads off to complete the lesson by himself. The disruption is over.

Unlike the teachers in my previous examples, Mr. Jordan succeeds in a firm and respectful manner. He achieves all of his guidance goals and maintains positive relationships in the process. No lectures. No humiliating consequences. No flip-flopping and no angry power struggles. He simply gives the boys the information they need to cooperate and then follows through based on their choice. Let's take a closer look at his methods by examining a diagram of the interaction (see Figure 6.4).

Notice how short this diagram is. Effective guidance requires less time and energy and achieves better results. Mr. Jordan is working with the plan. He knows what he's going to do, and he's prepared for whatever resistance he may encounter.

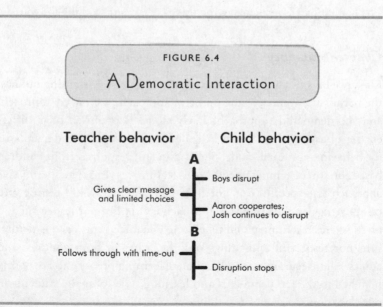

FIGURE 6.4

A Democratic Interaction

Teacher behavior   **Child behavior**

A

Gives clear message
and limited choices   Boys disrupt

                                   Aaron cooperates;
                                   Josh continues to disrupt

B

Follows through with time-out

                                   Disruption stops

He begins at point A by giving the boys a clear message about what he expects. He tells them they should be working quietly on their writing assignment. Then he gives them some choices. He asks whether they would like to work quietly at their seats or at the back tables. Both boys say they want to work at their seats. So Mr. Jordan tells them they will have to move if there is any further disrupting.

Now the boys have all the information they need to make an acceptable decision. They know what's expected and what will happen if they choose not to cooperate. The way things are set up, they cannot avoid learning the lesson Mr. Jordan intends.

What happens? Aaron decides to cooperate, but not Josh. He decides to test and continues disrupting. So Mr. Jordan simply follows through. In a matter-of-fact manner, he asks Josh to take his work to the back table and finish up. Josh gets a very clear message. Mr. Jordan is teaching his rules effectively.

Can you imagine how much more rewarding your teaching would be without all the reminders, threats, lectures, and power struggles? The goal is achievable (see Table 6.3). The methods are simple and easy to learn. The hardest part is recognizing the things that aren't working for you.

Chapter Summary

Most teachers teach their rules from one of four basic training models: the permissive approach, the punitive approach, the mixed approach, and the democratic approach. Each model is premised on a different set of assumptions about how children learn rules and standards for behavior, and each model elicits different responses from children based on their temperaments and learning styles. The permissive approach is respectful but not firm and often provokes testing and power struggles. The punitive approach is firm but not respectful and often incites resentment and rebellion. The mixed approach is neither firm nor respectful and brings out the worst in both children and adults. All three training models violate learning theory and are poorly matched to the temperaments and learning styles of many students in our classrooms.

Fortunately, there's an alternative to the ineffective extremes of

TABLE 6.3

The Democratic Approach

Teacher's beliefs	• Children are capable of solving problems on their own. • Children should be given choices and allowed to learn from the consequences of their choices. • Encouragement is an effective way to motivate cooperation.
Power and control	• Children are given only as much power and control as they can handle responsibly.
Problem-solving process	• Cooperative. • Win-win. • Based on mutual respect. • Children are active participants in the problem-solving process.
What children learn	• Responsibility. • Cooperation. • Independence. • Respect for rules and authority • Self-control.
How children respond	• More cooperation. • Less limit testing. •Resolve problems on their own. • Regard teacher's words seriously.

punishment and permissiveness. The democratic approach combines firmness with respect and achieves all of our guidance goals. It stops misbehavior. It teaches responsibility and it conveys in the clearest way the lessons we want to teach about our rules and authority. The teacher's job is to guide the learning process by providing clear messages about classroom rules and expectations and supporting those rules with instructive consequences when children decide to test. The teacher is prepared to teach rules the easy way or the hard way, how ever children choose to learn. The methods are well matched to the full range of temperaments and learning styles.

If this chapter has fulfilled its mission, you should recognize your limit-setting approach. Do you tend to be permissive? Punitive? Or use the mixed approach? If you fall into any of these categories, you already know that your limit-setting approach is a bad match with as much as 45 percent of the students in your classroom. The democratic approach to classroom discipline will provide you with the good match you're looking for. It's time to add some new tools to your discipline tool kit.

Classroom Dances: Ineffective Discipline in Action

Teachers who operate with unclear or ineffective limits develop their own special dance of miscommunication, which they perform over and over again when their rules are tested or violated. There's a permissive version of the dance that's wordy and drawn out and a punitive version that's angrier and more dramatic. Some teachers do a little of both. All dances are exercises in ineffective limit setting that lead to escalating conflicts and power struggles. Over time, the dances become such a familiar and deeply ingrained habit that teachers experience them as their normal way of doing things. They are not even aware they are dancing.

Teachers such as the ones we'll follow in this chapter can easily become stuck in these destructive patterns of communication. Without awareness and new skills, there's no way out. They have no choice but to continue dancing the only dance they know. Awareness is the key to breaking free.

If you suspect that you've been dancing with your students, this chapter will help you break free. You'll learn how your dances begin, how they end, and what keeps them going. Most important, you'll learn how to step off the dance floor so you can move on to more effective forms of communication. Let's look at how one frustrated teacher discovered her dance.

A Permissive Dance

Barbara, a third-grade teacher, was on the verge of burnout when I first met her. Her third year of teaching was starting off as rough as the previous two. The thought of facing another year full of conflicts and power struggles was more than she could bear. Depression was sinking in. Her principal suggested that she give me a call.

"I became a teacher because I like kids," Barbara said when she arrived at my office, "but I don't enjoy them much anymore. I treat them with kindness and respect, but some of them just tune me out and do what they want. I nag them all day long. They're wearing me out!"

She didn't realize it, but Barbara was stuck in an escalating pattern of conflicts and power struggles that she believed the kids were causing. My first task was to help her recognize her dance.

"Pick a typical misbehavior in your classroom and describe, in a very step-by-step manner, exactly what you say and do when your students behave this way."

"The most persistent problem I face is all the talking and clowning around that goes on while I'm teaching. This drives me up a wall."

"What do you do when this happens?" I asked. As she described what

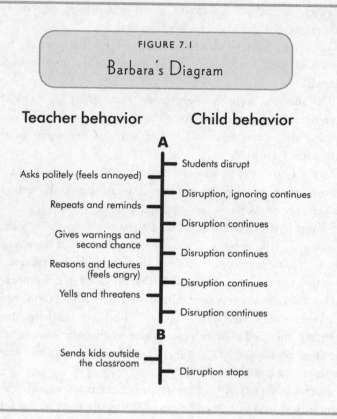

FIGURE 7.1

Barbara's Diagram

Teacher behavior   **Child behavior**

A

Asks politely (feels annoyed) — Students disrupt

Repeats and reminds — Disruption, ignoring continues

Gives warnings and second chance — Disruption continues

Reasons and lectures (feels angry) — Disruption continues

Yells and threatens — Disruption continues

Disruption continues

B

Sends kids outside the classroom — Disruption stops

usually happens, I diagrammed each step in the interactional sequence. Visual diagrams are an effective way to help teachers get acquainted with their dances. When Barbara finished, we both took a moment to reflect on her diagram (see Figure 7.1).

"Look familiar?" I asked.

"I must go through that ten times a day," said Barbara. "See what I mean when I say I nag them all day long?" She looked exhausted.

"Yes, that's quite a dance," I replied, giving it the label it deserved. I could understand why she felt so worn-out.

Performing classroom dances is like saving stress coupons. If we collect enough of them in the course of a day or a week, we get a prize—

headaches, stomachaches, and a variety of other upsets, even depression and burnout. Barbara's coupon book was full.

"Let's make sure we've captured everything that happens in your diagram," I said. "At what point in the dance do you begin to feel annoyed?"

"I'm annoyed from the beginning," she replied. "I know they're not going to cooperate, but I don't show my anger until later on. I try reasoning and lecturing, then I wear down, and my anger comes out. That's when I get loud."

At the beginning of Barbara's diagram, I wrote the words "feels annoyed," then, after her lecturing step, I wrote the words "feels angry." The sequence of events was now complete.

I summarized what Barbara's diagram was telling us. "It seems that the more you talk, the more the kids tune you out and the angrier you become. Your dance continues until you can't take it anymore. Then you stop it with your action step." Barbara nodded in agreement.

Her diagram was revealing. She started off with a polite request to stop. Her requests were usually ignored. Then she tried repeating and reminding, followed by warnings and second chances. The misbehavior continued. So she shifted gears again and tried reasoning and lecturing. The resistance continued.

The more she talked, the angrier she became until reasoning and lecturing turned into yelling and threats. When she reached her breaking point, she made disruptive students stand outside the classroom, ending the dance. Repeat offenders were sent to the office.

I returned to Barbara's diagram and drew a circle around all the steps that used words. This took up nearly all of her diagram. I labeled these "verbal steps." Then I drew a box around the step that involved action and labeled this "action steps." This box occupied only a small portion of her diagram (see Figure 7.2).

"Which steps take up most of your time and energy and cause you the greatest frustration?" I asked. She pointed to her verbal steps.

"Now, which steps stopped the misbehavior?" I asked. She just looked at me and smiled. She didn't need to answer because the answer stood right in front of her. Her diagram was proof that she spent most

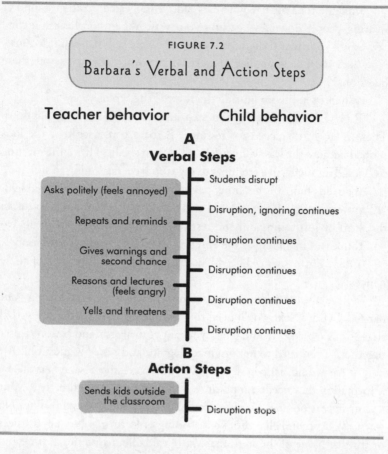

FIGURE 7.2

Barbara's Verbal and Action Steps

Teacher behavior   **Child behavior**

A
Verbal Steps

Students disrupt

Asks politely (feels annoyed)

Disruption, ignoring continues

Repeats and reminds

Disruption continues

Gives warnings and
second chance

Disruption continues

Reasons and lectures
(feels angry)

Disruption continues

Yells and threatens

Disruption continues

B
Action Steps

Sends kids outside
the classroom

Disruption stops

of her time and energy doing things that didn't work. Barbara looked confused and relieved at the same time.

"I thought I was supposed to do all that stuff," she confessed as she pointed to the circled portion of her diagram. "I thought I was giving them every opportunity to cooperate, but I can see I was giving them opportunities *not* to cooperate."

This insight would be her ticket out of the dances. The hardest part was now behind her. She recognized what wasn't working for her. My next task was to help her understand the type of research she was encountering.

"Imagine that you're eight years old," I suggested. "You're skillful at wearing people down and getting your way. When you hear someone say 'Stop,' your first thought is 'Or what? What will happen if I don't?' Now let's look at your diagram. At what point do you answer these questions?"

"When I send them outside the room," she replied.

"Right," I said. "Your action step answers their research questions. There is no further need for testing." Barbara could see that the kids pushed because she was willing to bend. When she held firm, the pushing stopped. Her ineffective attempts to say stop were beginning to sink in.

"The kids probably get other payoffs from your dances," I suggested. "If you were only eight years old and you could get an adult to do all this stuff by just tuning out and resisting, would you feel powerful? Do you think you might enjoy the entertainment and negative attention?"

"Okay, I'm convinced," said Barbara. "How do I get out of these dances?"

"You've already taken the most important step by recognizing your dance," I said. "Next, you'll need to eliminate all your ineffective verbal steps. Your dances will end when you put your words and actions closer together." I returned to her original diagram and posed a question.

"What would happen if you gave your aggressive researchers all the information they needed at point A, and then moved on directly to your action step at point B if they tested? No repeating. No reminding. No warnings or second chances. No reasoning or lecturing. No raised voices or threats. None of the steps that waste valuable instructional time and wear you out. Your new message might sound like this: 'Guys, you can follow along quietly, or you'll have to spend some quiet time by yourselves. What would you like to do?' "

"I'm ready to give it a try," Barbara replied. Her new diagram soon looked like Figure 7.3. So can yours.

A Punitive Dance

Punitive dances tend to be louder, angrier, and more dramatic than their permissive counterparts. The steps are different, but the dances are just

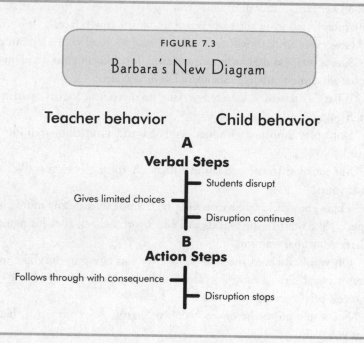

FIGURE 7.3

Barbara's New Diagram

Teacher behavior   Child behavior

A

Verbal Steps

Students disrupt

Gives limited choices

Disruption continues

B

Action Steps

Follows through with consequence

Disruption stops

another variation of the basic classroom power struggle. They begin with unclear or ineffective messages about rules. They're fueled by anger and resistance, and they lead to escalating conflicts and power struggles.

I recall one punitive dance I witnessed firsthand when a sixth-grade teacher invited me to her classroom to observe one of her disruptive students. "Try to arrive about forty-five minutes before we break for lunch," Sharon suggested on the phone. "Richard usually blows about that time."

She was right. Within minutes of my arrival, Richard disrupted the class. I watched him position several textbooks near the edge of his desk. Then, while Sharon was explaining a math problem at the board, he gave the books a nudge with his elbow. The ensuing crash got everybody's attention.

Sharon turned and glared at him. Her jaw was set. Her hands were on her hips. "That was real smart, Richard!" she said with a disgusted look on her face. "Why don't you grow up and cooperate for a change?" She wrote his name on the blackboard under the frown face.

"Give me a break. It was an accident," said Richard with a sly smile.

"Sure it was," said Sharon sarcastically. "Just like all your accidents. I know what you're doing." She glared at him again.

"What?" Richard countered, trying to keep the verbal sparring match going.

"Don't play innocent with me," said Sharon. "I'm sick of your lousy attitude."

"My lousy attitude!" exclaimed Richard, rolling his eyes. "What about yours?"

"That's enough!" said Sharon sharply. "I won't tolerate any more disrespect." She went to the blackboard and wrote a check after his name. "That's your final warning."

"Oh yeah!" Richard sneered. "What are you going to do? Take my recesses away?" It was only Tuesday, but Richard had already lost all of his recess privileges for the week.

"No. You'll go to the office," replied Sharon. "Keep it up if that's what you want."

"It's better than being here!" Richard shot back.

"I'm glad you like it, " countered Sharon, "because that's where you're going." She handed him three sheets of paper. "Don't come back until these pages are full of sentences saying 'I will not be disrespectful to my teacher.' " Richard gave her a defiant look as he headed out the door.

When the bell rang for recess, Sharon and I had an opportunity to talk. "See what I have to put up with?" she began. "He makes me so angry! I never would have talked to my teachers the way he talks to me."

"Was his behavior today typical of what happens?" I asked.

"Yes," she replied, "but he usually stops when I threaten to send him to the office. He hates that almost as much as being sent home. Nothing else seems to matter to him. I've taken away all of his recesses and free activity time, even his field trips."

"Have you spoken with Richard's parents?" I inquired.

"Yes. We're using a daily behavior report card system," she replied. "Each day, I send a behavior report card home to his parents. If he gets sent to the office, his parents make him spend all of his after-school time in his room. No TV, no video games, and no play privileges."

"Has that helped?" I asked.

"We thought it would," said Sharon, "but his behavior is worse, not better." They were digging themselves in deeper with their drawn-out consequences.

I was curious about how Sharon perceived her guidance methods. "What do you usually do when Richard misbehaves?" I asked.

"The first time, I write his name on the board and call his attention to his behavior and give him a chance to correct it. The second time, I write a check after his name as an additional warning. The third time, he loses a recess. The fourth time, he loses all of his recesses for the day. If he misbehaves again that day, and he usually does, then he loses all of his recesses for the week. Next, I send him to the office to write sentences or an apology letter. If Richard is sent to the office twice on the same day, the principal suspends him for the rest of the day. He has been suspended three times this year."

The methods Sharon described were only a partial description of what I observed. "Is she aware of what she's doing?" I wondered. It was time to hold up a mirror and help her see the methods she actually used.

"Sometimes visual diagrams give us a clearer picture of what's going on," I suggested. "Earlier, when Richard misbehaved, I recorded what he said and did. Then I recorded your responses. May I draw a descriptive diagram of the interaction?" Sharon nodded.

I went to the blackboard and drew a diagram of the interaction I observed, explaining each step as I went. When I finished, I stood back and gave Sharon a chance to check it over (see Figure 7.4).

"Did I do all of that?" she asked in disbelief, as she pointed to the long series of verbal steps in her diagram. "It seems so angry."

"I call them classroom dances," I said. "The dance you do with Richard is an angry one. You both took quite a few shots at each other." My suspicions were confirmed. She wasn't aware of all the steps she used.

"Let's make sure we've captured everything that happens in your dance," I said. "At what point do you become angry?"

"I'm angry in the beginning," Sharon admitted. "I know what

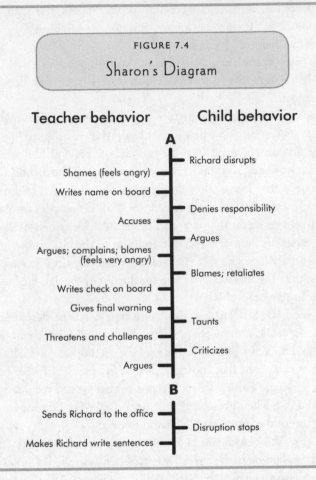

FIGURE 7.4

Sharon's Diagram

Teacher behavior   **Child behavior**

A
                                  Richard disrupts

Shames (feels angry)

Writes name on board
                                  Denies responsibility

Accuses
                                  Argues

Argues; complains; blames
(feels very angry)
                                  Blames; retaliates

Writes check on board

Gives final warning
                                  Taunts

Threatens and challenges
                                  Criticizes

Argues

B

Sends Richard to the office
                                  Disruption stops

Makes Richard write sentences

usually follows, but I become angriest when he argues and talks back." I returned to her diagram and wrote the words "feels angry" at the beginning of the interaction and the words "feels very angry" during the arguing and verbal sparring.

Sharon's diagram was now complete, so I summarized what it was telling us. "Richard is skillful at hooking you into verbal sparring matches. The more you talk, the more resistance you encounter, and the angrier you become. Your dance continues to heat up until you finally stop it with your action step.

"Let's take a look at the various steps in your dance," I suggested. I returned to Sharon's diagram and drew a circle around all the steps that relied primarily on words. I labeled these "verbal steps." They took up most of her diagram. Next, I drew a box around all of the steps that involved action, labeling them "action steps." They took up a small section at the end of her diagram (see Figure 7.5).

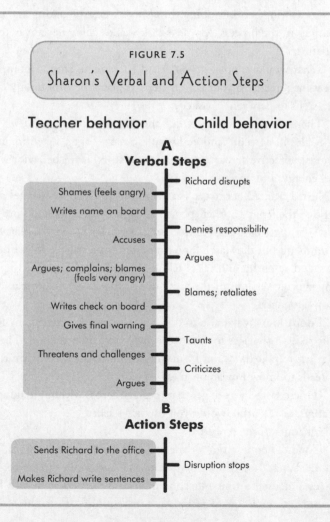

FIGURE 7.5
Sharon's Verbal and Action Steps

Teacher behavior   **Child behavior**

A
Verbal Steps

- Richard disrupts
Shames (feels angry)
Writes name on board
- Denies responsibility
Accuses
- Argues
Argues; complains; blames
(feels very angry)
- Blames; retaliates
Writes check on board
Gives final warning
- Taunts
Threatens and challenges
- Criticizes
Argues

B
Action Steps

Sends Richard to the office
- Disruption stops
Makes Richard write sentences

"You use two types of steps to stop Richard's misbehavior: verbal steps and action steps." I said. "Which one always stops his misbehavior?"

"My action steps," Sharon replied.

"Right," I said. "Sometimes he stops when you threaten to send him to the office because he knows from experience that your action steps will follow."

Sharon understood where I was heading. She could see that the last few steps in her diagram were the only ones Richard regarded seriously. She was wasting her time doing things that weren't working and becoming angry in the process. My next task was to show her a way to avoid the dance.

"What would happen if you asked Richard to stop at point A and then went directly to your action steps at point B without any of these other steps in between?" I asked.

"There would be less arguing," she replied.

"Right," I agreed. "And you would be less angry. By eliminating all of these ineffective verbal steps, you could stop his misbehavior with less time, energy, and upset."

Next, I wanted her to see that the long-term consequences actually extended the length of their power struggles. "Let's look at your action steps," I suggested. "Your action steps stop Richard's misbehavior for the moment, but they last a long time, sometimes all week. He becomes angry and resentful and takes it out on you. Then you end up doing many shorter versions of the same dance that end with threats instead of consequences."

"I don't know what else to do," she confessed. "He usually loses all of his recess privileges for the week by Monday afternoon. There isn't much left to take away, but I can't allow him to get away with it, either. He needs to know I mean business." I agreed.

"If there were a way to get that message across without making Richard angry or resentful, would you use it?" I asked.

"Of course," she replied.

"Good. Then let's put a different ending on your diagram," I suggested. "What would happen if you changed your threats to limited choices and used a time-out consequence if he persisted with his disruption? No more loss of recess time or sending him to the office. No more writing sentences or apology letters. No daily behavior reports. And no consequences at home for misbehavior at school. Your new message might sound like this: 'Richard, stop disrupting, please, and follow along quietly, or you'll have to spend some quiet time by yourself. What would you like to do?' "

"It sounds so easy," laughed Sharon.

"The methods are easy compared to what you have been doing," I replied, "and you can use them with your other students as well. The hardest part will be stopping yourself from doing the dance. Richard will probably do his best to get you back out on the dance floor."

"What should I do if he argues or talks back after I give him limited choices?" Sharon asked.

"Don't take the bait," I replied. "Use the cutoff technique." I explained how it works. "If Richard really wants to discuss the matter further, arrange a time during his lunch time or after school to do so. The time for discussion is not when your rules are being tested or violated."

"And if he persists?" she asked.

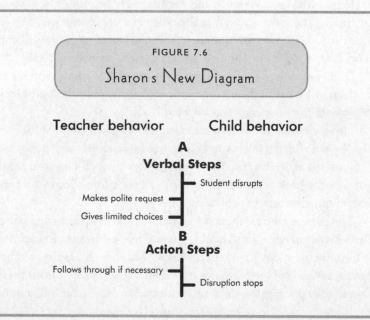

FIGURE 7.6

Sharon's New Diagram

Teacher behavior   Child behavior

A
Verbal Steps
                              Student disrupts
Makes polite request
Gives limited choices

B
Action Steps
Follows through if necessary
                              Disruption stops

"Then follow through with a time-out so he experiences what you said," I replied. "No dance. That's a clear signal."

"Sure, I can do that," Sharon replied, eager to get started.

We spent an hour that afternoon practicing the skills she needed to end her dances. She learned how to say stop in clear and respectful terms and how to use limited choices and the cutoff technique when she encountered testing or resistance. Logical consequences and time-outs replaced the drawn-out consequences she used earlier. She explained the new plan to Richard's parents, and they agreed to put it into effect the next day. Sharon's new diagram soon looked like Figure 7.6. So can yours.

A Mixed Dance

Mixed dances come in various forms. Some start off punitive and end up permissive when teachers compromise their limits or give in altogether. Others start off permissive and end up punitive when teachers react in anger and impose harsh or drawn-out consequences.

Jerry, a fifth-grade teacher, did the latter. He held the school record for sending the most students to the office in a single semester. The feat wasn't winning him many supporters. Parents were beginning to complain. The vice principal at his school suggested he give me a call.

"I can only take so much," Jerry complained. "The kids push me too far. That's why I send them to the office. There wouldn't be a problem if they would just cooperate and do what I ask."

He invited me to observe his class, and I agreed to do so the next day. We scheduled a follow-up conference for later that afternoon.

I arrived at Jerry's class five minutes after the bell rang and took a seat near the back of the room. The kids were curious about who I was. Several turned around to check me out.

Things were calm for the first few minutes, and then the testing started. Two girls began talking and passing notes. Their talking was loud enough to disturb others, but Jerry kept on teaching as though nothing was happening. He ignored their disruption altogether. The girls continued to talk. Occasionally one giggled, then turned around and looked at me, and then giggled some more. Jerry kept on teaching. Not a word was said.

When the girls saw that I wasn't going to intervene, they became bolder. They talked louder and giggled more. One of them passed a note to a boy and waited for his reaction. He read it and acted shocked, which triggered a new round of giggling. Jerry glanced in their direction several times but kept on teaching. The only change I could observe in his behavior was a slight amplification of his voice as he attempted to be heard above their chatter.

"This is interesting," I thought. "Does he eventually give them a signal?'"

On the other side of the room two boys were flicking bits of mud that had fallen off their shoes at each other. The game was great entertainment for several others nearby who chuckled each time a shot missed and nodded approval when shots were on target. Jerry seemed aware of what was going on but didn't say a word. He kept on teaching.

Finally, one of the boys did something Jerry couldn't ignore. One student pressed a muddy shoe against another boy's trousers and left a large print. Jerry looked at both of them impatiently.

"Come on, guys," he pleaded. "We only have thirty-five minutes to go. Can't you save the horsing around for after class?" The two settled down for the moment. Jerry returned to his teaching. Five more minutes passed, then there was another disturbance. One of the girls who had been passing notes earlier began gesturing excitedly to the boy sitting next to her. Everyone was watching. Jerry stopped once again and looked at her impatiently.

"Jana, would you get yourself under control, please?" he requested politely. "I don't want to have to ask you again." He waited for Jana to settle down. She did, and he resumed his lesson. Meanwhile, the mud-flicking game started up again on the other side of the room.

Jerry looked frustrated. "How much longer can he hold out before he gives a stronger signal?" I wondered. Jana answered my question. Without warning, she jumped out of her seat and tried to intercept a note passed to Mark. The whole class watched the two girls wrestle for the note. Jerry exploded.

"I've had it!" he shouted. "Jana and Shannon, you're out of here." He handed them both passes to the office. "Mark, you'll be joining them shortly if you don't settle down."

A tense silence fell over the class. Glances were exchanged, but no one disrupted. Even the mud-flicking game stopped. They knew he had reached his limit.

When I arrived for our afternoon conference, Jerry was still angry. "See what I have to put up with?" he said.

"Yes," I agreed. "They pushed you pretty far. Do you usually handle disruptions the way you handled them today?" I asked.

"Yes," he replied, "but they don't usually push me to the point where I have to send them to the office. That only happens a few times each week." Jerry was willing to overlook a lot. I wondered whether he was aware of the mixed messages he sent his students. I decided to check it out.

"May I draw a diagram of the interactions I observed in your class?" I asked. He nodded. When I finished, we both paused to look at it.

"Look familiar?" I asked.

"It sure does," he replied. "That's what I go through all day long."

"I call them classroom dances," I said. "Your dance starts off politely and ends up with an angry explosion. Were you aware of all the disruptions that took place before Jana and Shannon wrestled for the note?" Jerry nodded that he was.

"When did they begin to bother you?" I asked.

"I was annoyed when Greg wiped his muddy shoe all over Randy," Jerry replied. "And I was annoyed with Jana when she made all those dramatic hand gestures and showed off for Mark. But Jana and Shannon went much too far when they started wrestling for that note. That's when I lost it."

I returned to Jerry's diagram and wrote the words "feels annoyed" after the incidents he described and the words "feels very angry" after the wrestling incident. Jerry's diagram was now complete (see Figure 7.7).

I summarized what his diagram was telling us. "The kids test you with various forms of disruption, but your first response is to ignore their misbehavior. You overlook as much as you can until you become annoyed. Then you try pleading, cajoling, and polite requests. The disruption continues. When it reaches the point where you can't take it any longer, you stop it with your action step." He nodded in agreement.

"At what point in the diagram is their disruptive behavior unacceptable to you?" I asked. He looked at me as if I were crazy.

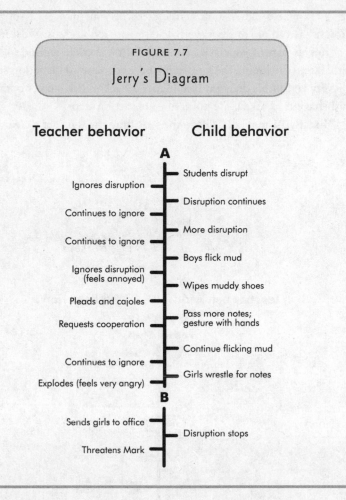

FIGURE 7.7

Jerry's Diagram

Teacher behavior	Child behavior
A	
	Students disrupt
Ignores disruption	
	Disruption continues
Continues to ignore	
	More disruption
Continues to ignore	
	Boys flick mud
Ignores disruption (feels annoyed)	
	Wipes muddy shoes
Pleads and cajoles	
	Pass more notes; gesture with hands
Requests cooperation	
	Continue flicking mud
Continues to ignore	
	Girls wrestle for notes
Explodes (feels very angry)	
B	
Sends girls to office	
	Disruption stops
Threatens Mark	

"It's never okay to disrupt," he replied.

"I agree with you, in theory," I said, "but let's look at the rule in practice. If their disruptive behavior was not okay at the beginning of class, then why did you allow it to continue for twenty-five minutes before you finally decided to stop it?"

Jerry didn't have an answer, but he understood what I meant. He could see that he was sending a mixed message.

"Let's take a closer look at the steps in your dance," I suggested. "You use two types of steps: verbal steps and action steps. We'll include ignoring as part of your verbal steps." I drew a circle around all of his verbal steps, including the ignoring, and a box around his action steps at the very end of his diagram (see Figure 7.8). "Which steps stopped the misbehavior?" I asked. He pointed to his action steps.

"Exactly," I replied. "That's the first time the kids get a clear signal

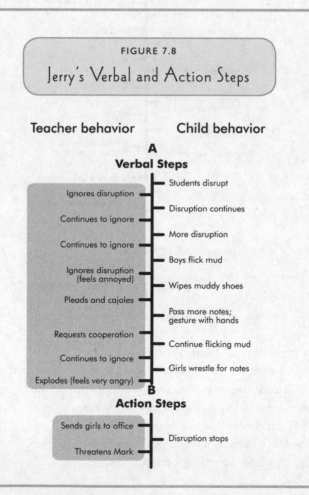

FIGURE 7.8

Jerry's Verbal and Action Steps

Teacher behavior   Child behavior

A
Verbal Steps

Ignores disruption ——— Students disrupt

——— Disruption continues

Continues to ignore ———

——— More disruption

Continues to ignore ———

——— Boys flick mud

Ignores disruption
(feels annoyed) ———

——— Wipes muddy shoes

Pleads and cajoles ———

——— Pass more notes;
gesture with hands

Requests cooperation ———

——— Continue flicking mud

Continues to ignore ———

——— Girls wrestle for notes

Explodes (feels very angry) ———

B
Action Steps

Sends girls to office ———

——— Disruption stops

Threatens Mark ———

that you expect their disruption to stop. None of the circled steps has any lasting impact on their behavior. How do the kids know how far they can go before they've gone too far?"

"They don't know," Jerry admitted. He could see that was why they keep pushing. "How do I get out of this dance?" he asked.

"The solution is simple," I said. "Since the kids want to know how far they can go, what would happen if you gave them the information they want the first time they disrupt? Your new message might sound like this: 'You can stop disrupting, or you'll have to spend some quiet time by yourself. What would you like to do?' "

"There would be much less disruption," replied Jerry, "but I still would be sending kids to the office."

"Then let's use a more effective action step," I suggested. I showed him how to use the Two-Stage Time-Out procedure. He introduced it to his class the next day. As expected, his aggressive researchers tested it out to see whether it worked. It did. They soon learned that disruptions would no longer be tolerated. Jerry's new diagram looked like Figure 7.9.

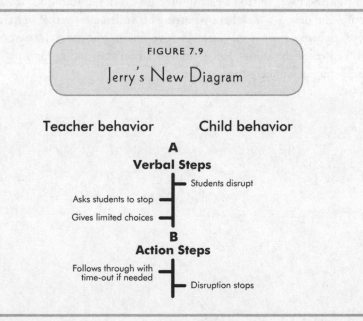

FIGURE 7.9

Jerry's New Diagram

Teacher behavior   Child behavior

A
Verbal Steps

Students disrupt

Asks students to stop

Gives limited choices

B
Action Steps

Follows through with
time-out if needed

Disruption stops

Chapter Summary

Classroom dances are destructive patterns of communication and problem solving that play out over and over again when classroom rules are tested and violated. For some students, the dances are a great source of live entertainment or "a reinforcement error" because they actually encourage unacceptable behavior. Students are the producers and directors, and teachers are the actors and actresses. For teachers, classroom dances are anything but fun. They're a major source of stress and wear and tear that leads to burnout.

Classroom dances come in many forms. There's a permissive version and a punitive version, and some teachers do both. All dances begin with unclear or ineffective messages about our rules. They're fueled by anger and misunderstanding, and they all lead to escalating conflicts and power struggles. Over time, classroom dances become such a familiar and deeply ingrained habit that teachers experience them as their normal way of doing things. They are not even aware that they are dancing. Awareness is the key to breaking free.

The best way to stop a classroom dance is not to start one. Teachers can avoid dances altogether by starting off with a clear verbal signal and by supporting their words with effective action. The process is easy once you discover the things you're doing that aren't working for you. The next chapter will help you do that.

Soft Limits Invite Testing and Power Struggles

Many teachers hold up the wrong signals to stop misbehavior in the classroom. They don't realize that their stop signs don't really require stopping or that their attempts to say no sound like "yes," "sometimes," or "maybe" to their students. Their limits are soft, not firm, and the kids know it. Soft limits invite testing and power struggles. They are the cause of countless classroom dances.

Recognizing the signals that aren't working for you is another important step for getting off the dance floor. If you're suffering from a bad case of soft limits, this chapter will be part of the remedy. Let's get acquainted with soft limits, the signals that don't work for us.

Soft Limits: When No Means Yes, Sometimes, or Maybe

Raymond, age nine, knows he's not supposed to eat snacks during class, but when his teacher isn't looking, he pulls out a bag of corn chips

and starts crunching away. He's halfway through the bag before his teacher notices what's going on.

"Raymond! You know you're not supposed to eat during class," she says with disapproval. "Put that bag away, please, and wait until lunch."

"Sorry," says Raymond, as he sticks the corn chip bag back in his desk.

A few minutes pass before Raymond tries again. When his teacher's back is turned, he sneaks a few more chips out of the bag and chews them softly, one at a time. No one notices, so he grabs a small handful. He gets caught a second time.

"Raymond!" says his teacher with exasperation. "Are you eating chips again? I thought I told you not to." He looks apologetic. "If I let you eat during class, then I have to let everybody do it," she explains. "It's not fair to others. I really wish you would put them away and wait for lunch."

"Okay," says Raymond contritely. He puts the chips back in his desk.

Raymond's teacher is using soft limits. She believes her message is getting across, but what did Raymond experience after all the reasons and explanations? It wasn't stopping. Instead, he finished most of the bag!

What did Raymond learn from this experience? He learned that eating snacks during class is really okay if he can endure his teacher's annoying comments. His teacher sent Raymond a different message than she intended.

Soft limits are rules in theory, not in practice. They invite testing because they carry a mixed message. The verbal message seems to say stop, but the action message says that stopping is neither expected nor required. Raymond understood this clearly and responded the way most drivers do when the light turns yellow. He acknowledged his teacher's signal but continued on his way. Raymond and his teacher will likely have many more of these encounters as long as she uses soft limits.

From a training perspective, soft limits do not accomplish any of our basic goals. They don't stop misbehavior, they don't encourage acceptable behavior, and they don't promote positive learning about our rules or authority. They simply don't work. Worse yet, they frequently achieve the opposite of their intended effect by inviting testing and power struggles. Soft limits are the cause of most classroom dances.

Soft limits come in a variety of forms. They can be ineffective verbal messages or ineffective action messages. Sometimes they are both at the same time. All share the common message that compliance is neither expected nor required. Let's look at some typical examples.

Wishes, Hopes, and Shoulds

Rhonda, age four, knows she's not supposed to use painting materials in the carpeted areas of her classroom but both easels are in use, and she really wants to paint. She grabs a brush and a tray of paints and heads to the nearest table. Her picture is nearly complete when the teacher discovers what's going on.

"Rhonda, you know you're not supposed to use paints near the carpets. You might spill."

"I'll be careful," says Rhonda.

"I know you will," says her teacher, "but accidents can happen even when you're careful. That's why we put the easels in the tiled area. I really wish you would put the paints away and finish your picture later when an easel is free."

"Okay," replies Rhonda, but she continues to paint.

Her teacher waits, but nothing happens. So she tries again. "Rhonda, do you know how difficult it is to get paint stains out of the carpet? I hope you put the paints away before there is an accident."

"I'm almost done," says Rhonda, as she dabs the brush into the blue paint jar.

"Rhonda! I'm starting to get mad," exclaims her teacher. "Is that what you want? Please do what I ask before I get even madder." Rhonda paints quickly.

Did you hear a clear message that Rhonda was required to stop painting? Rhonda didn't, and she responded the way many children do when they receive this type of mixed signal. Wishes, hopes, and shoulds are another way of saying "Stopping is nice, but you really don't have to until you're ready." Compliance is optional, not required. Often, when children confront this type of signal, they test for clarification. That's what Rhonda did when she ignored her teacher and continued painting.

Repeating and Reminding

Math is Chad's least favorite subject. While his teacher explains equations at the board, Chad pulls out a comic book and starts reading. His teacher notices.

"Chad, I think it would be a good idea if you put that away," suggests the teacher. Chad places the comic under one of his books and looks up attentively. As soon as his teacher returns to the lesson, Chad pulls the comic out and continues reading. Several minutes go by before he's discovered.

"Chad, how many times do I have to tell you?" asks his annoyed teacher. "Put the comic book away!"

Chad puts the comic away and waits a full fifteen minutes before he pulls it out again. This time he conceals it under his binder and looks up periodically to give the impression he's really paying attention. His teacher isn't fooled. He walks over to Chad's desk and lifts up the binder.

"That's enough!" says the teacher. "Put the comic in your backpack, or you can give it to me and pick it up after school." Chad puts the comic in his backpack.

When Chad ignored the first request, nothing happened, so he decided to test and try again. The second request followed the same pattern. If the teacher did not mean what he said the first two times, why should Chad take his words seriously the third time? He doesn't.

Teachers who repeat and remind are teaching kids to ignore and tune out. Like many students who wonder how far they can go, Chad doesn't comply with his teacher's request until he has to.

Speeches, Lectures, and Sermons

Robin, a fifth grader, strolls into class from recess five minutes late. "Where have you been, Robin?" asks her annoyed teacher. "The bell rang nearly five minutes ago."

"I had to use the restroom," Robin replies.

"You need to take care of bathroom trips before the bell rings," admonishes her teacher. "I don't appreciate your lack of consideration. I've already given directions for the next assignment, and now I have to repeat them just for you. You're holding everybody up. What kind of a class would this be if everyone showed up when they felt like it? It isn't fair to others. Now take your seat, please, so we can get started."

Did you hear a clear message that showing up late would not be tolerated? Robin didn't. Will the lecture help her arrive on time in the future? Probably not.

What did Robin learn from all of this? She learned that showing up late is really okay if she can tolerate her teacher's lectures. This is not a bad deal for someone who wants to avoid classwork and extend recess time. Robin knows from experience that she can count on her teacher to provide a set of personal instructions when she arrives late.

Warnings and Second Chances

It's a sunny day, and Mrs. Adams decides to take her second graders outside and read them a story. When everyone is seated, she begins. Within minutes, several students begin horsing around.

"Carlos and Daniel, would you like to sit together?" asks Mrs. Adams. They both nod. "Then you will have to follow along quietly. That's a warning."

She resumes her story. A few moments later, the boys poke and tickle each other again. Mrs. Adams puts her book down. "Guys, didn't I ask you to follow along quietly?" she asks. They both nod. "Well, I meant it, too. This is your final warning." She returns to her story.

This time, things are quiet for a full five minutes, and then Daniel lets out a yelp. "He pinched me!" complains Daniel.

"It was an accident," says Carlos.

Mrs. Adams isn't sure what happened. "Okay, this is your last chance," she says. "If I hear any more disruptions, I'm going to separate you. I really mean it. Do you understand?" The boys nod. She resumes her story.

Do you think she has seen the last of their disruptions? Not likely. The boys violated her rule three times, and each time they received a warning and another chance. They'll probably continue to test until they receive a signal that requires stopping.

Cooperate, Okay?

Three-year-old Shelly knows she's supposed to put her materials away when she's finished with them, but she leaves her completed puzzle on the floor and begins playing in the sand trays. Her teacher notices.

"Shelly, you left your puzzle on the floor," says the teacher. "You're supposed to put it away before you begin something new. Okay?"

Shelly acknowledges her teacher's words but continues to play with the sand trays. Her teacher tries again. "Shelly, if everybody left their projects lying around, our classroom would be a mess. Please pick up the puzzle and put it away, okay?" This time, Shelly doesn't even look up.

What does it mean when we ask a child to do something and then add "okay?" at the end of our request? Okay with whom? The child? Or the teacher? What happens if it's not okay with the child? Does that mean cooperation is optional? And who decides? Shelly seems to have made up her mind. When we add "okay?" to the end of our requests, we obscure the clarity of our message.

Statements of Fact

The bell rings, and Mr. Gilbert moves to the front of the class to begin his lesson. He's ready, but many of his students are not. They talk and joke around. Several haven't even made it to their seats. Mr. Gilbert waits patiently.

"I'm ready to start," he announces, but his words have little impact. The kids continue to talk. Mr. Gilbert waits a little longer. "It's too noisy. I can't get started until it's quiet," he says. The talking continues. Mr. Gilbert is angry. "I'm waiting," he says impatiently.

Did you hear a message that said his students were required to stop talking and get in their seats? Neither did they. Many continued to test for that message. Mr. Gilbert is not likely to get the cooperation he expects until he gives a clearer signal. Statements of fact do not convey the intended message.

Ignoring the Misbehavior

Kyle, a sixth grader, enjoys being the class clown. Each day he pulls a series of gags and stunts to amuse his classmates. His teacher is not amused. She finds his behavior irritating and tries to ignore it in the hope that it will go away. She encourages his classmates to ignore him, too, but Kyle shows no sign of slowing down. He blurts out and disrupts all day.

"When will he ever learn?" his teacher asks herself.

Is the absence of a green light the same as a red light? If it were, Kyle would have stopped his disruption and clowning long ago. When we ignore misbehavior, we are really saying "It's okay to do that. Go ahead. You don't have to stop." That's the message Kyle follows.

If Kyle's teacher wants to stop his clowning, she needs to give him the right signal. She needs to say stop with her words and, if needed, follow through with her actions by temporarily removing Kyle from his audience. Kyle will learn his teacher's rule when he experiences the consequences of his unacceptable behavior.

Reasoning and Explaining

A group of fourth-grade boys has invented a variation of the game of tag. When someone is tagged, the tagger yells out for the others to pile on the new person, who becomes "it." The game is great fun, but not very safe. When the yard duty teacher sees what's happening, he intervenes.

"Guys, that game doesn't look safe. Someone could get hurt. You can play tag without piling on."

"Come on, Mr. Kearney," pleads one boy. "No one is going to get hurt. We'll be careful."

"I know you will," replies Mr. Kearney, "but the blacktop is hard, and Christopher could have been hurt when you guys piled on him. I'm concerned."

"But Christopher didn't mind," says one boy. "Yeah, he liked it," says another. Christopher nods in agreement.

"Well, it's still not a good idea," says Mr. Kearney. "It's best that you stop."

The boys grumble a little but head off. A few minutes pass, then Mr. Kearney hears "Pile on Jared!" This time he sees the same group of boys piling on Jared. Mr. Kearney calls them over.

"Guys, didn't I ask you not to do that?"

"You said it wasn't okay on the blacktop," says one boy. "We're on the grass. It's safe here."

"Piling on is not safe anywhere," insists Mr. Kearney. "Someone might get hurt. You guys would feel terrible if that happened and so would I. That's why we don't allow rough games on the playground. They lead to problems. Do you understand?"

The boys nod and head off once again. This time, they select an area well away from Mr. Kearney before they resume the game. Mr. Kearney decides to check it out. Sure enough, the boys are at it again. He calls them over.

"Guys, you don't seem to understand what I've been trying to tell you," says a frustrated Mr. Kearney. "That game is dangerous. I'm not going to wait for someone to get hurt before it stops. If I see any of you piling on again, you'll spend the rest of your recess on the bench." No one wants to spend his recess on the bench. The game stops.

Mr. Kearney believes he said *stop* each time he gave reasons and explanations about the dangers of piling on, but what did the boys experience? They didn't stop. Cooperation was optional, not required. The boys knew it and continued to pile on until they experienced a signal that required them to stop.

Is there a time for giving reasons and explanations? Yes, but that time is not when our rules are being tested or violated. When children test or go too far, they need to know the consequences of their behavior. Reasons and explanations do not provide them with the data they need to complete their research.

Bargaining and Negotiating

Lynn, a fifth grader, knows she's supposed to turn in her biography assignment on Wednesday, but it's Monday and she hasn't even started. She asks for a deadline extension.

"Mr. Edwards, may I have a few extra days to complete my biography assignment?" Lynn asks.

"You've had three weeks," says Mr. Edwards. "That should have been plenty of time for a project under six pages."

"I know, but it's taking longer than I expected. May I turn it in on Monday?" she asks.

"No, but you can turn it in on Friday for full credit," he replies.

"Oh, please, Mr. Edwards!" Lynn pleads. "I'll do a better job if I can have a few more days. May I have the weekend, please?"

"Okay," concedes Mr. Edwards, frustrated by his weakening position, "but just this once. Next time, you'll have to finish on time like everybody else."

Did you hear that getting assignments in on time was expected and required? Lynn didn't. Her teacher was willing to bargain and negotiate about the due date for the assignment. In effect, Mr. Edwards is saying "My rules are negotiable. Let's make a deal." Lynn tested to see how far she could go.

To children, negotiable feels a lot like optional. By the time the negotiation session is over, Lynn understands the real rule is "Complete your assignments on time unless you can talk your way out of it." Teachers who bargain and negotiate over their rules invite children to test and redefine those rules.

Arguing and Debating

Andre, a second grader, knows he's supposed to clean around his desk before he leaves in the afternoon, but he tries to sneak out the door unnoticed. His teacher calls him back. "Andre, you can't leave until you pick up around your desk and put your books and papers away," she says.

"I don't see why I have to clean up when Shelton doesn't," says Andre.

"Shelton's desk is clean, and he put his books away," replies the teacher. "That's what you need to do, too."

"Well, it didn't look that way yesterday," argues Andre, "and you let him go. It's not fair."

"We're not talking about Shelton," replies his teacher. "We're talking about you, and you know what you have to do."

"You're not fair," Andre complains, looking for a little bargaining room. "Why do I have to do things others don't have to do?"

"I'll keep a closer eye on Shelton's desk from now on," says the teacher, "and I'll make sure he follows the rules just like you."

"Well, they're stupid rules!" says Andre.

"Stupid or not, they won't change all year," says the teacher. She walks to her desk and begins to correct papers. When Andre realizes that he can't talk his way out of it, he heads over to clean up his desk.

What was not happening while the arguing and debating was going on? Of course, Andre was not cleaning up his desk. That won't happen until the argument is over. Some arguments can last a long time.

What is the message Andre's teacher sends by arguing and debating over her rules? Isn't she saying that her rules are subject to further discussion and debate? That's what Andre thinks. She invited resistance and a power struggle by allowing Andre to test her limits and prolong his resistance.

Pleading and Cajoling

It's snack time, and four-year-old Trent decides to amuse his friends by spitting gobs of chocolate pudding onto the table.

"Oh, gross!" says the girl sitting next to him, but Trent keeps it up. *Plop.* Another gob hits the table. His teacher intervenes.

"Come on, Trent," she says. "It's not nice to eat like that. The kids think you're gross. Show me you can eat like a big boy." The words barely leave her lips when the next gob hits the table. *Plop.* Trent smiles mischievously.

"Okay, Trent, you've had your fun. Now let's eat the right way, okay?" she pleads. But Trent is having a ball. He spits out two more gobs. "You usually have such good table manners," she says. "We all would feel better if you stopped that."

Did Trent hear a message that stopping was expected and required? No. He heard a lot of pleading and cajoling and a message that said it would be nice if he stopped. Trent thinks it would be nice if he doesn't. If Trent's teacher really wants him to stop, she needs to say stop clearly with her words and remove the pudding if he doesn't. Without a clear signal, he's not likely to give up his game.

Bribes and Special Rewards

Every day Mr. Sawyer complains in the staff lounge about one of his disruptive fifth graders. "Why don't you offer him some special rewards for better classroom behavior," suggests a well-meaning colleague. "Maybe you can buy his cooperation."

Mr. Sawyer is desperate. He decides to give it a try. The next day after school, he calls Carl to his desk and asks about the things Carl enjoys most. Carl shares the typical list—pizza, ice cream, video games, baseball cards, skateboarding, and street hockey.

"How would you like to earn a pack of baseball cards every day at school?" Mr. Sawyer asks. Carl perks up. "All you need to do is complete a whole day without disrupting class," says Mr. Sawyer. "Do we have a deal?" Carl nods.

The agreement results in a dramatic turnaround in Carl's behavior. He earns four packs of cards the first week and five packs during weeks two and three. Carl likes the new arrangement, but Mr. Sawyer is having second thoughts. By the end of the third week, he has paid out nearly twenty dollars. Carl's cooperation is expensive.

"None of my other students have to be paid to cooperate," Mr. Sawyer thinks. "Carl has already shown that he can do it. I shouldn't have to pay him any longer." The more he thinks about it, the madder he becomes. He decides to revise the terms of their agreement.

When Carl comes up to collect his cards the next day, Mr. Sawyer says, "Carl, I don't think we need to do this anymore. You've shown that you know how to cooperate."

"No way!" says Carl. "I'm not doing it unless you give me the cards." Carl's cooperation stopped as soon as the reward was withheld.

When we offer children bribes and special rewards in return for cooperation, aren't we really saying with our actions that we don't expect them to cooperate unless we pay them off? That's what Carl thought. Bribes and special rewards are another form of soft limits.

Unclear Directions

Mrs. Robie, a sixth-grade teacher, selects two students to return an overhead projector to the school's equipment room. She suspects they may try to stretch the trip out longer than it should be. "Don't take too long," she says as they leave the room. "I want you back on time."

What does "too long" mean to a couple of sixth graders who enjoy being out of class? Five minutes? Ten minutes? Fifteen minutes? And who decides? Isn't Mrs. Robie making an assumption that she and her students share the same belief about how long the trip should take?

Unclear or open-ended directions invite testing and set up both students and teacher for conflict. If Mrs. Robie expects the students back in five minutes, she should say, "I expect you back in five minutes."

Saying Shh . . . When Students Blurt

Mr. Jacobs, a first-grade teacher, begins his morning circle sharing activity when he hears Antonio talking to Stephen. Mr. Jacobs puts his index finger to his lips and says, "Shh . . ." The boys quiet down briefly.

A short time later, another student starts to talk.

"Shh," says Mr. Jacobs again. The student stops talking briefly. The sharing activity resumes. Things go smoothly for a few minutes, then Antonio blurts out another comment to Stephen.

"Shh," says Mr. Jacobs, with an annoyed look on his face. Antonio stops talking for the moment. The activity continues for another two or three uninterrupted minutes. Mr. Jacobs asks the class a question and waits to pick someone, but Antonio blurts out the answer.

"Shh," says a visibly annoyed Mr. Jacobs. "We're supposed to raise our hand when we want to speak."

What does *shh* mean anyway? Does it sound like a yellow light to you? It certainly didn't stop Antonio.

If Mr. Jacobs wants students to stop talking and blurting out during instruction, he needs to state his rule with a clear message such as "We don't blurt during instruction" and support his rule with an effective action step by separating the student from his or her audience each time he or she blurts or interrupts. For repeat offenders, Mr. Jacobs may need to arrange individual training sessions during recess to practice the important skill of raising a quiet hand to speak.

Ineffective Role Modeling

Mr. Allen, a third-grade teacher, sees two boys in the hallway yelling, threatening, and calling each other names. They're squared off and ready to fight. He intervenes.

"Knock it off!" he shouts, as he pushes the boys apart. "You're both acting like a couple of punks. If you want to make fools out of yourselves, do it on your own time. Now get to class before I send you to the office!" Reluctantly the boys head their separate ways.

What did the boys learn from this encounter? They attempted to resolve their conflict with yelling, threatening, and name-calling. What did Mr. Allen do? He resolved the conflict with yelling, threatening, and name-calling. In effect he was teaching them to do the very thing he was reprimanding them for.

Inconsistency Among Staff

When it comes to teaching rules and the lessons of classroom management, our guidance practices are all over the map. Some teachers overlook and ignore blurting out, disruption, clowning around, and talking during instruction. Others do not. Some require students to pull colored behavior cards for misbehavior. Other teachers write students' names on the board under the frown face, send them to the office, make them pick up trash, take away favorite privileges and activities for long periods of time, or ask parents to come to class and sit with the child for a day.

When discipline practices vary from teacher to teacher, inconsistency is the norm. Students receive a series of mixed messages and confusing lessons about school rules and expectations. Inconsistency sets everyone up for conflict. Inconsistency among staff is the biggest soft limit on most school campuses.

Inconsistency Between the Classroom and the Office

There are two minutes until recess, and Madison, a second grader, has art supplies spread out all over her desk.

"You can't go out for recess until you put your art supplies away," says the teacher as she passes by Madison's desk. Madison tries to bargain her way out of it.

"If I do it now, I'll be the last in line for hopscotch. Why can't I do it after recess?" Madison pleads. Her teacher holds firm. When the bell rings, Madison tries to sneak out. Her teacher intercepts her at the door.

"Not so fast, Madison," says the teacher. "First, you need to put your things away."

"I won't do it!" says Madison defiantly.

"That's up to you, but you can't leave for recess until you do," says the teacher.

"I still won't do it," says Madison.

Her teacher is not about to spend her break period arguing with Madison. She gives Madison some choices.

"You can clean it up now or work the problem out with Mr. Thomlin, our principal, if you prefer," says the teacher. She escorts Madison to the office and explains the situation to Mr. Thomlin.

When she's finished, Mr. Thomlin calls Madison into his office and listens to her side of the story. "I don't see what difference it makes if she picks up before or after recess," Mr. Thomlin thinks. He decides to let her off the hook. "Okay, this time, I'll let you go out to play, but it's important to cooperate with your teacher. Now run along."

What did Madison learn? In effect, two sets of rules are operating: the teacher's rules that say pick up your mess before you can go out to play and the principal's rules that say you don't have to if you have a good reason not to. Which set of rules will prevail?

What do you think Madison will say next time her teacher wants her to pick something up before recess? Sure, she'll probably play the principal against the teacher by saying "Mr. Thomlin says I don't have to do it."

If Mr. Thomlin decides to hold firm next time, Madison will probably say, "Last time you said that I didn't have to do it." Inconsistency between the classroom and the office sets up students for testing and teachers, parents, and the principal for conflict.

EXAMPLES OF INEFFECTIVE VERBAL MESSAGES (SOFT LIMITS)

"Would you cooperate just once in a while?"

"Come on, get your act together!"

"Would you do me a favor and pay attention?"

"Can't you see I'm trying to teach a lesson?"

"You'd better shape up."

"I don't care for your attitude."

"I don't believe it. You actually did what I asked."

"Would you like it if I interrupted you?"

"Stop acting like a jerk!"

"Is it asking too much to have a little cooperation?"

EXAMPLES OF INEFFECTIVE ACTION MESSAGES (SOFT LIMITS)

- Allowing students to walk away from a mess
- Cleaning up students' messes for them
- Overlooking misbehavior when you're in a good mood
- Overlooking misbehavior to avoid embarrassment
- Giving in to persistent nagging
- Giving in to a tantrum

TABLE 8.1

Comparison of Firm and Soft Limits

	FIRM LIMITS	SOFT LIMITS
Characteristics	• Stated in clear, direct, concrete behavioral terms. • Words supported by actions. • Compliance expected and required. • Provide information needed to make acceptable choices and cooperate. • Provide accountability.	• Stated in unclear terms or as mixed messages. • Actions do not support intended rule. • Compliance optional, not required. • Do not provide information needed to make acceptable choices.
Predictable outcomes	• Cooperation. • Decreased limit testing. • Clear understanding of rules and expectations. • Regard teacher's words seriously.	• Resistance. • Increased limit testing. • Escalating misbehavior, power struggles. • Ignore and tune out teacher's words.

	FIRM LIMITS	SOFT LIMITS
What children learn	• No means no. • "I'm expected and required to follow the rules." • "Rules apply to me like everyone else." • "I am responsible for my own behavior." • Adults mean what they say.	• No means "yes," "sometimes," or "maybe." • "I'm not expected to follow the rules." • "Rules are for others, not me." • "Adults are responsible for my behavior." • Adults don't mean what they say.

Chapter Summary

Limits come in two basic varieties, soft and firm (see Table 8.1). Soft limits are rules in theory, not in practice. These ineffective teaching tools contribute to miscommunication and testing as children attempt to clarify what we mean. Soft limits take many forms. They can be ineffective verbal messages or ineffective action messages. Sometimes they are both. All soft limits are mixed messages that invite power struggles and dances.

Firm Limits: Clear Signals
Students Understand

A clear message begins with our words, and most often that's where communication breaks down because we say or do more than is needed. Anger, drama, strong emotion, or failing to provide students with all the information they need to make an acceptable choice can sabotage the clarity of our message and reduce the likelihood of cooperation.

It's not only what we say that matters; it's how we say it. Our words are an important part of our overall limit-setting message.

This chapter will show you how to use your words in the clearest and most understandable way. By following a few simple guidelines, you'll learn how to give your aggressive researchers and fence-sitters a firm, limit-setting message and provide them with the information they need to make an acceptable choice and cooperate.

Guidelines for Giving Clear Messages

The key to giving a clear message with your words is to say only what needs to be said in a clear, firm, and respectful manner. The following tips will help you get started.

KEEP THE FOCUS OF YOUR MESSAGE ON BEHAVIOR.

Keep the focus of your message on what you want the child to do or stop doing, not on attitude or feelings or the value of the child. Remember, our goal is to reject unacceptable behavior, not the child performing the behavior. Messages that shame, blame, criticize, or humiliate are easily personalized. They reject the child along with the behavior and obscure the clarity of the guidance message. The focus is misdirected. A clear behavioral message is less likely to be perceived as a personal attack.

For example, if Tommy, age seven, decides to push another student in line, a clear message is "Tommy, we don't push others in line. Please go to the back of the line."

A poorly focused message is "Hey Tommy! How do you think that feels? Would you like to be pushed? What would our lines look like if everybody pushed and shoved others all the time? Now knock it off!"

BE DIRECT AND SPECIFIC.

A clear message should inform children, directly and specifically, about what you want them to do or not to do. If necessary, be prepared to tell them how and when you want them to do it. The fewer the words, the better.

For example, if you want Kyle, age nine, to clean up his desk before he leaves for home, your message should be "Kyle, pick up thoroughly around your desk before you leave. That means picking up all the crayons, pencils, or any other items that are on the floor, and putting away all your books and papers. If that's not finished, you won't be able to go."

Avoid indirect messages such as "Kyle, I hope you do a better job picking up around your desk today." What is "a better job"? And who decides? You or Kyle? What happens if your definition is different from his? Without a direct, specific message, Kyle's performance may fall short of your expectations.

USE YOUR NORMAL VOICE.

The tone of your voice is important. Ideally, your tone should be positive or neutral. Your normal voice tone expresses control, whereas your raised voice sends the opposite message—loss of control. Your tone should convey that you are firm, in control, and resolute in your expectations that the children do what you've asked. The best way to communicate this expectation is simply to state your message matter-of-factly in your normal voice.

Firm limits are not stated harshly. There is no need to yell, scream, or use anger or strong emotion to convince children that you really mean what you say. Your actions will convey your resolve more powerfully than words.

Maintaining a matter-of-fact attitude in guidance situations is easy for some teachers, but not for others—particularly those who grew up in homes where yelling, screaming, and angry dances were commonplace. The urge to yell becomes a deeply ingrained habit and a nearly automatic response in conflict situations. These old habits won't disappear overnight just because you're inspired to do things differently. You have to work at it. Managing anger is a skill you can learn, but like most skills, the learning process requires time, patience, and lots of practice. The more you practice, the faster your new skills will improve.

USE NONTHREATENING BODY LANGUAGE.

Our body language also conveys a message about our comfort level, feelings, and expectations in guidance and discipline situations. When our body language is congruent with a neutral or positive verbal message, we increase the likelihood that our message will be received in a supportive and instructive manner.

Threatening body language, on the other hand, increases the likelihood of a defensive response. Glaring or staring at students, standing too close, standing rigidly with arms crossed, or looking down on students are examples of intimidating body language that raises the threat level and increases the likelihood of a defensive response from students.

How can we avoid giving unintended threatening messages with our body language? Many find it helpful to practice keeping arms relaxed at their sides and delivering their message in a matter-of-fact tone. When students are seated, practice sitting or kneeling comfortably to deliver your message. Sitting and kneeling are not attack positions.

SPECIFY THE LOGICAL CONSEQUENCE FOR NONCOMPLIANCE.

Strong-willed children and fence-sitters want to know the bottom line, or how far they can go. That's why they test our rules and authority so frequently. When they hear a request for their cooperation, they're thinking "Or what? What are you going to do if I don't?" We can prevent a lot of testing and power struggles by simply providing students with the information they need from the beginning. This is not a threat. You're just being clear. You're simply providing the information your students need to make an acceptable choice to cooperate.

For example, if you ask Larry, a second grader, to put away his toy during class time, but you expect him to test, your message should be "Larry, put away the toy, please. If you have it out during class again, I'll keep it in my desk until the next parent-teacher conference."

Now Larry has all the information he needs to make an acceptable choice. He may still decide to test, but if he does, all you have to do is follow through with a logical consequence and take the toy. This is the data Larry needs to determine that you mean what you say.

EXAMPLES OF EFFECTIVE VERBAL MESSAGES (FIRM LIMITS)

"Stop pushing, please."

"It's not okay to interrupt."

"I expect you back in five minutes."

"If you wipe the glue stick on others, I'll have to take it away."

"You can play by the rules or find another game to play."

"If you shove, you'll have to go to the back of the line."

"You won't be ready to leave until your desk is clean."

"You can sit together quietly or sit apart quietly."

"You can finish your assignment during class time or during recess."

EXAMPLES OF EFFECTIVE ACTION MESSAGES (FIRM LIMITS)

- Using a time-out consequence for persistent disruption
- Removing a toy from a child who does not put it away when asked
- Revoking a play privilege temporarily for failing to play by the rules
- Separating a child from others for misbehaving in the cafeteria
- Temporarily removing a privilege for abusing that privilege
- Holding students accountable for cleaning up their messes

Chapter Summary

A clear limit-setting message begins with our words, and most often, that's where communication breaks down. Anger, drama, strong emotion, threatening body language, or failing to provide students with all the information they need can sabotage the clarity and meaning of your message. A clear message is not harsh, and it's not a lecture. We don't need a lot of words, and we don't need drama or strong emotion to show that we mean what we say. We only need to be clear.

A firm, limit-setting message should focus on behavior, not on attitude or feelings. It should be specific and direct, stated in a matter-of-fact manner with positive or neutral body language, and it should specify the consequences for noncompliance so students have all the information they need to make an acceptable choice to cooperate. Firm limit-setting messages reduce testing and dances and set up instructive learning experiences.

10

Ending Power Struggles
Before They Begin

If tuning out were an Olympic event, nine-year-old Travis would be a gold medal contender. He knows how to ignore directions better than any student in his class, and he can hook almost any teacher into a power struggle. Once he hooks them, he's a master at wearing them down with arguments and debates. Travis has perfected his skills with years of practice at home.

What Travis doesn't realize is that his current teacher has figured out his game. She read a book about classroom dances and recognizes his tactics for what they are. She's ready to stop his dances before they begin. She gets her chance the next day.

When Travis is supposed to be working at his seat, he gets up, walks to the back of the room, and turns on the computer. Then he begins playing a game.

"Travis, you need to finish your paragraphs before you're ready for computer time," says his teacher. Travis doesn't respond. He continues playing.

"She'll remind me a few more times," he says to himself, "then she'll get upset and give me a final warning before I have to return to my seat. I'll probably get a full game in."

Not this time. His teacher walks over to the computer. "Travis, what did I ask you to do?" she inquires matter-of-factly.

Travis is dumbfounded. "What is going on?" he wonders. "No reminders or lectures? No final warnings or instructions?" He can't believe it. She places her hand on the keyboard and waits for his response.

"You said I need to finish my paragraphs before any computer time," he replies.

"Right," she says, with her hand still on the keyboard. "Now do it, please."

But Travis isn't ready to give up so easily. He tries a different tactic. "I don't see why I can't finish the game I've already started," he says, looking for a little bargaining room. He presents the bait skillfully, but his teacher doesn't bite.

"We're finished talking about it, Travis," she says matter-of-factly. "If you bring it up again, the computer won't be available to you for the rest of the day. If you really want to know why you can't use the computer now, we can arrange a time to discuss it after school or during one of your recesses." Travis doesn't want to know why that bad. He heads back to his seat to finish up.

As the example illustrates, the best way to stop a classroom dance is not to start one. We need to begin with a clear verbal message, avoid the bait students use to hook us, and be prepared to move quickly to logical consequences if needed. Travis's teacher does this effectively. You can, too, but if you've danced in the past, don't expect your students to give up their testing quickly.

Your aggressive researchers will likely challenge even your clearest verbal messages and do everything they can to get you back out on the dance floor. You'll probably be tempted to go along with it, too. This chapter will help you resist the urge. You'll learn how to recognize the bait, avoid the hook, and stay off the dance floor. Let's begin with the typical bait we encounter in the classroom and explore how best to avoid it.

When Students Tune Out, Check In

One of the best ways to hook teachers into power struggles is to tune out and ignore their requests. When this happens, teachers wonder, "Did my message get across? Am I being ignored? Is it time to move on to a logical consequence?"

The check-in procedure is a simple way to answer these questions without getting hooked into the old repeating-and-reminding routine. When in doubt, check in with the child by saying one of the following:

"What did I ask you to do?"
"Did you understand what I said?"
"Were my directions clear?"
"Tell me in your words what you heard me say."

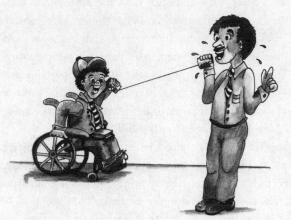

For example, morning snack is over, and it's time for Mrs. Jansen's preschoolers to get ready to go out to the playground. "Put your napkins, wrappers, and other garbage in the waste can," she says. Most of them do, except for Stacey, who just looks at her blankly and then heads to the door with her classmates.

"Did she hear what I said?" wonders Mrs. Jansen. "She doesn't act like she did." Mrs. Jansen is tempted to ask Stacey a second time when she remembers the technique she learned in the book—when in doubt, use the check-in procedure. She gives it a try.

"Stacey, what did I ask you to do before you go outside?" asks Mrs. Jansen.

"Pick up my mess," replies Stacey.

"Then do it, please," says Mrs. Jansen matter-of-factly. Stacey goes back to pick up her mess.

In this case, Stacey was limit testing. She had the information she needed but chose to ignore it. She fully expected to hear a lot of repeating and reminding before she would actually have to pick up her mess, if she would have to pick it up at all. The check-in procedure (see Figure 10.1) helped her teacher clarify that they were communicating, avoid a dance, and eliminate the payoffs for tuning out all at the same time.

Now let's consider another scenario. Let's say that when Mrs. Jansen checks in with Stacey, she responds with the same blank stare because she really has tuned out completely. What should Mrs. Jansen do?

She should give Stacey the information that Stacey missed the first time and preview her action step. Mrs. Jansen's message might sound like this: "Put your napkins, wrappers, and other garbage away before you go outside. You won't be ready to leave until that job is finished." Now Stacey has all the information she needs to make an acceptable choice. All Mrs. Jansen needs to do is follow through.

The check-in procedure also can be used in situations where children respond to our requests with mixed messages; that is, they give us the right words but the wrong behavior. Sam, a fifth grader, is an expert at this. He sits in class and doodles when he's supposed to be writing a short plot summary. There are thirty minutes left before recess. The teacher notices his lack of progress.

"Sam, you have thirty minutes to finish up," he says as he passes by Sam's desk.

"I will," says Sam, but ten minutes go by, and he hasn't written a sentence. He hopes to avoid the assignment altogether or talk his way out of it when the bell rings. His teacher suspects this also and decides to check in.

"Sam, what did I ask you to do?" inquires his teacher.

"I'll finish up," says Sam in a reassuring voice.

The teacher clarifies Sam's message. "Your words say that you will, but your actions say you won't. Let me be clearer. You won't be ready to leave until you finish your plot summary. I'll be happy to stay with you after school if you need more time to finish up." Now his teacher's message is very clear.

"Darn! It didn't work," Sam says to himself. He gets out a clean piece of paper and hurries to complete the assignment before the bell rings.

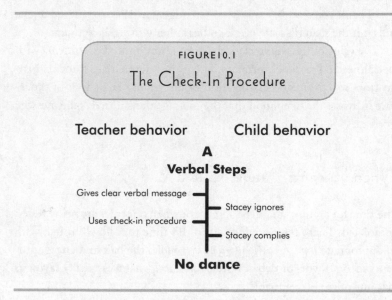

FIGURE 10.1

The Check-In Procedure

Teacher behavior   **Child behavior**

A

Verbal Steps

Gives clear verbal message

Stacey ignores

Uses check-in procedure

Stacey complies

No dance

The Whole-Class Check-In

The whole-class check-in procedure is an effective way to provide individual students with the information they require without embarrassing them in front of their classmates. We recommend using the procedure with distractible students, ADD students, and students with auditory processing problems or learning disabilities. Consider the following situation.

Mrs. Claridge gives her fourth graders instructions for a writing assignment when she notices Celia, an ADD student, looking around trying to figure out what to do. She didn't fully understand the directions. The last thing Celia wants to do is raise her hand and say, "Mrs. Claridge, I'm the only one who doesn't know what to do again." Mrs. Claridge does her best to save Celia some embarrassment by addressing her check-in to the entire class.

"Who can tell me what we're supposed to do?" asks Mrs. Claridge. Jacob raises his hand and repeats the directions for the benefit of all.

"Thank you, Jacob," says Mrs. Claridge. Celia looks relieved as she pulls out the materials she needs to begin her writing assignment.

The value of the whole-class check-in is not limited to students with special needs. Preschool, primary, and even intermediate students benefit from repetition and clarification of directions. The check-in procedure increases the likelihood that the message transmitted is the message received.

When Students Argue, Cut It Off

The time for arguing and debating is not when our rules are being tested or violated. That's the time for action. It's time to follow through with an appropriate logical consequence. If we take the bait and engage students in arguments or debates over our rules, what we're really saying is that our rules are negotiable.

To strong-willed students in particular, negotiable feels a lot like optional, and optional rules invite testing. Teachers who engage students in verbal sparring matches over classroom rules are opening themselves up for power struggles. How do we avoid the power struggle?

The cutoff procedure is a respectful method for ending an argument or discussion before it develops into a power struggle (see Figure 10.2). When students try to hook you into arguing or debating over your rules, end the discussion by saying one of the following:

"We're finished talking about it. If you bring it up again, then you'll have to spend some quiet time by yourself." (Follow through with a time-out consequence.)

"Discussion time is over. You can do what you were asked, or you can spend some quiet time by yourself getting ready to do it. What would you like to do?" (Follow through with a time-out consequence.)

For example, a group of sixth-grade boys play catch with a football on the blacktop area. Their errant passes barely miss younger children playing nearby. The yard duty teacher intervenes.

"Guys, it's not okay to play catch on the blacktop," says the teacher matter-of-factly. "You can play on the grass away from the younger children."

"We're not hurting anybody," says one boy.

"Why can't they move if they don't want to get hurt?" asks another.

The teacher isn't sure his message got across. He decides to check in. "Did you guys understand what I asked you to do?" he inquires.

"Yeah, but I don't see why we should," says one boy. The others nod in agreement.

"I'm not going to debate with them about why they should follow the rules," the teacher thinks. He decides to end this potential power struggle before it begins. "We're finished talking about it," he says. "If you pass the ball on the blacktop again, I'll have to take it away, and you'll spend the rest of the recess on the bench."

Now his message is really clear. The boys know their options. They have all the information they need to make an acceptable decision. Whether they cooperate or test, either way they will learn the rule he's trying to teach. No dances this time (see Figure 10.2).

Emily's teacher also uses the cutoff technique effectively when Emily, a fifth grader, arrives late to class and tries to talk her way out of a tardy slip.

"I was only a couple of minutes late, Miss Stevens," pleads Emily. "It won't happen again. I promise."

"I hope not," replies Miss Stevens, "but you still need to pick up a tardy slip before I can let you back in class."

"It's not fair!" insists Emily, hoping for a little bargaining room. It nearly works. Miss Stevens is about to argue the issue of fairness when she remembers the technique she read about in the book.

"We're finished talking about it, Emily," says Miss Stevens matter-of-factly. "If you want to discuss it further, we can arrange a time after you pick up your tardy slip." That wasn't what Emily wanted to hear. Reluctantly she heads to the office.

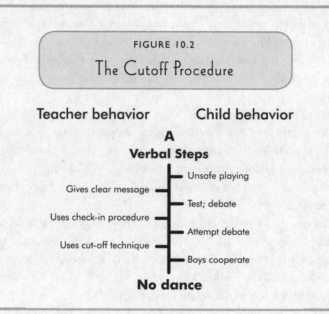

FIGURE 10.2

The Cutoff Procedure

When Students Become Upset, Cool Them Down

Effective problem solving is difficult for anyone to do, adults or children, in an atmosphere of anger and frustration. The cooldown is an excellent method for restoring self-control and keeping both sides off the dance floor until the time is right for problem solving. The procedure is easy to carry out. In situations of anger or upset, separate yourself from the child by saying one of the following.

> When both sides are upset: "I think we both need a little time to cool down. Have a seat at the back table. We'll talk about it during our next break."

When the child is upset: "You look angry to me. You can cool down at the back table or in Mrs. Kenner's classroom next door. What would you like to do?"

When the teacher is upset: "I'm feeling angry, and I need some time to cool down. You can read quietly at your desk while I get myself under control, or you can put your head down for five minutes."

Be sure to allow sufficient time for all parties to restore control before attempting further problem solving. People recover at different rates. Don't assume the child has calmed down because you have. If communication breaks down a second time, use the procedure again. Use it as often as you need it. The following example illustrates how it works.

Brett, age nine, lives in a home where discipline involves a lot of yelling, name-calling, threats, and angry accusations. Often he arrives at school upset and on the defensive. Even minor corrections can set him off. That's what happens when his teacher tries to refocus him during a math exercise.

"Brett, turn around in your seat, please," says the teacher matter-of-factly. "You only have ten minutes to finish the worksheet."

"Why don't you say something to Greg!" shouts Brett. "He talked to me first. Why do I always get blamed?" Brett's face is flushed with anger, but his teacher knows what to do.

"Brett, you look pretty angry," she says in a calm voice. "I'll set the timer for five minutes. Take some time to cool down."

Brett picks up his pencil and worksheet and heads to their prearranged cooldown area at the back table. He grumbles and complains the whole way there, but the five minutes helps. When the timer goes off, he's under control and ready to rejoin the class. No angry dances this time. Brett is learning a tool for managing his angry feelings.

Sometimes teachers need time to cool down more than their students do. That's what Mr. Conner discovered when he became a teacher. His quick temper caused a lot of angry dances. He was wearing down when one of his colleagues suggested he give me a call.

"The kids know my buttons," Mr. Conner confessed. "They push the hardest when they know I'm close to losing it. I think they enjoy watching me blow up."

I asked him to describe what his students did to push his buttons. Then I asked him to describe, from beginning to end, what he did in response to their behavior. As he spoke, I diagrammed the interaction on the board (see Figure 10.3).

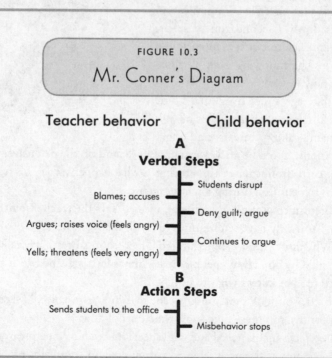

FIGURE 10.3

Mr. Conner's Diagram

Teacher behavior   **Child behavior**

A
Verbal Steps

Students disrupt

Blames; accuses

Deny guilt; argue

Argues; raises voice (feels angry)

Continues to argue

Yells; threatens (feels very angry)

B
Action Steps

Sends students to the office

Misbehavior stops

Mr. Conner's diagram revealed an angry, punitive dance. The dance usually began with a minor disruption, and Mr. Conner usually responded with blaming and accusations. When his students denied their guilt or attempted to argue, which they usually did, he became angry and raised his voice. The more they argued, the angrier he became. Before he knew it, he was shouting and threatening to send them to the office. It was clear from Mr. Conner's diagram that he didn't know how to stop his dances short of an angry explosion. He needed a way to restore self-control before things went too far.

I showed him how to start off with a clear message and how to use the cutoff technique and time-out procedure when students tried to hook him into arguments. Now he was prepared to interrupt his dances, but he still needed a tool to restore his self-control. I introduced the cooldown and encouraged him to use it whenever he felt hot. We arranged a follow-up conference two weeks later.

"How did it go?" I asked when Mr. Conner arrived for our follow-up. He looked more relaxed.

"The methods worked," he said. "When my students try to hook me into arguments, I tell them we're finished talking about it and send them to the classroom next door for a time-out if they persist. If I feel hot, I take out a book and read quietly for five minutes, and I ask my students to do the same. No yelling. No threats. No shouting. The kids know things are different. They don't try to push my buttons as often." Mr. Conner had some new tools for stopping his dances and staying under control. His new diagram looked like Figure 10.4.

When Students Challenge, Give Limited Choices

Bev and Sandy, third graders, sit next to each other in their desk group. They're good students, but they also like to talk, which has become a problem. Their teacher gives them some choices.

"Bev and Sandy, you can sit together quietly, or you can sit apart quietly. What would you like to do?"

"We'd like to sit together," says Sandy. Bev nods in agreement.

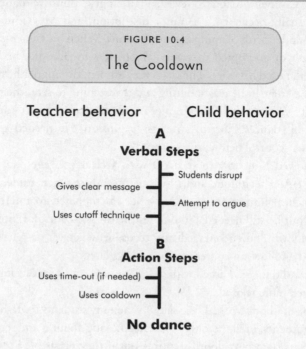

FIGURE 10.4

The Cooldown

Teacher behavior   Child behavior

A
Verbal Steps

Students disrupt

Gives clear message

Attempt to argue

Uses cutoff technique

B
Action Steps

Uses time-out (if needed)

Uses cooldown

No dance

They made their choices. Now, all their teacher has to do is follow through.

Bev and Sandy's teacher is using *limited choices,* a highly effective method for handling testing and avoiding power struggles while teaching responsibility and problem solving. The way this teacher sets the situation up, the girls cannot avoid being responsible for their choices and behavior. The rule is clear, and so is the consequence for noncompliance. The girls have all the information they need to make an acceptable choice to cooperate.

Let's say, for the sake of argument, that the girls make a poor choice and continue talking. What should the teacher do? She should follow through with a logical consequence and move the girls apart. Either way, the girls will learn the intended lesson. Both choices, acceptable or unacceptable, lead to effective learning.

GUIDELINES FOR USING LIMITED CHOICES

The following guidelines will help you use limited choices most effectively.

LIMIT THE NUMBER OF CHOICES YOU PRESENT.
Limit the options to two or three, and be sure the desired corrective step is one of them. For example, if you don't want your students to wear hats in the classroom, you might say, "You can wear hats in the corridors or anywhere on the school grounds, but not in the classroom. If you wear them in the classroom, they're going to remain in my desk for the rest of the week. You can take them home on Friday."

When students attempt to introduce other choices that are not acceptable, you should respond, "These are your only choices. What would you like to do?" Strong-willed students often try to turn limited choices into one of their favorite games, Let's Make a Deal. Hold firm with the choices you offer.

REMEMBER, THE CHOICES ARE YOUR LIMITS.
State them firmly with no wiggle room, or you may invite limit testing. For example, if you don't want students to tilt backward in their chairs, you should say, "You can sit the right way, with all four legs on the floor, or we can put the chair up for the next ten minutes and you can sit on the floor or stand next to your desk. What would you like to do?"

HOLD STUDENTS ACCOUNTABLE FOR THEIR DECISIONS.
After presenting limited choices, ask the student, "What would you like to do?" This question places the hot potato of responsibility in the student's lap, not yours.

FOLLOW THROUGH WITH A LOGICAL
CONSEQUENCE FOR NONCOMPLIANCE.
For example, if you say, "You can play tetherball by the rules or find another game to play," and the student continues to play unfairly, you simply follow through and restrict the student from playing tetherball.

EXAMPLES OF LIMITED CHOICES

The following examples illustrate some of the many ways limited choices can be used. Often, this guidance procedure leads to an acceptable choice, but I've also included examples where students respond with testing or defiance so you can see how to follow up with an instructive logical consequence.

It's lunchtime, and Harry, a preschooler, tries to amuse his friends by taking bites of his peanut butter and jelly sandwich and opening his mouth to reveal the contents. His teacher asks him to stop, and he does for a while but then starts again. His teacher gives him some choices.

"Harry, you can sit with the group if you eat your lunch the right way. If you don't, you'll have to eat by yourself at the back table. What would you like to do?" she asks. Eating alone is no fun. Harry decides to cooperate.

Jessica, a third grader, is a talented jump roper, but she isn't very tolerant of others with less skill. Sometimes, when others attempt difficult tricks, Jessica swings the rope extra fast to end their turn. When the yard duty teacher sees what Jessica is doing, she intervenes.

"Jessica, you can play the right way or find another game to play," says the teacher. "What would you like to do?"

"I'll play the right way," says Jessica, but a few minutes later, she's back to her old tricks. This time the teacher follows through with a logical consequence.

"You'll have to find another game to play for today," says the teacher matter-of-factly. "You can try jump rope again tomorrow." Jessica will probably think carefully next time she decides to end someone's turn.

Maria, a sixth grader, refuses to go to the time-out area after being disruptive. Her teacher gives her some choices.

"Maria, you can spend ten quiet minutes at the back table or twenty minutes in Mr. Dickson's class next door. What would you like to do?"

"Ten is better than twenty," Maria thinks. Reluctantly, she heads to the back table.

It's the third week of school, and Manny, a second grader, continues to disrupt class every day. His teacher has used time-out consistently, but the pattern continues. She suspects she may need assistance from Manny's parents. After class, she presents Manny with some choices.

"Manny, I've tried to help you stop disrupting for three weeks, but we haven't made much progress. Can we work this out between the two of us, or do we need some help from your parents?" Manny is sure he doesn't want his parents involved.

"I think we can work it out," he says.

"I hope so," says the teacher, "but if we can't, I'll have to schedule a conference with your parents." Now the consequence for continued disruption is clear. All Manny's teacher needs to do is follow through.

Sid, a sixth grader, knows it's not okay to wear a bandanna in class but does it anyway. When his teacher asks him to take it off, he refuses. She gives him some choices.

"You can put the bandanna away, or you can work it out with Mr. Clayborn, our vice principal," she says matter-of-factly. "What would you like to do?" Sid knows what will happen if he has to deal with Mr. Clayborn. Reluctantly, he removes the bandanna.

When Students Posture with Defiance, Give Choices

Sometimes, the behavior teachers interpret as defiance is actually extreme limit testing or noncompliance that can be resolved without using the office or administration for backup support. How can you determine whether you're confronting actual defiance or just extreme noncompliance? Give the student a few simple choices that clarify the situation. Consider the following.

Randal, a sixth grader, has been disruptive all morning. When his teacher asks him to take his books and go to the time-out area, he refuses.

"I'm not going," says Randal, "and you can't make me." He has just painted himself into a corner. His teacher gives him some choices.

"Randal, if you refuse to go to time-out, then you're defying me, and if you defy me, I have no choice other than to call the office and have you escorted out. Is that really what you want? I'll give you a minute to think about it." Randal's teacher has given him an option other than being escorted out of the class if he chooses to use it. All eyes are on Randal.

"Okay, I'll go to time-out," Randal says reluctantly. He picks up his books and heads off to the time-out table.

In this case, the office isn't needed. This is an example of extreme limit testing, not defiance. Randal was hoping his teacher would give in or put on an entertaining floor show. When he realized neither of these things would happen, he chose the next best option—cooperation. The lesson wasn't lost on others.

Now let's consider the other possible scenario. When Randal's teacher offers him the same choices, this time he refuses to budge. What should she do? Of course, she should follow through. She should call the office and have Randal escorted out of class. Randal will likely make a different choice next time he considers defying his teacher's authority.

When Students Dawdle, Use a Timer

There are twenty minutes until recess, and Karen, a fourth grader, still has thirty math problems left on her worksheet. When the teacher passes by Karen's desk, he sees her doodling on her workbook. He's been through this dawdle drill before.

"Karen, you need to finish your worksheet before you go out to recess," says her teacher.

"I will," says Karen, who pretends to get busy but, as soon as her teacher leaves, resumes doodling. She hopes to avoid the assignment altogether. There are fifteen minutes left until recess. Her teacher suspects what she's up to. When he cruises by to check on her progress, his suspicions are confirmed. He places a timer on her desk and sets it for fifteen minutes.

"If the worksheet is not complete when the timer goes off," says the teacher matter-of-factly, "I'll find you a comfortable spot on a bench so you can finish it during recess."

"Darn!" Karen grumbles to herself. She can't see any way out of it. She scrambles to finish the worksheet before recess.

Ignore Attitude, Not Misbehavior

Grumbling, mumbling, eye rolling, door slamming, looks of impatience, and stomping off in a huff are tempting baits that are hard for many teachers to resist. If we bite and respond on the child's level, then we're back in the dance, and what have we taught? A lesson in disrespect? They already know that. When students try to hook you with their disrespectful attitude, remember Anthony's teacher in the next example.

Anthony, a sixth grader, knows he's not supposed to read comic books during class time, but when his teacher isn't looking, he decides to do it anyway. She sees him and intervenes.

"Anthony, hand over the comic book, please," she says in a firm, matter-of-fact voice.

Anthony gives his teacher a look of disgust, rolls his eyes, mumbles something under his breath, and starts to complain.

"It's not fair," he says. "Last year, Mr. Rosen allowed us to read comic books in class after our work was done. I don't see why I have to follow your stupid rule."

Anthony's teacher holds firm and waits. "I'm the adult. He's the kid," she reminds herself. "I'm not going to get hooked by his bad attitude."

When Anthony sees she isn't going to budge or dance, reluctantly he makes the right choice and hands over the comic book.

"Thank you, Anthony," says the teacher.

Anthony did his best to hook his teacher with his disrespectful attitude, but she didn't take the bait. Instead she held her ground, maintained her composure, and remained focused on getting what she wanted—his cooperation.

Does ignoring a disrespectful attitude mean that it's okay? No, it's not okay. It doesn't feel good, and we don't like it. But if you reward a disrespectful attitude by responding to it, you'll likely see a lot more of it. Avoid the reinforcement error. Be the adult. Don't bite, but if it happens repeatedly, you can arrange Recess Academy to practice the skill of being respectful.

When does attitude cross the line and become misbehavior that shouldn't be ignored? This is a judgment call every teacher must make in the moment. We can offer some guidelines to keep you on track. Mumbling, grumbling, eye rolling, looks of disgust, and even sticking out the tongue are baits we generally ignore. Profanity, name-calling, insults, hurtful statements, or rude gestures cross the line. We respond to these with time-outs.

Hold Firm: No Second Chances

Do your students sometimes evade your consequences by pleading for a second chance or by promising not to do it again after they have misbehaved? If so, do you go along with it? Teachers who do go along set themselves up for further testing and power struggles. When children give you the right words but the wrong behavior, hold firm and follow through. Let's look at how Dean's teacher does this.

Dean, a fourth grader, sits at his table group and gives another student a kick under the table. The student lets out a loud "Oww!" His teacher comes over to investigate.

"Dean kicked me," the student complains. He lifts up his trouser cuff to reveal a visible red mark.

"I barely touched him," says Dean. "It didn't hurt. Besides, he had his legs spread out on my side of the table."

"It's not okay to kick others," says his teacher, matter-of-factly. She sends him to the back table for a time-out. "You can return to your desk in ten minutes."

"I won't do it again," Dean says contritely. "Can I have another chance?"

His teacher holds firm. "That's a good choice for next time," she says. "This time you need to go to the back table."

Alexis, a third grader, had a similar experience when she tried to stretch a five-minute bathroom trip into a fifteen-minute excursion. After class, her teacher takes Alexis aside.

"Alexis, you know the rule. Bathroom passes are five minutes," says the teacher. "Unless you have a note from your parents, you're going to have to take your bathroom trips before or after class. Your five-minute bathroom privilege will be restored next quarter."

"Come on, Mrs. Donaldson," says Alexis contritely. "I forgot. I won't do it again. I promise."

Her teacher holds firm. "That's a good choice for next quarter," she replies. No second chances and no dances. Alexis will probably think carefully before she tries to take advantage of that privilege.

When Teachers Lose Their Cool, Apologize

Mr. Timmons's day starts off bad and gets worse. He wakes up with a sore throat that isn't bad enough to call in sick. When he arrives at school, his usual parking spot is taken, and he has to park in the reserve lot across the street. It's raining. When he arrives at his classroom, he finds a note on his desk informing him that the film on Egypt he planned to show after lunch didn't arrive from the media center. He has to revise his lesson plan. To top things off, Curtis, his most challenging student, acts out most of the morning and provokes others in his table group. Mr. Timmons loses control.

"What's wrong with you, Curtis?" he shouts. "I'm sick and tired of your bratty attitude day after day. You act like a two-year-old." Mr. Timmons was about to say something even more hurtful when he realized what he was doing and stopped himself.

"Have a seat at the back table, Curtis," Mr. Timmons says. "I need some time to cool down."

After a five-minute cooldown, Mr. Timmons goes to the back table to apologize.

"I'm sorry for the hurtful things I said," he begins. "I lost my temper, but that's no excuse for treating you disrespectfully. Will you accept my apology?" Curtis nods and returns to his seat.

Providing guidance for strong-willed children is challenging and exhausting work. From time to time, we all lose our patience, react in frustration, and say or do things we later regret. How should we handle this when it happens?

An apology is the best way to begin. The gesture conveys all the right messages. It shows children how to be respectful of others' feelings. It teaches them how to heal the little hurts in relationships that often lead to resentment and power struggles. Most important, an apology from a caring adult gives children permission to be human and the courage to try harder.

Some teachers believe that apologizing to students is a sign of weakness that diminishes the child's respect for adult authority. My years as a counselor have shown me that just the opposite is true. To children, an apology is not a sign of weakness. It's a sign of strength that inspires them to try harder. Children respect adults who have the courage to be human and take responsibility for their imperfections and mistakes.

Misbehavior Is About the Student, Not the Teacher

When your students misbehave, do you sometimes ask yourself, "Why is he doing this to me?" If so, you're probably personalizing the testing, which sets both of you up for power struggles. Aggressive research is tiring, but most of the time it's not intended to be a personal attack. Tyrone, a third grader, is a good example of a student who wears teachers down with his aggressive research.

Tyrone's teacher has asked him repeatedly not to wear his Rollerblades into the classroom. The wheels leave scuff marks on the floor, which makes extra work for the custodian. Sometimes, when Tyrone is running late and thinks his teacher isn't looking, he sneaks into the classroom with his Rollerblades on to avoid a tardy slip. On this occasion, he gets caught.

"Tyrone! Why are you deliberately disobeying me?" asks his annoyed teacher. "You know I don't allow Rollerblades in the classroom. They leave marks that are hard to clean up."

"I was being careful," Tyrone replies. "I didn't think you'd mind if I didn't leave any marks."

"Well, I do mind," says his teacher. "It's not considerate. The custodian has enough work to do without cleaning up your messes. Do you understand? Now take them off and give them to me. You can have them back on Friday."

"That's not fair!" protests Tyrone. "I won't do it again. Can't I have one more chance?" he pleads.

"You can next week," replies his teacher. "Hand them over, please."

"You're mean!" Tyrone grumbles as he passes over his Rollerblades.

Tyrone's testing is not intended to be an attack on his teacher's authority. In fact, his testing is not about her at all. It's about him and how he learns. Tyrone needs to collect a lot of evidence in the form of experience before he's convinced that her rules are mandatory, not optional. Persistent testing is part of his normal learning process.

Tyrone's teacher was on the right track when she took away his Rollerblades for violating her rule, but she turned an instructive guidance experience into a power struggle when she personalized his testing.

If you tend to personalize your students' misbehavior, try to hold on to the bigger picture. Aggressive research is part of a normal learning process for strong-willed kids. We set ourselves up for power struggles when we take students' testing personally.

Chapter Summary

Let's reflect on the new tools you've added to your guidance toolbox thus far. In the last chapter, you learned how to be clear with your words, but sometimes even the clearest message isn't enough to prevent students from hooking us into power struggles. In this chapter, you learned some practical strategies for ending power struggles and classroom dances before they begin. You learned how to check in when kids tune out, how to cut it off when kids try to argue or debate, how to cool kids down when they get angry or upset, how to give limited choices when children test or challenge, and how to use timers when children dawdle and procrastinate. You know how to ignore the tempting attitude bait that students use to hook you, how to hold firm when kids plead for second chances, and how to avoid personalizing students' misbehavior.

You're as prepared as you can be to use your words effectively, but your words are only the first part of your overall message. When students continue to test, then it's time to act. Consequences are the second part of your overall message. They speak louder than your words. It's time to get acquainted with your next set of tools.

Logical Consequences: Structured Learning Experiences

Thus far, you've added some important tools to your classroom management tool kit. You've learned how to give a clear limit-setting message with your words and how to stop power struggles before they begin. These steps provide students with the verbal information they need to make an acceptable choice to cooperate, but as you know, your words are only the first part of your total message.

Your students may still decide to test, and when they do, the time for talking is over. It's time to act. You need to answer their research questions with instructive action messages they really understand. Logical consequences are the second part of your limit-setting message. They speak louder than words.

Logical consequences are structured learning opportunities. They are arranged by the adult, experienced by the child, and logically related to the situation or misbehavior. When used in a firm but respectful manner, logical consequences set the gold standard for effective classroom guidance and discipline.

The key to using logical consequences effectively is knowing *how, when,* and *where* to use these wonderful tools. That's what this chapter will show you how to do. We'll take all the guesswork out of the process by providing you with a framework or reference guide for making decisions about what logical consequences to use in specific situations. By the time you're done, you'll know how to get the most instructional value from your logical consequences and what consequences to use in specific situations ranging from typical low-level classroom behavior problems to the "911" calls to the office for backup support.

Let's look at how one teacher uses a logical consequence to handle an incident of negative attention-seeking behavior. It's music time in Mrs. Kellerman's third-grade class. The kids have been practicing the song "Hot Cross Buns" with their recorders all week. They've nearly mastered it. The practice goes well until Lisa decides to prolong the rehearsal. Each time she reaches a certain point in the song, she blasts away with a high note.

The first time, everyone laughs, even Mrs. Kellerman. They think it's an accident. The second time, only Lisa laughs. Mrs. Kellerman gives her some choices.

"Lisa, you can practice the right way, or you'll have to put away your recorder and sit quietly while the rest of us practice. What would you like to do?"

"I'll practice the right way," says Lisa. The practice resumes. When the class reaches that familiar point in the song, Lisa can't resist. She lets out another high note.

"Put your recorder away, Lisa," says Mrs. Kellerman matter-of-factly. "You can join us for music again tomorrow."

Lisa's teacher is using a logical consequence to support her rule about cooperating during music. Because Lisa chose not to cooperate with her teacher's request, she temporarily lost the privilege of practicing recorder with the class. Her teacher's message is clear: Use the recorder the right way, or put it away. The consequence is directly related to Lisa's choice and her behavior. In effect, she chose the consequence she experienced.

How to Use Logical Consequences

Logical Consequences have their greatest impact when they are immediate, consistent, temporary, carried out with nonthreatening body language, and followed with a clean slate. The following guidelines will help you stay on target.

USE YOUR NORMAL VOICE.

Logical consequences are most effective when carried out in a matter-of-fact manner with your normal voice. Angry, dramatic, or emotionally loaded tones convey overinvolvement on your part. The message is more likely to be perceived as a personal attack. When this occurs, an instructive lesson can backfire into a power struggle and generate resentment. Our goal is to discourage the unwanted behavior, not the child performing the behavior.

THINK SIMPLY AND LOGICALLY.

Some adults have difficulty with logical consequences because they think too abstractly and try to come up with the perfect consequence for the situation, or they don't think at all, react in anger, and use a punitive consequence that causes anger and resentment. Punitive thinking is not logical thinking. The intent is to overpower and force compliance.

When you think in concrete, logical terms, an appropriate consequence usually jumps out at you. For example, most misbehavior involves at least one of the following circumstances: children with other children, children with adults, children with objects, children with activities, or children with privileges. In most cases, you can apply a logical consequence by separating one child from another, a child from an adult, a child from an object such as a jump rope, a child from an activity such as a game, or a child from a privilege. Take a moment and ask yourself, "What's happening here?" Then follow through. It's easier than you might think.

FOLLOW THROUGH DIRECTLY.

Logical consequences are "action messages." They must be experienced to have their desired effect. When students test or violate rules, the time for talking is over. It's time to follow through directly. Consider the following.

Thad and Byron, two sixth graders, are supposed to be working on a science experiment. Instead they pinch each other with tweezers from their dissection kits. Their teacher intervenes directly with logical consequences.

"Put away the tweezers," she says matter-of-factly. "Thad, please sit at the back table for the next ten minutes, and Byron, you can sit in the empty chair next to my desk. You both can have your tweezers back in ten minutes if you use them the right way."

By separating them from their dissecting tools and each other, the teacher succeeds in stopping their misbehavior and teaching the intended lesson.

USE TIMERS FOR DAWDLERS, PROCRASTINATORS, OR TIME WASTERS.

Stopwatches and timers are highly effective behavior management tools in situations where students test and resist limits by dawdling or procrastinating. Liz and Becky are a good example. These two fourth graders live for recess. When the bell rings, they're the first ones out the door, and they are the last to return when recess ends. It's the last part that has become a problem, but their teacher has a plan for holding them accountable.

The next time the girls arrive late from recess, their teacher greets them at the door with a stopwatch. She clicks the watch as they walk through the door and announces, "You both owe me forty seconds from your next recess. You can leave forty seconds after everyone else."

Forty seconds may not sound like much of a consequence, but it can be an eternity to two fourth graders who want to be the first ones out the door. After several of these experiences, Liz and Becky started returning to class on time.

USE LOGICAL CONSEQUENCES AS OFTEN AS NEEDED.

How many academic lessons do you teach with 100 percent mastery the first time you teach it? Not many, we suspect. The same point applies to teaching the complicated lesson of classroom management. We teach the lesson, practice the skills, review the lesson, and practice the skills some more. Mastery is seldom 100 percent. Some students learn quickly. Others require more repetition and practice. Some require a great deal of repetition and practice. All of these learning styles are normal.

We know that approximately half the students in our classrooms will need to experience repeated consequences before they learn to follow our rules and respect our authority on a regular basis. If we are going to teach this lesson effectively, we must be prepared to use our tools as often as needed. If we need to repeat the same consequence many times a day for the same misbehavior, we shouldn't assume the consequence is ineffective. More likely, we're dealing with an aggressive researcher or fence sitter who requires more data before he or she is convinced we really mean what we say. We need to be prepared to teach the lesson the way our students need to learn it, the "easy way" with our words or the "hard way" with logical consequences. Let the learning process run its course.

Punitive Thinking is not Logical Thinking

If you've relied upon punitive guidance practices in the past, you will have to guard against using logical consequences in a punitive manner. Punitive consequences may stop misbehavior, but they seldom teach or inspire acceptable behavior from students. Why? Because students often perceive punitive consequences as a personal attack, and this is where the lesson ends. Punitive consequences do not inspire cooperative, respectful relationships between teachers and students.

If you suspect you have punitive tendencies in disciplinary situations, check your thinking. Remember, punitive thinking is not logical thinking. When students misbehave, do you ask yourself, "What do they like? What do they care about? I'll show them! I'll take it away!" If you're thinking along these lines, you probably have punitive tendencies and your guidance lessons are likely to break down.

If you're still in doubt, check the types of consequences you use. Simplistic progressions of consequences that follow a three-, four-, or five-step procedure almost always fall into this punitive category. The color-coded behavior card system is a good example. The first card is usually associated with a warning. The second card usually corresponds to the loss of recess or some desired privilege. The third card usually corresponds to further loss of privileges. The fourth card often corresponds to a note or call home to the parents, and the fifth card results in a referral to the office.

The consequences at each step in the guidance process are typically unrelated to the misbehavior. For example, a student might receive a warning for disruption, lose a recess for distracting others, and lose all recesses for the day for making bathroom sounds during a lesson. If we want students to stop distracting or disrupting, doesn't it make more sense to separate the students temporarily from his or her peers or provide practice sessions for mastering the important skill of not disrupting?

EXAMPLES OF INEFFECTIVE PUNITIVE CONSEQUENCES

- Making students stand in a corner.
- Making students write sentences (for example, "I will not . . .").
- Making students pick up trash on school grounds.
- Taking away favorite privileges for long periods of time.
- Using time-out as jail for long periods of time and without a timer.
- Giving F grades on assignment for disrupting during the assignment.
- Taking away recess, field trips, or privileges for misbehavior in class.
- Asking parents to take away privileges at home for misbehavior in class.
- Writing students' names on the board under the frown face.
- Sending home negative daily behavior reports.
- Making students do extra schoolwork as a punishment.
- Criticizing, shaming, or embarrassing students in front of their peers.
- Assigning unrelated consequences for classroom misbehavior.

Where to Use Logical Consequences

Logical consequences have instructive applications in a wide variety of situations: in the classroom, in the office, on the playground, and in the cafeteria. The Setting Limits Program provides a series of guidance posters to help staff use logical consequences in each of these settings.

Logical Consequences in the Classroom

Let's begin by looking at some of the many possibilities for using logical consequences in the classroom. Most of these procedures are designed to address low- and mid-level behavior problems and are inexpensive in terms of the drain they place on your time, energy, and resources. All of the procedures are easy to carry out.

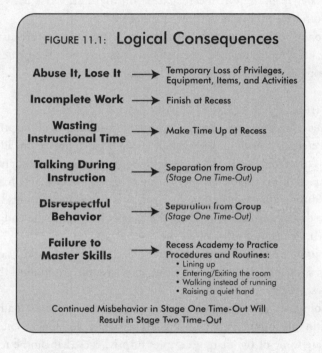

FIGURE 11.1: **Logical Consequences**

Abuse It, Lose It ⟶ Temporary Loss of Privileges, Equipment, Items, and Activities

Incomplete Work ⟶ Finish at Recess

Wasting Instructional Time ⟶ Make Time Up at Recess

Talking During Instruction ⟶ Separation from Group *(Stage One Time-Out)*

Disrespectful Behavior ⟶ Separation from Group *(Stage One Time-Out)*

Failure to Master Skills ⟶ Recess Academy to Practice Procedures and Routines:
  • Lining up
  • Entering/Exiting the room
  • Walking instead of running
  • Raising a quiet hand

Continued Misbehavior in Stage One Time-Out Will Result in Stage Two Time-Out

WHEN STUDENTS BRING UNACCEPTABLE ITEMS TO CLASS.

Logical consequence: Separate the student from the item temporarily. The students in Miss Lowe's sixth-grade class know they're not supposed to bring magazines, comic books, pocket video games, or a variety of other items to class, but Katelyn sits in the back row and thinks she won't get caught. She pulls out a teen magazine, conceals it under her notebook, and tries to read it while Miss Lowe teaches. Katelyn gets caught.

"Katelyn, please put the magazine on my desk," says Miss Lowe. "You can have it back at the end of the week."

Comic books, cards, toys, candy, and electronic devices are just a few of the many items teachers need to remove to support their rule about not bringing those items into the classroom.

WHEN STUDENTS MISUSE OR ABUSE PRIVILEGES.

Logical consequence: Temporary loss or modification of the privilege. Mr. Peters, a fourth-grade teacher, has a liberal policy on allowing friends to sit together in the same desk group, that is, until students take advantage of his policy. Garrett is one of those students. He has been warned three times during the first week about talking with his buddy, Miles, during instruction. When the class is released at the end of the day, Mr. Peters meets Garrett at the door.

"Sitting near our friends without talking is not easy to do," says Mr. Peters. "You're going to have to sit in another table group until the end of the semester."

Computer privileges, classroom jobs, leadership roles, bathroom and drinking fountain privileges, recess privileges, and lunchroom privileges are some of the many examples of privileges that can be revoked temporarily when students misuse or abuse them.

WHEN STUDENTS WASTE OR MISUSE INSTRUCTIONAL TIME.

Logical consequence: Make up the wasted time. What is the single most valuable resource during the instructional day? It's time, of course. This precious commodity is always in short supply.

Who controls the use of time in the classroom? In theory, teachers do. But in reality, students often control a significant portion of classroom time with limit testing, misbehavior, or by failing to follow classroom rules and procedures. The competition for time between students and teachers is perhaps the biggest drama that plays out in the classroom on a daily basis.

Is there a way teachers can take back control of this precious resource? Yes. Time can be used as a logical consequence. The value of instructional time comes into perspective for students when it is contrasted against the time they really value—before school time, after school time, recess, lunch, and breaks. This is "prime time" for students. Students who waste instructional time should be held accountable for making up that time on their time. When students have to pay out of their own pockets, they start to take instructional time more seriously

WHEN STUDENTS TALK OR DISRUPT
DURING INSTRUCTION.

Logical consequence: Separate the students who are talking or use a Stage One Time-out.

Selena, a second grader, is supposed to work on a penmanship activity at her desk but chooses to talk with the student sitting next to her instead. Her teacher gives her some limited choices.

"Selena, you can work quietly at your desk or work quietly next to my desk. What would you like to do?" says her teacher.

"I'll be quiet," replies Selena, but less than five minutes pass before Selena talks to her neighbor again. Her teacher follows through with a logical consequence.

"Selena, bring your paper, workbook, and pencil and have a quiet seat next to my desk," her teacher says, matter-of-factly. Now, Selena has to work quietly.

WHEN STUDENTS TREAT OTHER STUDENTS OR THEIR
TEACHER DISRESPECTFULLY.

Logical consequence: Separate the disrespectful student from his or her peers or teacher temporarily with a Stage One Time-out.

Brenda, a fifth grader, goes to the blackboard to correct a punctuation error in a sentence. As she returns to her seat, several classmates notice she failed to add quotation marks in the sentence.

"Nice try, Brenda," says one of her classmates sarcastically. The teacher intervenes.

"Collin, it's not okay to treat anybody disrespectfully in this classroom," says the teacher. "Have a seat at the back table. You owe Brenda an apology." The teacher sets the timer for 10 minutes. Collin heads to the back table.

WHEN STUDENTS TRY TO HOOK US INTO ARGUMENTS.

Logical consequence: Use the cut-off technique and separate yourself from the child temporarily.

Roberta, a sixth grader, wants to leave class early to get a good seat at a spirit rally. When her teacher denies the request, Roberta does her best to turn a no into a yes.

"Come on, Mr. Richards," pleads Roberta. "Be fair!"

"You'll have plenty of time to get a seat if you leave with everyone else," he replies.

"Yeah, but not a good seat," argues Roberta. "I don't want to sit in the very back. What's the big deal, anyway?" Her voice has a sarcastic tone. Mr. Richards decides to cut off the discussion.

"We're finished talking about it," he says. "If you bring it up again, you'll have to spend some time by yourself."

"Why?" Roberta protests. "Are you afraid you might be wrong?"

"Take your books and have a seat at the back table," says Mr. Richards. "I'll let you know when it's time to rejoin the group." He said the discussion was over, and he backed up his words with a time-out.

WHEN STUDENTS ARRIVE TO CLASS UNPREPARED.

Logical consequence: Teach responsibility with a classroom rental center.

Miles, a third grader, arrives to class without his textbook, writing paper, or a pencil. When it's time to begin an assignment, Miles raises his hand.

"Mrs. Thomas, I don't have a book, paper, or anything to write with," he says.

She signals him to come over to a table provisioned with class supplies.

"Welcome to my rental center," she says. "Collect what you need and take it back to your desk. The rent today will be wiping off the blackboard and emptying the pencil sharpener before you leave for recess."

Sure, Miles's teacher could have given him the items he needed, but who would have been responsible for solving the problem? Classroom rental centers are an effective strategy for holding students responsible for arriving to class prepared.

WHEN STUDENTS MAKE MESSES.
Logical consequence: Have them clean it up.
Todd and Kirk, two sixth graders, write graffiti in the boy's bathroom and get caught. Graffiti has been a serious problem at their school. A lot of money has been spent on cleaning it up. The staff is concerned, but they are divided about the best way to deal with the problem.

The principal wants to send a strong message to other students. He suggests suspending the boys for a week and turning the matter over to the police.

The vice principal thinks the principal's plan is too harsh. "They need to understand the seriousness of what they did," he says. He recommends four weeks of mandatory counseling.

The classroom teacher has another idea. He proposes a logical consequence. "Todd and Kirk helped make the mess. Shouldn't they clean it up?" He suggests giving them some choices. "They can put in twenty hours of their own time cleaning up graffiti or they can be suspended and the matter can be turned over to the authorities." Everyone likes the plan.

When they present the choices to the boys and their parents, they all decide to avoid the hassle of dealing with school authorities and put in twenty hours of cleanup. This lesson won't be lost on others.

WHEN STUDENTS ARE DESTRUCTIVE.
Logical consequence: When possible, have them repair, replace, or pay for the damaged items.
Sondra, a fifth grader, is a determined campaign manager. She'll do

almost anything to get her candidate elected, including tearing up posters of a rival candidate. She does this and gets caught. The principal calls her to the office.

"I know you want to help your friend, but destroying posters of other candidates isn't the best way to go about it," says the principal. "Nadia is missing fourteen posters. I asked her to give me one to use as a model. You need to bring in fourteen more just like it tomorrow and help her put them up before class."

WHEN STUDENTS DON'T RAISE THEIR HAND DURING INSTRUCTION.

Logical consequence: Use the Blurt Box

Cole, a fourth grader, sits on the carpet with his classmates as his teacher reads a story about raccoons. Occasionally, she pauses to ask some questions.

"What foods do raccoons like to eat?" asks the teacher. She waits for a quiet hand.

"Oh, I know," Cole blurts excitedly. "They like berries and bugs and bird eggs." His teacher doesn't look pleased.

"Cole, you need to raise your hand if you want to share something," says his teacher. She writes his name in the Blurt Box on the chalkboard then returns to her story. After a few minutes, she pauses again.

"Why do raccoons spend so much time around lakes and streams?" asks the teacher.

"They eat frogs and fish," Cole blurts again. "Oops!" he says to himself.

"Cole, it's not okay to interrupt without raising a quiet hand," says his teacher. "Please have a seat at the time-out desk." She sets the timer for five minutes and writes a check after Cole's name in the Blurt Box. Cole heads to the time-out desk.

His teacher continues reading the story, pausing occasionally to ask more questions. She chooses students who raise a quiet hand. Five minutes pass. Cole rejoins his classmates on the carpet.

"What is special about the front paws of raccoons?" asks the teacher. Cole knows the answer. He can't resist.

"They can grab things like people," he says proudly, then realizes his mistake.

"Cole, what are we supposed to do when we want to say something?" she asks as she writes a second check after his name.

"Raise my hand," replies Cole.

"Right," says his teacher, matter-of-factly. "We'll practice that skill at Recess Academy next recess." She writes Cole's name in the box on the chalkboard labeled "Recess Academy." "Please take your things and have a seat at the time-out desk." She sets the timer once again for five minutes. Cole heads to the time-out area.

When students are released for recess, Cole's teacher asks him to return to the carpet area. "We're going to practice the important skill of raising a quiet hand." She begins to read story about raccoons once again, then pauses to ask a question. Cole nearly blurts out the answer when he stops himself and raises his hand.

"Good job!" says his teacher. He answers and she proceeds with her story. They repeat the procedure three more times during the next five minutes.

"You handled that great!" says his teacher with an appreciative smile. "You can join your friends at recess." She erases his name from the Blurt Box and box for Recess Academy. Cole may need more of these training opportunities before he fully masters the important skill of raising a quiet hand, but the training procedure will surely lead to the desired outcome.

Blurting out during instruction is the single most recurring problem behavior in most classrooms. No other classroom misbehavior comes close to rivaling it. For the vast majority of students like Cole, blurting out is simply a bad habit that can be remedied with effective limit setting. For a few students, however, blurting out may be a symptom of an impulse control disorder such as ADD or ADHD that is less responsive to limit setting due to the neurological nature of the disorder.

Does this mean we should avoid using the Blurt Box as a limit-setting procedure for students with ADD or ADHD? No. Students with special needs don't require different discipline. They just require more of it. Teachers need to be patient and adjust their expectations for a slower

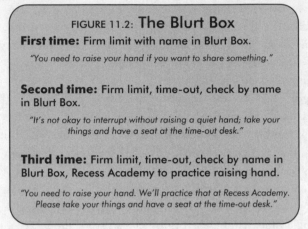

FIGURE 11.2: **The Blurt Box**

First time: Firm limit with name in Blurt Box.

"You need to raise your hand if you want to share something."

Second time: Firm limit, time-out, check by name in Blurt Box.

"It's not okay to interrupt without raising a quiet hand; take your things and have a seat at the time-out desk."

Third time: Firm limit, time-out, check by name in Blurt Box, Recess Academy to practice raising hand.

"You need to raise your hand. We'll practice that at Recess Academy. Please take your things and have a seat at the time-out desk."

training process. Also, they may need to make some modifications and accommodations in how they carry out some of their limit-setting procedures.

The Blurt Box is an effective training procedure for managing blurting and teaching students the important skill of raising a quiet hand. Here are some guidelines for carrying out this procedure.

- The first blurt: The first time a student blurts say, "You need to raise a quiet hand if you want to share something." Then write the student's name in the Blurt Box.
- The second blurt: The second time a student blurts, say, "It's not okay to speak without raising a quiet hand and being called on. Please take your things and have a quiet seat at the time-out desk." Place a check after the student's name in the Blurt Box. Set the timer for five or ten minutes depending on the child's age and grade level and follow through with a Stage One Time-out.
- The third blurt: The third time a student blurts, say, "You need to raise a quiet hand when you want to share something. We'll practice that skill at Recess Academy." Place a second check after the student's name in the Blurt Box. Set the timer once again and

follow through with a Stage One Time-out. The third occurrence makes the student an automatic candidate for Recess Academy.

- Further blurts before Recess Academy: Follow the procedure above for each subsequent blurt. Place a check after the student's name and follow through with a Stage One Time-out. Repeat occurrences are telling you the student requires additional training.

- Practice the skill during Recess Academy. Practice sessions should be held for three to five minutes at a time. Stay positive during practice sessions and express your confidence that the student can and will master the skill. Acknowledge successful efforts. When students begin Recess Academy with more than two checks after their name, consider lengthening the practice sessions in three-minute increments. This practice is not recommended for students with ADD or ADHD. Once the skill has been practiced in Recess Academy, erase the student's name from the Blurt Box and Recess Academy box. The process starts over. Start each day with a clean slate.

LOGICAL CONSEQUENCES IN THE OFFICE

Imagine a line that separates two categories of consequences: those that place a minimal drain on time, energy, and resources, and those that are more expensive in terms of the drain they place on time, energy, and resources. Most logical consequences used in the classroom fall in the first category. They are designed to manage low- and mid-level behavior problems or 90–95% of the misbehavior on most school campuses. We are about to cross the line.

The next category of consequences is reserved for the 5–10% of students who show extreme, persistent, or intensive-level behavior problems and sometimes require backup support from the office. Most are carried out by school administrators and require considerable time, planning, and assistance to successfully execute. From a financial perspective, these consequences are the most expensive discipline procedures used on campus in terms of the drain they place on time, energy, and expensive school resources.

Before using any costly procedure, there are some questions we should ask. First, is the misbehavior severe enough to warrant an expensive consequence? Second, have we exhausted all the less expensive options to resolve the problem? Third, are the people we need to assist us willing and available to help?

If the answer to any of these questions is no, then we should continue our guidance efforts at a less expensive level. When we involve administrators, counselors, or others in the guidance process before they are needed, we drain valuable school resources and risk alienating our colleagues and parents in the process. Expensive consequences should be used judiciously. With this in mind, let's examine some of these expensive, but potentially effective, procedures.

After-School Detention as a Logical Consequence

After-school detention is a logical consequence for handling problems such as tardies or wasted time. As Nick discovers in the following example, the procedure provides accountability for those students who want to move on to more pleasurable activities at the end of their day.

Nick, a sixth grader, arrives late for class for the third time during the semester. When he goes to the office to pick up a tardy slip, he's informed that he must put in one hour of after-school detention as a consequence.

"That sucks!" Nick says to himself. "I was planning to go skateboarding with my friends." After-school detention gave Nick a new reason for arriving at class on time.

In this case, Nick is held accountable for wasting time by making up that time after school. Lunch detentions are another option. Detentions are most effective when the student has something constructive to do such as reading or catching up on homework. The referring teacher should provide a study packet. Detentions are not appropriate for young students and first-time incidents.

On-Campus Suspension as a Logical Consequence

Some misbehavior, such as extreme defiance, disruption, or aggressive behavior, requires removing students from the classroom for more than brief periods. In these situations, on-campus suspension (OCS) can be an effective logical consequence. Consider the following example.

Darrell, a fifth grader, knows it's not okay to wear hats in the classroom but decides to challenge the school rule and do it anyway. He arrives at class with his hat on and waits for the teacher to ask him to take it off. When she does, he explodes.

"Buzz off!" he shouts. "I don't have to follow your stupid rules or take any garbage from you or anybody else." He slumps back in his chair defiantly.

"Pick up your books and take them with you to OCS, Darrell," says the teacher matter-of-factly. "You can join us again after lunch if you're willing to take your hat off." She hands him a slip with the time on it and sends him to the on-campus suspension center for the rest of the morning. Darrell was hoping his protest would be his ticket home for the day. When he arrives at OCS, he decides to stick with his original plan and keeps his hat on.

"You know the rules, Darrell," says the OCS supervisor. "If you don't take it off, I'll have to send you to the vice principal's office. He'll probably send you home for the day."

"Go ahead. Make my day," Darrell says to himself. He knows his parents can't afford to take any time away from work. He'd love to spend his day hanging out at the mall. He leaves his hat on.

When Darrell arrives at the office, the vice principal has a good idea about what's going on. He gives Darrell some choices. "You can spend the rest of the morning in OCS with your hat off, or you can spend the rest of the day in OCS with it on. What would you like to do?"

These were not the choices Darrell expected. He takes a moment to consider what his day would be like in OCS. No visiting with friends on the playground or during lunch. He would eat lunch by himself, take periodic bathroom breaks, and spend most of his day catching up on assignments or doing homework. Reluctantly, Darrell takes off his hat and heads to OCS for the rest of the morning.

As the example illustrates, on-campus suspension has many advantages. It stops the immediate misbehavior. It removes the audience and payoffs for misbehavior, and it maintains the student in an instructional setting to the greatest extent possible. The message to Darrell was clear:

You will stay at school. You can cooperate in class and enjoy your usual privileges and the company of your peers, or you can work quietly by yourself without your peers or usual privileges. The best option is not difficult to figure out.

Although OCS is best suited for larger schools with a high incidence of misbehavior, the procedure can be adapted for smaller schools. Spending the balance of the day in a fellow teacher's classroom works well in many cases. The procedure is flexible. Some schools use OCS as a second-stage time-out area.

The primary disadvantage of OCS is cost. An on-campus suspension center is expensive to operate. It requires a full-time staff position to supervise students, an available classroom, and a set of record-keeping procedures to track referrals, arrivals, departures, and no-shows. The following guidelines will help you set up an on-campus suspension program.

GUIDELINES FOR OPERATING OCS

- Select an appropriate place for OCS. The room should be large enough for students to sit well apart from one another.
- Provide work folders. OCS should be a quiet place for students to work. Referring teachers should send work folders with their students.
- Hold referring teachers accountable. OCS referral forms should include a section for the teacher to complete indicating all prior steps taken to resolve the problem. The referral should clearly indicate that OCS is an appropriate consequence for the student's misbehavior.

Off-Campus Suspension As a Logical Consequence

The effectiveness of this procedure depends on cooperation between home and school, which is also the biggest limitation of the procedure. Administrators can exclude a student from campus, but they have no control over what happens when the student leaves. Enforcing the consequence is the parents' job. Parents must be willing to enforce the consequence for it to be effective. Administrators should routinely ask parents if they are available to supervise their children during the days they are suspended and at home. If the parents are not available, an on-campus suspension might be a preferable option.

When parents are not willing or able to enforce the consequence, many students view the suspension as a vacation day and welcome opportunities for more. In effect, the consequence becomes a reinforcement error or a reward for continued misbehavior. When parents are willing to enforce the consequence, off-campus suspension can be instructive. Consider the following example.

Chase, a third grader, decides to play a joke on the girl sitting in front of him. As she begins to sit down, he pulls out her chair, and she falls backward. The joke isn't funny. She has a gash on the back of her head that probably requires stitches.

The teacher asks Chase to collect his books and assignments and sends him to the office with a note. The principal promptly calls his parents and informs them that Chase has been suspended from school for the rest of the day.

"How can we help him learn from this experience?" asks Chase's mom. The principal offers some helpful tips.

"Suspensions are most effective when children spend a quiet day in the house without the privileges they would normally enjoy. No TV, video games, riding bikes, playing in the neighborhood, or hanging out with friends, at least not during school hours. They should spend their time catching up on missed schoolwork, reading, or doing other quiet activities. Tomorrow, Chase can return to school with a clean slate."

In this case, cooperation between home and school ensured the success of the procedure. The off-campus suspension provided Chase with the instructive lesson he needed.

Saturday School As a Logical Consequence

Saturday school can be an effective logical consequence for handling problems with tardies, cuts, or truancy. The message is clear: Make up the time you missed. Although the program requires costly supervision, room space, and record keeping, much of the costs can be recovered through the additional aid generated by student attendance.

The biggest disadvantage of Saturday school is that the consequence cannot be enforced without parent support. When parents are willing to hold their children accountable, a day or two of Saturday school can be very instructive. Consider the following.

Julie and Miranda, both fifth graders, decide to hang out at the mall during the first half of their day. When they arrive at class after lunch, they are called to the office.

"May I see the excuse notes from your parents so I can admit you to class?" asks the office clerk. Neither girl has a note or a good excuse. The clerk alerts the vice principal who gives the girls some choices.

"You both will have to make up your truancies with half a day of Saturday school. There are two Saturdays left in the month. Which one would you like?" Julie and Miranda know their parents will support the consequence. They'll probably think carefully next time they consider spending class time at the mall.

LOGICAL CONSEQUENCES FOR THE PLAYGROUND

Logical consequences also are effective tools for supporting rules and procedures on the playground, but before we examine the many possible applications, let's prevent the problems that are preventable by revisiting the issue of structure. Clearly defined rules and procedures are as important on the playground as they are in the classroom. When students, teachers, yard duty supervisors, and administrators operate under a common set of rules and procedures, the playground becomes a much more orderly and cooperative place for all involved. Here are some simple ways to improve the structure of the playground:

- Teachers, yard duty supervisors, and administrators should agree on a common set of playground rules and procedures and post those rules and procedures on the playground, in the classrooms, and in the school handbook that goes home to parents.
- Teachers and yard duty supervisors should be trained to carry out playground procedures and to use appropriate logical

consequences to consistently enforce playground rules and
procedures.

- Every school should have clearly defined procedures for entering
  and exiting the playground in a safe and orderly manner. Teachers
  should practice these procedures with their students during the first
  two weeks of school and periodically as needed.
- The school principal should review playground rules and
  procedures with students during school assemblies at the beginning
  of the year. Teachers should do the same in their classrooms during
  the first few weeks of school and periodically as needed.
- Students who repeatedly violate playground rules and procedures
  are good candidates for Recess Academy. They should review
  playground rules and practice the skills they haven't mastered with
  their teacher.
- Every playground should have suitable areas for time out. Benches,
  tables, or other seating areas work fine.

When to Use Logical Consequences on the Playground

Logical consequences have instructive applications in a wide variety of
playground situations. The following are just a few of the many possibilities.

WHEN CHILDREN MISUSE SCHOOL EQUIPMENT.
Logical consequence: Loss of equipment for that recess.
Derek, a third grader, knows it's not okay to swing on the tetherball rope
but does it anyway and gets caught.

"Stop swinging on the tetherball rope, Derek," says the yard duty
teacher. "You need to find another game to play. You can try tetherball
again next recess."

WHEN CHILDREN DON'T PLAY GAMES BY THE RULES.
Logical consequence: Find another game to play for that recess.
Holly, a fifth grader, prides herself as one of the best hopscotch

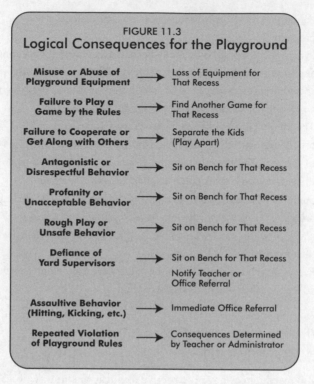

FIGURE 11.3
Logical Consequences for the Playground

Misuse or Abuse of Playground Equipment →	Loss of Equipment for That Recess
Failure to Play a Game by the Rules →	Find Another Game for That Recess
Failure to Cooperate or Get Along with Others →	Separate the Kids (Play Apart)
Antagonistic or Disrespectful Behavior →	Sit on Bench for That Recess
Profanity or Unacceptable Behavior →	Sit on Bench for That Recess
Rough Play or Unsafe Behavior →	Sit on Bench for That Recess
Defiance of Yard Supervisors →	Sit on Bench for That Recess Notify Teacher or Office Referral
Assaultive Behavior (Hitting, Kicking, etc.) →	Immediate Office Referral
Repeated Violation of Playground Rules →	Consequences Determined by Teacher or Administrator

players in the whole school. She seldom steps outside the lines, but when she does, sometimes she refuses to give up her turn. That's when other students complain.

"Holly refuses to give up her turn," a student complains to the yard duty supervisor. The other girls waiting in line agree.

"You'll have to find another game to play the rest of the recess, Holly," says the yard duty supervisor. "You can play hopscotch again next recess if you play by the rules."

WHEN CHILDREN FAIL TO COOPERATE WITH OTHERS.

Logical consequence: Separate the kids (make them play apart). Kurt and Thomas, two second graders, tattle and complain about each other to the yard duty supervisor three times during the same recess. Kurt is about to make it number four.

"Thomas won't stop knocking down my sand castles," complains Kurt.

"I couldn't help it," argues Thomas. "He builds his castles too close to mine." The yard duty supervisor intervenes.

"Sometimes it's hard to play together even when we want to," she says, matter-of-factly. "You guys are going to have to play apart for the rest of this recess. If either of you bothers the other again, you'll have to spend the rest of the recess on the bench."

WHEN CHILDREN SHOW ANTAGONISTIC OR HURTFUL BEHAVIOR.

Logical consequence: Sit on the bench for the rest of the recess.

Several students alert the yard duty supervisor to a problem going on in the four-square area. When the supervisor arrives on the scene, she hears Alexas, a fifth grader, berating another student and using profanity.

"It's not okay to use profanity or to talk to others in hurtful ways," says the yard duty supervisor. "Alexas, you need to sit on the bench for the rest of the recess." Alexas heads off to the bench for a time-out.

WHEN CHILDREN USE ROUGH OR UNSAFE PLAY.

Logical consequence: Sit on the bench for that recess.

The yard duty supervisor notices a spirited soccer game in progress and observes Justin, a fourth grader, deliberately trip another student. The yard duty supervisor intervenes.

"It's not safe to trip others when they're running," he says. "You need to take a seat on the bench for the rest of the recess." Justin will probably think carefully before he decides to trip other students.

WHEN CHILDREN DEFY THE YARD DUTY SUPERVISOR.

Logical consequence: Sit on the bench for the rest of the recess, or if the student decides not to cooperate, notify the student's teacher or the principal.

The bell rings, beginning recess. The students know they are supposed to walk, not run, to the playground. Austin, a fifth grader, decides to ignore the rule and sprint for the field. He nearly crashes into a group of younger students when the yard duty supervisor stops him.

"You need to return to the edge of the blacktop and walk onto the playground," she says. Austin has other ideas.

"You're not my teacher. I don't have to do what you say," he says defiantly. He continues to run. The yard duty supervisor follows him to the field.

When she catches up with him, she intervenes again.

"The rule is walk, not run. You need to return to the edge of the blacktop and walk out again the right way," she says.

"No way," says Austin defiantly.

"Then you'll have to spend the rest of your recess on the bench," says the yard duty supervisor.

"No way!" says Austin. "I'm not going to waste a perfectly good recess on the bench." The yard duty supervisor holds firm.

"If you don't do what I ask, then you're defying me, and if you defy me, I have no choice but to report you to your teacher or the principal. Is that really what you want?" she asks. Now Austin's defiance doesn't seem like such a good idea. He thinks it over for a moment.

"Okay," Austin says reluctantly. "I'll go back and walk."

"That's a good choice for next time," says the supervisor. "This time, you're going to have to spend the rest of your recess on the bench." Austin is about to argue the matter, then reconsiders.

"Okay, I'll sit on the stupid bench." He heads toward the bench.

WHEN CHILDREN SHOW ASSAULTIVE BEHAVIOR.

Logical consequence: Immediate referral to the administrator for further consequences. In these situations, loss of recess is only the beginning step. The next level of intervention is usually dictated by state educational code or school discipline policy.

WHEN CHILDREN REPEATEDLY VIOLATE PLAYGROUND RULES OR PROCEDURES.

Logical consequence: Should be determined by the student's teacher or administrator. Many teachers find that Recess Academy is an effective logical consequence when students need time to practice important skills or procedures. Administrators often choose to suspend recess privileges for days or even weeks in situations involving safety issues or defiance. Consider the following example.

The bell rings, ending recess. All students are expected to freeze until the yard duty supervisor blows the whistle releasing them to line up with their classmates. Conner, a second grader, hates to freeze. He wants to be first in line to lead his class back to the classroom. The yard duty supervisors have intervened repeatedly, but Conner doesn't seem to get the message.

Eventually the problem is reported to Conner's teacher, who decides Recess Academy is the next appropriate step. When the bell rings for the next recess, the teacher pulls Conner aside.

"Conner, we're going to practice the important skill of freezing." She asks him to go to the carpet area and role-models a good freeze position. She holds the position for twenty seconds, the time the yard duty supervisors usually take before blowing the release whistle.

"Now, you try it," she says. Conner kneels down in the freeze position. His teacher starts the timer and holds him in that position for the full twenty seconds.

"Good job!" she says. "You did that perfectly. Now, let's try a few more." She pretends to ring the bell. Conner freezes and she starts the timer. After twenty seconds, she releases him. They repeat the procedure three more times.

"You did those very well," says his teacher. "There are five minutes left for this recess. Go out and join your classmates. When the bell rings, I'll come out to watch you freeze." Conner heads to the playground.

When the bell rings, Conner kneels down and waits for the yard duty supervisor to blow the release whistle. When he arrives at the lineup area, his teacher catches his eye. "Good work," she says proudly. "Would you lead the class back to the classroom?"

LOGICAL CONSEQUENCES FOR THE LUNCHROOM

If you anticipated starting off with structure for the lunchroom, you're right on target. A few clearly defined rules and procedures ensures an orderly and cooperative eating experience for students and an easier

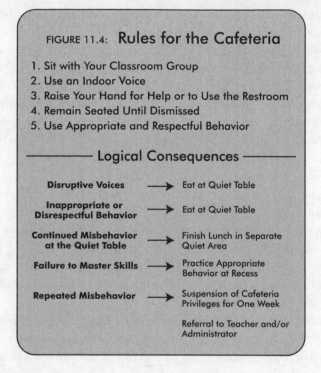

FIGURE 11.4: **Rules for the Cafeteria**

1. Sit with Your Classroom Group
2. Use an Indoor Voice
3. Raise Your Hand for Help or to Use the Restroom
4. Remain Seated Until Dismissed
5. Use Appropriate and Respectful Behavior

———————— **Logical Consequences** ————————

Disruptive Voices ⟶	Eat at Quiet Table
Inappropriate or Disrespectful Behavior ⟶	Eat at Quiet Table
Continued Misbehavior at the Quiet Table ⟶	Finish Lunch in Separate Quiet Area
Failure to Master Skills ⟶	Practice Appropriate Behavior at Recess
Repeated Misbehavior ⟶	Suspension of Cafeteria Privileges for One Week
	Referral to Teacher and/or Administrator

supervision task for lunchroom supervisors. Two structural components are essential: orderly procedures for entering and exiting the lunchroom and a separate quiet table for students to finish their lunch when they choose to be disruptive or inappropriate. See Figure 11.4, which should be helpful.

When to Use Logical Consequences in the Lunchroom

After rules and procedures have been introduced to students, the next step is for lunchroom supervisors to consistently enforce those rules and procedures with logical consequences. Consider the following.

WHEN STUDENTS USE LOUD OR DISRUPTIVE VOICES.
Logical consequence: Eat at the quiet table.

Sonia, a fifth grader, loves to talk, but sometimes her talking turns to shouting and disturbs others. A few minutes into lunch period, Sonia's voice can be heard above all others. A lunchroom supervisor intervenes.

"Sonia, what kind of voice do we use in the lunchroom?" he asks.

"An indoor voice," she replies. "I won't do it again," Sonia pleads.

"That's a good choice for next time," replies the supervisor. "This time, you have to finish the rest of your lunch at the quiet table." Sonia heads off to the quiet table to finish her lunch.

WHEN STUDENTS USE INAPPROPRIATE OR
DISRESPECTFUL BEHAVIOR.

Logical consequence: Eat lunch at the quiet table.

Ruben, a sixth grader, thinks it's funny to open his mouth revealing chocolate pudding and then spit gobs of pudding on his tray. His classmates think it's gross and complain to the lunchroom supervisor.

"Take your tray and finish your lunch by yourself at the quiet table," the supervisor says, matter-of-factly. "You can join your classmates at your class table tomorrow if you eat the right way." Ruben picks up his tray and heads to the quiet table.

WHEN STUDENTS CONTINUE TO MISBEHAVE AT THE
QUIET TABLE.

Logical consequence: Finish lunch in a separate quiet area and/or practice appropriate behavior during Recess Academy.

When Ruben arrives at the quiet table, he decides he's not finished with his quest for negative attention. He unwraps his sandwich from the plastic bag, blows it up with air, and pops it against the table. This gets everyone's attention. The lunchroom supervisor intervenes a second time.

"Put your tray up and have a quiet seat against the wall next to the door," she says. "I'll let you know when it's time to leave." At the end of lunch, she releases the rest of his class, then returns to inform Ruben he can join them on the playground. If this happens again, next time Ruben will practice eating appropriately during lunch Recess Academy.

REPEATED MISBEHAVIOR.

Logical consequences: Suspension of lunchroom privileges for one week and/or referral to school administrator for further consequences. Ruben is a very aggressive researcher and decides to repeat his disruptive behavior in the lunchroom, not once, but several times. Each time, the supervisor reports the incident to Ruben's teacher, and each time, Ruben's teacher has him practice eating appropriately during lunch Recess Academy. The procedure seems to work. He has four cooperative lunches in a row. On the fifth day, however, Ruben decides to throw an empty milk carton and hits another student in the back. The supervisor calls the office, and the principal arrives to escort Ruben out of the lunchroom.

When they arrive at the office, the principal informs Ruben that he has lost his lunchroom privileges for the one week. He will have to eat all of his lunches by himself in the office. Then, the principal asks Ruben an important question.

"Do you think we can work this out here between ourselves, or do we need some help from your parents?" Ruben doesn't want that kind of attention.

"I think we can work it out here," Ruben replies.

"Good," says the principal with a smile of appreciation. The next logical consequence is in place if Ruben decides to test.

Selecting the Appropriate Logical Consequence

If you were not familiar with logical consequences before reading this book, it may take some time for you to feel comfortable using these tools. In the beginning, you may have difficulty deciding what logical consequence to use in specific disciplinary situations. The Setting Limits Program takes the guesswork and the angst of decision making out of the process by providing you with a handy Companion Guide for selecting the appropriate logical consequence for nearly every classroom behavior problem.

The full range of classroom behavior problems can be represented in a three-tier pyramid diagram (see Figure 11.5). Tier 1 of the diagram

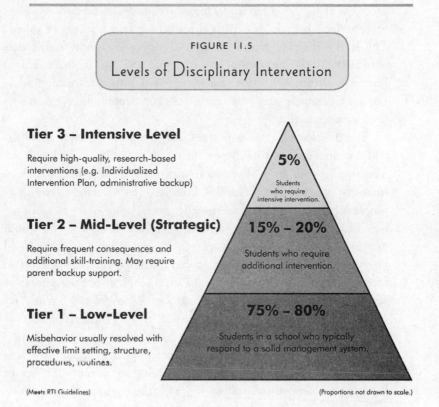

FIGURE 11.5

Levels of Disciplinary Intervention

Tier 3 – Intensive Level

Require high-quality, research-based
interventions (e.g. Individualized
Intervention Plan, administrative backup)

5%

Students
who require
intensive intervention.

Tier 2 – Mid-Level (Strategic)

Require frequent consequences and
additional skill-training. May require
parent backup support.

15% – 20%

Students who require
additional intervention.

Tier 1 – Low-Level

Misbehavior usually resolved with
effective limit setting, structure,
procedures, routines.

75% – 80%

Students in a school who typically
respond to a solid management system.

(Meets RTI Guidelines)   (Proportions not drawn to scale.)

represents low-level classroom behavior problems. Research shows that
approximately 75–80 percent of behavior problems can be resolved at
this level by improving the structure of your classroom, your procedures
and routines. What does it mean if you're spending most of your time
managing problems at this level? Most likely, it means that structure in
your classroom has not been fully established. This is where you need to
devote your time and energy.

Tier 2 of the diagram represents mid-level behavior problems and
accounts for approximately 15–20 percent of classroom misbehavior.
This number will go up in poorly managed classrooms. Most of the

problems at this level fall under the category of "disruptive behavior" or behaviors that interfere with the teaching and learning of others. This level is the playground for aggressive researchers and fence-sitters particularly in classrooms that lack structure and effective limit-setting. Problems at this level often require repeated consequences and additional skill training and may require backup support from parents or from administrators.

Tier 3 of the diagram represents intensive-level behavior problems and accounts for less than 5 percent of all school behavior problems. This number will go up in schools with many poorly managed classrooms or an ineffective discipline policy. Often students who display problem behavior at this level present special behavioral or emotional needs that exceed what can be adequately addressed with classroom management practices alone. They require high quality, research-based interventions such as individual behavior support plans, 504 plans, special education support services, or psychological support services in addition to administrative backup support. Many of the disciplinary interventions at this level are determined by school district discipline policy or state educational codes.

How is the three-tier pyramid diagram helpful to classroom teachers? The diagram is a starting point for helping you identify the type of behavior problem you're confronting and the appropriate level of disciplinary intervention. Most important, the diagram gives you the big picture of what's going on so you can view classroom behavior problems in their proper context. Some behavior problems feel more serious than they really are, particularly when students succeed at hooking us on an emotional level. The diagram provides a reality check. It helps you select the appropriate logical consequence for the problem.

Once you've identified the level of the problem you're confronting, you can use our Setting Limits Companion Guide in appendix 1 to find the appropriate logical consequence or limit-setting procedure to use in each situation. The Companion Guide includes a list of typical problem behaviors and corresponding logical consequence at each tier of the diagram. For each problem behavior, we provide the appropriate logical consequence and what to do for repeat occurrences.

Chapter Summary

Logical consequences are structured learning experiences. They are arranged by the adult, experienced by the child, and logically related to the event or misbehavior. Logical consequences set the gold standard for effective guidance and discipline. They accomplish all of our guidance goals. They stop misbehavior. They support rules and teacher authority, and they promote cooperative relationships between teachers and students. Get to know them. Make friends with them. They are your ticket to credibility in the classroom, in the office, on the playground, and in the cafeteria.

Logical consequences are easy to use if we think in simple, logical terms and follow some general guidelines. Most incidents of misbehavior involve at least one of the following circumstances: children with other children, children with adults, children with objects, children with activities, or children with privileges. In most cases, we can apply a logical consequence by temporarily separating one child from another, a child from an adult, a child from an object (such as a toy), a child from an activity (such as a game), or a child from a privilege (such as using the playground). Your aggressive researchers and some fence-sitters will need generous helpings of logical consequences to learn to respect your authority and follow your rules.

The key to using logical consequences effectively is knowing *how,* *when,* and *where* to use them. The three-tier pyramid for disciplinary intervention and corresponding Setting Limits Companion Guide make this task easy for you. Once you identify the problem behavior, you can quickly determine the appropriate logical consequence or procedure to use and what to do with repeat occurrences. Chapters 12–16 will provide more detailed information regarding how to use the consequences and procedures specified in the Companion Guide.

Recess Academy:
Strategic Training for Mastering Skills

How much time do you spend disciplining your students for the predictable misbehaviors they do repeatedly throughout the week? I'm talking about tilting back in their chairs, talking during instruction, leaving seats without permission, interrupting, chewing gum, disrupting, running in the hallways, entering and exiting the classroom in a disorderly manner. These are the predictable friction points for most students and their teachers.

You can stop these misbehaviors with logical consequences, but consequences alone may not be sufficient for teaching your students the skills they need to behave more appropriately in the future. How do you get off the discipline treadmill? You have to go to the next step in the guidance process. You have to teach them the skills they need to behave more acceptably. Recess Academy is the skill-training component of the logical consequence. What makes it a logical consequence? The training session is carried out on the student's time. Recess time is prime time for students. When they have to master social skills on their time, the importance of the lesson comes into focus. Even brief lessons, carried out strategically, can have a big impact.

Recess Academy is your ticket off the discipline treadmill. This highly effective procedure is designed to address the repetitive, low-, and mid-level problem behaviors that can plague us throughout the year. As the following example illustrates, the procedure works great with aggressive researchers, limit testers, and students who simply lack skills and are stuck in bad habits.

It's the third week of school in Mrs. O'Hair's fourth-grade class. Like most effective teachers, she devotes time each day to teaching her rules and procedures, but she knows that some of her students will require additional training. Marcus, Patrick, and Holly are three of those students.

Marcus's name has been in the Blurt Box since flag salute. He has two checks after his name and he's about to get his third. Patrick has lost his chair six times this week for tilting. It's only Wednesday. Holly is a very aggressive researcher with a surly attitude. She has a bad habit of leaving her seat without permission. All three have their names on the board in the box labeled "Recess Academy." They are about to receive some additional training for basic skills they haven't mastered during class time. As their classmates line up for recess, Mrs. O'Hair makes an announcement.

"Marcus, Patrick, and Holly, please remain in your seats and take out your reading books. You'll be joining me today for Recess Academy." When the last student leaves, Mrs. O'Hair explains her lesson plans.

"Marcus, you and I will be working on raising a quiet hand and not blurting out during instruction," Mrs. O'Hair begins. "What does a quiet hand look like?" Marcus raises his hand to demonstrate. "Good! Begin reading chapter four in your book. In a few minutes, I'll ask you some questions about the story. Each time I do, I want you to raise a quiet hand and wait to be called on before you answer. Is that clear?" Marcus nods. Mrs. O'Hair turns to Patrick.

"Patrick, you need to practice sitting in your chair the right way. That means all four legs on the floor without tilting, the same way I'm sitting." Mrs. O'Hair role-models the correct behavior. "Is that clear?" she asks. Patrick nods.

"Good," says Mrs. O'Hair. "Begin reading chapter four. I'll let you know when the practice session is over." Mrs. O'Hair turns her attention to Holly.

"Holly, what are you supposed to do if you want to leave your seat during class time?" she asks.

"Raise my hand and ask for permission," Holly replies, rolling her eyes.

"Right," Mrs. O'Hair replies. "You need to practice sitting in your seat without leaving for the next five minutes." She sets the timer for five minutes. "Begin reading chapter four. When the timer goes off, I expect you to raise your hand to ask permission to leave. Is that clear?"

"This is really stupid," complains Holly. "I already know how to raise my hand and ask permission to leave my seat." She rolls her eyes again and lets out a sigh of disgust. The last thing Holly wants to do is lose five minutes of her valuable recess time. Mrs. O'Hair doesn't take the bait.

"Good, then this should be an easy practice session," she replies.

Two minutes pass before Mrs. O'Hair asks Marcus a question about the story. Marcus raises his hand before answering. When Mrs. O'Hair calls Marcus's name, he answers.

"Good job!" says Mrs. O'Hair with an appreciative smile. She notices Patrick is sitting in his chair the right way and reading quietly. Holly hasn't even opened her book, but she is still seated and rolling her eyes.

Mrs. O'Hair repeats the procedure with Marcus two more times. Each time, Marcus raises his hand and waits to be called before responding. Patrick and Holly are still parked firmly in their seats.

When the timer goes off, Mrs. O'Hair thanks Marcus for his good efforts and erases his name from the Blurt Box and box for Recess Academy. Marcus heads out to recess. Patrick is still sitting in his chair the right way.

"Good work, Patrick!" says Mrs. O'Hair. She erases Patrick's name from the Recess Academy box and excuses him for recess. Then she turns her attention to Holly, who is still seated with a quiet hand in the air but still rolling her eyes and looking disgusted. Mrs. O'Hair acknowledges her quiet hand.

"May I leave for recess?" asks Holly.

"Yes," says Mrs. O'Hair with an appreciative smile, "and thank you for your cooperation." The lesson was successful. Holly demonstrated the appropriate skill. Mrs. O'Hair succeeded because she kept the focus of the training session where it belonged—on Holly's behavior, not her attitude. Holly heads out to the playground to enjoy her ten remaining minutes of recess time. Mrs. O'Hair still has time to use the restroom and pick up some materials in the staff room.

Five minutes may not seem like much time to practice important skills, but brief practice sessions can seem like an eternity to students who are eager to enjoy the best part of their day. The underlying message is clear: Master the skills during class time or practice mastering the same skills during recess. When students pay out of their pockets, the importance of mastering skills and the value of instructional time come into focus.

Situations for Using Recess Academy

Recess Academy is a strategic skills-training procedure reserved for the small group of students in the classroom who fail to master basic skills and procedures that are taught on a whole-class basis. Usual participants include aggressive researchers or hard-way learners, students who lack basic skills, students who have learned bad habits, and students with special needs who require more training. The following are just some of the many skills that can be taught during Recess Academy.

Entering the classroom	Exiting the classroom
Raising a quiet hand	Lining up at the door
Sitting in a chair or desk	Sitting on the carpet area
Using an indoor voice	Practicing silent signals
Walking in the hallway	Asking for help
Responding to questions	Listening to directions
Maintaining good body space	Paying attention
Practicing not talking	Addressing other students
Practicing not chewing gum	Practicing cooperating
Practicing not interrupting	Reporting problems
Practicing problem-solving skills	Reviewing homework

Arranging Recess Academy

Recess Academy usually takes place in the classroom, but the procedure can be carried out anywhere training is needed—on the playground, in

the hallway, or in the cafeteria. Training sessions should be scheduled during the student's time, not during instructional time. Recess and noon periods work fine. Allow five to fifteen minutes depending upon the complexity of the skill that needs to be taught. Simple skills such as sitting appropriately, raising a quiet hand, or paying attention to directions can be taught in two to three minutes. More complex skills such as handling interpersonal problems may require the full fifteen minutes or longer.

How do students become candidates for Recess Academy? The procedure is designed to address repeated low- and mid-level behavior problems. Students with two or more checks after their name in the Blurt Box become automatic candidates. Other students who repeatedly fail to master classroom rules and procedures may also be candidates. The key word here is *repeated*. Repeated failure to master skills is the signal that more teaching and learning is needed. We're beyond simply telling them what to do. It's time to show them and provide repeated opportunities for them to practice and demonstrate they can carry out the skill successfully.

Training Is More than Providing Information

Sometimes teachers assume that telling students how to handle a situation is equivalent to teaching the skill. For many students, it's not.

Providing information is an important first step in the teaching process, but information alone is not enough to help many students master new or unfamiliar skills. They need to be shown what to do, and often they need practice and additional instruction before they can fully master the skills we're trying to teach.

Many children find themselves in situations like Kaley's, where they know what to do but not how to do it. They need more than information. Simply telling them to walk away from a fight, ignore someone who teases, or just say no when peers encourage them to cut class may not be enough. They need our help breaking the skill down into teachable pieces, role-modeling the acceptable behavior, giving them opportunities to practice, and catching them being successful. This is what Recess Academy is all about. If you follow these simple steps and allow your students to collect the data they need, they will arrive at the desired outcome. Let's look more closely at each step in the skill-training process.

Three-Step Procedure for Recess Academy

There are three basic steps to teaching most skills and procedures during Recess Academy:

1. Teach the skill. Define it, break it into parts, model, and demonstrate.
2. Practice the skill. Rehearse and practice the skill under supervision.
3. Reinforce the skill. Acknowledge, encourage, and reteach if needed.

STEP 1. TEACH THE SKILL

Step 1 involves defining the skill, breaking the skill down into teachable parts, explaining the skill in very concrete terms, modeling the skill, and demonstrating the skill in a step-by-step manner.

Breaking Skills into Teachable Parts

An essential part of teaching social skills is to make the skill understandable to the learner. This involves breaking it down into teachable pieces, then teaching the complete skill piece by piece. Let's look at how Sean's teacher does this during Recess Academy.

Sean, a third grader, has a habit of interrupting. When he was younger, his parents thought it was just a stage or phase that would pass with time. It didn't.

In fact, the problem got worse. Sean's parents decided it was time to do something about it. They tried complaining and criticizing him each time he interrupted. That didn't help. They told him to say "Excuse me" when he wanted their attention. That didn't help, either. Sean simply prefaced all of his interruptions with the words *excuse me* and continued to interrupt.

When Sean's frustrated parents shared their experiences with their son's teacher, she offered to help because the same problem was occurring at school. She used the Blurt Box and time-out, but she decided it was time to schedule a practice session during Recess Academy. The next time he interrupted, she followed through with a time-out and wrote his name in the Recess Academy box. She explained the lesson during recess.

"Sean, I have a plan to help you stop interrupting," she began. "Here are the steps I want you to follow. When you want my attention, but I'm talking or busy doing something, I want you to raise your hand quietly and make eye contact with me. Then I want you to wait for a pause in the conversation, say, 'Excuse me,' once, and wait to be recognized. When I look at you, it's your turn to speak." She models the procedure several times, then gives Sean a chance to practice it. "Do you understand how it works?"

Sean nods.

"Good," says his teacher, "because we're going to practice this skill from now on. When you forget and interrupt, I'll ask you to use the skills I described and try it again. If you interrupt intentionally, I'll ask you to take a time-out. If it happens a lot, we may need to practice this skill again in Recess Academy. Is this clear?" Sean nods again.

Sean gets his first practice opportunity the next morning. After recess, he runs into the classroom excitedly and interrupts his teacher, who's talking to the school's speech therapist. The teacher stops Sean before he completes his first sentence.

"What are you supposed to do when you want my attention?" she asks. Sean remembers.

"Now go back and try it again," says his teacher. Sean leaves the classroom and returns a few moments later. He approaches his teacher, who's still talking, makes eye contact, raises his hand, and waits for a pause in the conversation.

"Excuse me," says Sean. His teacher looks at him and smiles. "Thank you," says the teacher. "What would you like to say?" Sean and his teacher repeated this drill many times in the days and weeks that followed. No, things didn't always go smoothly. Breaking old habits is not easy. After a few weeks, Sean's successes outnumbered his failures. He was well on his way to mastering an important skill. Recess Academy helped Sean and his teacher get off the discipline treadmill.

Role-Modeling Corrective Behavior

Sometimes children need to see, hear, feel, and experience the skill we want them to learn before they are ready to master it. Role-modeling corrective behavior is a simple but powerful teaching technique during Recess Academy that is particularly well suited to younger children and hard-way learners. The method is concrete, easy to use, and has varied applications. It can be used to teach basic skills when no misbehavior is involved or to teach acceptable corrective behavior when misbehavior is involved.

When your focus is on teaching skills when no misbehavior is involved, use the following steps:

- Role-model the corrective behavior you want the student to use.
- Encourage the student to try it again using the corrective behavior.
- Catch the student using the skill correctly, and acknowledge the success.

For example, Miss Casey, a preschool teacher, wants her students to get ready to go outside. "It's time to pick up whatever you're using and put it away," she announces. "We need to get ready for recess."

Emma, age three, hears her teacher and hurriedly throws most of the blocks she's using into their container. Then she places the container on the shelf. "I'm ready," she says.

"Are you sure you're ready, Emma?" asks Miss Casey, noticing several blocks are still scattered on the floor and that Emma's carpet strip hasn't been put away. Emma nods.

"Well, you're close," says Miss Casey. "Let me show you what your area should look like when you're ready." She places a carpet strip down on the floor and pours out a container of blocks next to the carpet strip. While Emma watches, Miss Casey picks up all the blocks, puts them in the container, and returns the container to the shelf. Then she puts away the carpet strip.

"Does your area look like this?" asks Miss Casey. Emma shakes her head. "Then you need to finish the job. I'm sure you'll do fine." Emma does.

Now let's look at another application of this procedure. When teaching corrective behavior following an incident of misbehavior, use the following steps:

- Provide a clear, firm, limit-setting message.
- Role-model the corrective behavior.
- Encourage the child to try it again using the corrective behavior.
- Acknowledge effort and improvement.

For example, Joel, a fourth grader, has a very short fuse and is quick to react when annoyed. He becomes frustrated when the student behind him taps the back of Joel's chair. Joel can't concentrate on his work.

"Cut it out, butthead!" shouts Joel angrily. His teacher intervenes by separating the boys and informing them they will be joining her for Recess Academy next recess. She writes their names on the board in the box labeled Recess Academy.

"Joel, we don't talk like that in the classroom," begins the teacher after other students have left the room.

"Chris was tapping the back of my chair, and he has been bugging me all morning," complains Joel. "I'm sick of it!"

"What are you supposed to do when other kids bother or tease you?" asks the teacher. Joel looks at his teacher blankly.

"I don't know," he replies.

"Well, you could ask him politely to stop or ask me to help if he doesn't," says the teacher. "Watch how I do it." She turns to Chris and says, "Chris, please stop tapping my desk." She pauses briefly to let her words sink in, and then looks at Chris.

"Would that work, Chris?" she asks. Chris nods.

"Good!" says the teacher. " Now you try it, Joel. Tell Chris what he needs to know." Joel turns to Chris and demonstrates the skill. He carries out the skill perfectly.

"That's all there is to it," says the teacher. "Thanks, guys. I'm confident you will handle this better if it comes up again."

STEP 2. PRACTICE THE SKILL

We're all familiar with the old saying "Practice makes perfect." Practice is an important part of any skill-training process, and Recess Academy is the perfect place for practice. When students reach the point that they can demonstrate the skill you're trying to teach, the next step is to have them practice that skill under your guidance and supervision. Set up the practice situation and simply ask them to "try it again."

Try-it-again is a simple, concrete, and highly effective skill-training procedure that is used almost intuitively by preschool teachers. The applications of this procedure, however, extend well beyond the preschool level. Try-it-again is a very effective method for getting students of any age to practice new skills.

The procedure is easy to carry out. When a child fails to carry out a procedure successfully or after an incident of minor misbehavior, state a firm limit-setting message and encourage the child to carry out the corrective behavior by saying, "Try it again." The focus is on the corrective action. The child is simply given another opportunity to demonstrate that he or she can make a better choice and cooperate. Consider the following examples.

A group of fifth graders runs into the classroom yelling and creating a disturbance. Their teacher intervenes.

"Guys, we're supposed to use indoor voices in the classroom." She leads them outside. "Let's try it again the right way." Most of them do, except Leo and Dwight, who think it's fun to irritate the teacher. She gives most of the group an appreciative smile.

"Thanks for your cooperation," she adds. Then she writes Leo's and Dwight's names on the board in the Recess Academy box.

"You'll spend part of next recess practicing how to enter the classroom the right way."

Ryan, a second grader, is a tattler who capitalizes on every possible opportunity to tell on his classmates. His teacher wants him to take some responsibility for solving problems on his own. The next day, Ryan approaches her desk during a math activity to tattle on one of the students in his desk group. His teacher informs him it's time for him to learn some new skills other than tattling. She writes his name in the Recess Academy box and arranges a training session next recess. After his classmates leave for recess, the teacher calls Ryan to her desk, but before she can share her plan, Ryan tattles.

"Nikolas is humming while I'm trying to work," Ryan complains. "I can't concentrate. Would you tell him to stop?"

"Did you tell Nikolas his humming was bothering you?" asks the teacher. Ryan shakes his head. "Did you use your words and ask him to stop?" she adds. Ryan shakes his head again. "Well, those are the steps you need to take first before I become involved." She role-models the message Ryan should give Nikolas next time and gives Ryan several opportunities to practice his new skill. He carries out the skill flawlessly.

"Now you know what to do if this happens again," she says with a smile. She sends him out to join his classmates.

STEP 3. REINFORCE THE SKILL

After we've taught a new skill, and the student has practiced the skill under our supervision to the point of mastery, our next task is to get the student to perform the skill on a regular basis. We want the skill or procedure to become a routine. How do we motivate students to continue to use newly acquired skills? We need to help them feel good about their successful efforts, and we need to let them know that we feel good about their accomplishments. How do we do this? We simply give them what they want most—recognition and acknowledgment.

Skill acquisition is the primary developmental task of early and middle childhood. Children are naturally motivated to learn new skills and to have their successes recognized by the important adults in their lives. They don't require treats, toys, bribes, or special rewards to become more skillful. They're already motivated to show us what they can do.

Nothing poisons a potentially positive learning experience faster than criticism, shame, humiliation, or sarcasm. Sure, we may get the children to do what we want in the immediate situation, but do you think they will be motivated to do it on their own later on? Would you feel like cooperating with someone who treated you with disrespect?

Fortunately, there's a more effective alternative. One of the most powerful ways to motivate children to learn new skills is also one of the easiest. We simply catch them being successful and acknowledge it. Let's look at how one teacher does this.

It's the first week of school in Ms. Carter's second-grade class. She notices that one of her students has a bad habit of running to the door to line up for recess. She's afraid someone might get hurt. Each time she sees him run, she asks him to return to his seat and then walk to the door again. They've been through this drill about a half-dozen times before Ms. Carter decides to accelerate the process with Recess Academy. She writes his name on the board.

"Matt, you'll be joining me next recess for Recess Academy," says Ms. Carter. As his classmates are released to the playground, Ms. Carter turns her attention to Matt.

"How are we supposed to line up for recess?" she asks.

"We're supposed to walk to the door, not run," Matt replies.

"But that's hard to do when you really want to get out to play, isn't it?" Ms. Carter asks. Matt nods. "Let's practice lining up the right way. Watch how I do it." She sits at Matt's desk, gets up, and walks to the door.

"Now have a seat at your desk, then get up and walk to the door to line up," she says. Matt carries out the procedure flawlessly.

"Good job!" she exclaims. "Show me five good trips walking to the door, and you're ready for recess." Matt puts in five good trips and receives positive acknowledgment for each. Then Ms. Carter thanks him for his cooperation.

The next day when Ms. Carter announces that it's time to line up for recess, she sees Matt bolt from his seat and then catch himself. He returns to his seat and walks to the door.

"Thanks, Matt," says Ms. Carter with an appreciative smile. "I really like the way you handled that." Matt beams. He appreciates having his success acknowledged, and he's eager to show her more.

QUESTIONS AND ANSWERS ABOUT RECESS ACADEMY

Q: What does it mean when the same students repeatedly end up in Recess Academy?

A: The answer depends on the type of skill the students need to master. If the skill relates to carrying out a classroom procedure such as raising a quiet hand, lining up properly, not interrupting, sitting in desks acceptably, or paying attention to directions, most students master these skills within the first six to eight weeks of the school year if you enforce your rules and procedures with good consistency. Immature students, poorly socialized students, and some students with special needs require longer. If the problem does not improve after ten weeks, you should consider additional interventions. You may need backup support from the parents, or the student may need to be evaluated for a learning or impulse control disorder or some other developmental condition.

If the recurring problem includes misbehavior such as disruption, defiance, or aggressiveness toward others and persists for more than six weeks, you should consider seeking backup support from the parents, school administrator, counselor, or school psychologist.

Q: Will I need to use Recess Academy on a regular basis throughout the year?

A: In most cases, the answer is no. Recess Academy is designed to eliminate recurring behavior problems, not simply manage them. The procedure shouldn't be needed on a regular basis after it has done its job.

There are always exceptions. If you have a particularly immature or poorly socialized group of students in your classroom, you may need to spend more time shaping them up. Also, if you have more than the usual 10 percent of aggressive researchers in your classroom, you may need to spend more time with Recess Academy.

Q: Recess Academy takes place during the teacher's prime time. Teachers also need time to use the restroom, make calls, etc. Is this procedure fair to teachers?

A: The choice is yours. Pay up front or pay as you go. It's always more expensive to pay as you go. The problem is not going to go away because we decide not to deal with it. The time you invest up front will pay huge dividends later on. Also, the great thing about Recess Academy is that you don't have to give up much of your time. Brief lessons can have a huge impact.

Q: Can I still conduct Recess Academy if I have to supervise recess?

A: In most cases, the answer is yes. Simply ask the student or students to join you on the playground to practice the skill they need to master.

Q: Can I share Recess Academy duties with other teachers at my grade level?

A: Yes. This is a common practice at many of the schools that have adopted the Setting Limits Program. When teachers share or rotate the job, they may end up doing Recess Academy only one week or less out of the month.

Q: What does it mean if I have to use Recess Academy with nearly 20 percent of my class on a regular basis?

A: This probably indicates that your class lacks structure. In most cases, when we hear this question, we find that too little time has been devoted to teaching classroom rules and procedures on a whole-class basis.

Q: Is Recess Academy appropriate for preschool and kindergarten students?

A: Yes, but you should keep the lessons very brief (two to

three minutes) and use a great deal of positive reinforcement. We recommend relying more heavily on whole-class lessons, role-modeling, try-it-again, and enlisting assistance from parents before deciding to use Recess Academy.

Chapter Summary

Providing information is an important first step in the teaching-and-learning process, but information alone may not be enough. Sometimes children need to be shown what to do and given opportunities to practice before they can master the skills we're trying to teach. Recess Academy is designed for that purpose.

Recess Academy is a logical consequence and a skill-training procedure wrapped up in the same package. It is the method of choice for managing and eliminating low- and mid-level behavior problems before they develop into patterns. The procedure is effective with aggressive researchers, fence-sitters, students with special needs, students who have learned bad habits, and students who simply lack the skills to do what we expect.

Recess Academy is carried out in a three-step procedure: Teach the skill, practice the skill, and reinforce the skill. Step one involves defining the skill for the learner, breaking it down into teachable parts, explaining, role-modeling, and demonstrating. Step two involves rehearsal and practice. Successful repetition of the skill under the teacher's supervision is essential. Step three involves reinforcing the skill. The goal is to help students feel good about their accomplishments by recognizing and acknowledging their success. We encourage you to rely heavily on this procedure during the first six to eight weeks of the school year. Recess Academy is your ticket off the discipline treadmill.

Two-Stage Time-Out:
A Stop Signal Kids Understand

Mitch, a sixth grader, tries to spice up a social studies lesson with some clowning around. While his teacher writes at the board, Mitch pretends to conduct an orchestra. He gets a few laughs. The teacher catches a glimpse of what's going on.

"Have a seat please, Mitch," says the teacher matter-of-factly. Mitch sits down, but he isn't finished yet. He got a few laughs earlier, and he's hungry for more. When the teacher returns to the board, Mitch jumps up once again and begins conducting. More laughter. This time the teacher decides to put a little distance between Mitch and his audience.

"Take your books and have a seat at the back table, Mitch," says the teacher. "You can join us again in ten minutes." He sets the timer. Mitch heads to the back table.

Mitch is quiet for a few minutes and then renews his quest for attention. He drums on the table loud enough to distract others. This time the teacher decides to separate Mitch completely from his audience.

"Pick up your books and take them with you to Mrs. Currier's class," says the teacher. "You can join us again in twenty minutes." He won't find a receptive audience there. Mrs. Currier teaches second grade. Mitch digs in his heels.

"No way!" he protests. "I'm not going, and you can't make me." All eyes are on Mitch, who has just painted himself into a corner. His teacher remains calm. He knows what to do.

"Mitch, if you refuse to go to Mrs. Currier's class, then you're defying me, and if you're defying me, I have no choice but to call the office and have someone come and escort you out of the classroom. Is that really what you want?" his teacher asks matter-of-factly. "I'll give you a minute to think about it."

The teacher asks Mitch's classmates to take a minute to write their homework assignments from the board while he completes a referral to the office. Mitch considers his options. After a minute, the teacher rephrases his original question for Mitch.

"What would you like to do?" asks the teacher.

"Okay, I'll go to Mrs. Currier's classroom." The teacher hands Mitch a study packet as he leaves for Mrs. Currier's room. No payoffs for disruption this time. Mitch's goal was to get attention from his classmates, not from the office or his parents.

The teacher in the example above is using the Two-Stage Time-Out procedure to manage Mitch's disruptive behavior. This highly effective procedure is designed to keep disruptive students in instruction as much as they possibly can be and out of instruction only when they have to be. When a student is removed from instruction, we have two problems: a behavior problem and an academic problem. But sometimes students are so disruptive that teachers can't teach and students can't learn. When this happens, disruptive students need to be separated temporarily from their audience and from instruction. That's what Stage Two Time-Outs are all about. They protect the classroom from repeated disruption, and they preserve the classroom for learning.

In this chapter, you'll learn how to use both the stage-one and stage-two time-out procedures to manage a variety of mid-level disruptive behaviors. You'll learn how to set up time-outs, how to carry out the procedure, and how to overcome the typical obstacles teachers confront.

Time-Out Is Not Jail or Siberia

Time-out is a highly effective classroom management tool when it is used as intended—as a logical consequence. The consequence sends all the right signals to children. It stops their misbehavior. It removes them from their audience and payoffs for disruption, and it helps children restore self-control quickly so they can return to instruction.

Teachers like time-out because they can stop disruptive behavior quickly and effectively without losing valuable time for instruction. Administrators like time-out because it keeps disruptive students out of the office and allows teachers to manage the vast majority of disruptive behaviors at the classroom level. The procedure is easy to carry out and can be used at all grade levels.

Unfortunately, time-out has received some unfavorable press because the procedure has been so widely misused and misunderstood. Those who operate from the punitive model have used it as a jail sentence to force children into submission. The punitive version of time-out sounds something like this: "You sit in the corner and don't leave until I tell you to. I don't want to hear a peep out of you." Punitive time-outs can be quite lengthy, several hours or even days, and they are carried out in an atmosphere of anger or upset. The goal is to humiliate or shame students into cooperating.

When it comes to using consequences, punitive teachers go for maximal impact. They tend to omit stage one and move directly to stage two, creating an unnecessary academic problem in the process. Time-out is not jail or exile to Siberia.

On the other extreme, those who operate from the permissive model view time-out as a tool for the child to use at his or her discretion. The child decides when it starts, when it ends, or whether it even happens at all. The permissive version of time-out sounds something like this: "I think it would be a good idea if you take some quiet time by yourself for a while at the back table, okay? You can rejoin the group when you're ready." The child decides the length of time, which is usually quite brief. The goal is to persuade students into cooperating.

In actuality, neither of these methods is really time-out. Time-out is not jail, nor is it an optional consequence for students to use at their own discretion. When time-out is used in either of these ways, responsibility shifts in the wrong direction, and most of the training value of the consequence is lost.

Time-out is really time away from reinforcement or temporary loss of the "good stuff." In most classrooms, the good stuff consists of the many rewards of daily routines, such as being a member of the group, enjoying full privileges, participating in group activities, getting recognition and attention from others, and enjoying the freedom that goes with cooperation. The goals are to stop the misbehavior, restore self-control, and reintegrate the student into instruction as quickly as possible.

Does time-out still sound like jail? The two are similar to the extent that both provide a solid set of walls to stop misbehavior and remove reinforcement. There are also some major differences.

Time-outs are generally brief (three to twenty minutes) and are designed to keep students in instruction as much as they can be. The procedure can be used repeatedly, which provides many opportunities for teaching and learning. Jail sentences, on the other hand, tend to be lengthy (hours or days) and are designed to exclude students from instruction and learning. There are few, if any, opportunities for students to practice responsible corrective behavior in jail.

Guidelines for Using Time-Out

Time-out is a quick, simple, and easy-to-carry-out procedure that can be used with students of all grade levels (preschool through secondary) and in many different situations. The procedure is most effective when presented as a logical consequence and carried out in a firm, respectful, and matter-of-fact manner. The following guidelines should be helpful.

SELECT AN APPROPRIATE TIME-OUT AREA.

Selection of an appropriate place or places for time-out is critical to the success of the procedure. The best place for time-out within the classroom is an unoccupied desk, table, or three-sided study carrel positioned away from others near the periphery of the classroom. These areas separate disruptive students from their stage and audience temporarily.

What should we do when students persist with their disruption while in time-out? We have to become creative and select a second time-out area or stage two outside the classroom. Use a buddy teacher's classroom as the Stage Two Time-Out area.

Why not use the school office? The school office is one of the least suitable places for time-out. It's the hub of school activity with busy people and lots of interesting things going on. For many students, time-out in the office is like watching their own personal soap opera. The consequence is actually a reward, a big reinforcement error. Remember, time-out should be time away from reinforcement. You won't accomplish your purpose if you send a disruptive child to an entertaining area.

Some teachers send students outside the classroom to sit in the hallway for time-out. Is this a recommended practice? Time-outs in the hallway have several disadvantages. This procedure removes students from instruction, often needlessly, and the hallway creates problems with supervision. Most students can take time-out in the classroom without isolating them from instruction and without compromising your duty to keep them supervised. For those students who need more, the two-stage procedure is a better way to go.

Can time-out be used outside the classroom in settings such as the cafeteria, library, or playground? Yes. Select a chair, a bench, or some comfortable spot away from other children. Then keep track of the time.

USE A TWO-STAGE PROCEDURE
FOR PERSISTENT DISRUPTION.

What should you do when students continue to disrupt while in time-out? We recommend using the Two-Stage Time-Out procedure. A two-stage procedure is ideal for aggressive researchers because it provides escalating consequences for escalating misbehavior. Each stage further separates the disruptive child from his or her audience and from the payoffs for misbehavior. Each stage also provides more time for the child to restore self-control.

The procedure is very simple. Stage One Time-Outs take place in the child's immediate classroom for a predetermined period of time. Most students will decide to cooperate at this point. A few may decide to test, and when they do, you'll need a backup area outside your classroom for time-out. Stage Two Time-Outs should take place in a buddy teacher's classroom for twice the usual period of time. If your school has a supervised on-campus suspension center (OCS), that location is an excellent choice as a Stage Two Time-Out area. The only time we advance to stage two is when the student continues disrupting in stage one. Stage One Time-Outs stop disruptive behavior for the majority of students.

For kindergartners and preschool students, both Stage One and Stage Two Time-Outs should take place in the immediate classroom. Each time, you simply separate the child a little further from the group. For example, stage one might take place at an unoccupied worktable, and stage two might take place in a chair on the periphery of the classroom. The exceptions are when students tantrum or disrupt to the point where instruction is compromised. Then you have no choice but to move the students out of the classroom, preferably to another kindergarten classroom. In extreme cases such as loud tantrums and meltdowns you may require backup support from the office.

When choosing a buddy teacher, select someone who is familiar with the procedure and who is willing to carry it out in a firm, matter-of-fact manner. The ideal buddy teacher is someone with older or younger students to eliminate the possibility of a receptive audience. Generally, older students do not like to be in classrooms with younger students and vice versa. The buddy teacher's job is to provide a place for the child to sit during time-out, to supervise the child, and to keep track of time. This is not a time for interrogation ("What did you do this time?") or shaming ("Oh, no, not you again!"), nor should it be a rewarding or pleasurable experience. If the child cooperates during the time-out, the usual outcome, then he or she returns to class when the time is over.

INTRODUCE TIME-OUT TO YOUR
STUDENTS BEFORE USING IT.

You can prevent a lot of testing, resistance, and confusion if you introduce the time-out procedure to your students before using it, preferably during the first few days of school. Pose some hypothetical situations and walk your students through the complete procedure so they can see how it works. Consider the following sample introduction from an intermediate teacher to the class.

"I use the time-out procedure when someone disrupts class. Here's how it works. If I think you are unaware of your behavior, I will usually give you a warning such as 'Jimmy, you need to work quietly now,' so you can stop what you are doing. If you continue to disrupt, or if I'm sure you are aware of what you are doing, I will ask you to go to the time-out area. You can take your books and follow along with the lesson or just sit quietly. When the time-out is over, I will ask you to return to your seat. If you leave the area before the time-out is over, you'll have to go back, and the time will start over.

"If you continue to disrupt while in time-out, I will ask you to go to Mrs. Smith's class [buddy teacher] for twice the time. You can take your books and work quietly when you're there or just sit quietly. She will let you know when the time-out is over and you can return to class. Any questions about how time-out works?"

The Setting Limits Program has time-out guidance posters for the classroom (see Figures 13.1 and 13.2) for both primary (kindergarten through grade three) and intermediate level (grades four through six). We recommend you place these posters in visible areas and review them periodically with your students.

USE A TIMER.

Time-outs should always have a beginning and an end that is clear to all involved. Open-ended, vague, or arbitrary time limits such as "You can return when I think you're ready" or "Go to the time-out area for a while" set up both teacher and students for further testing and power struggles.

The best way to keep track of time is to use a time-out timer,

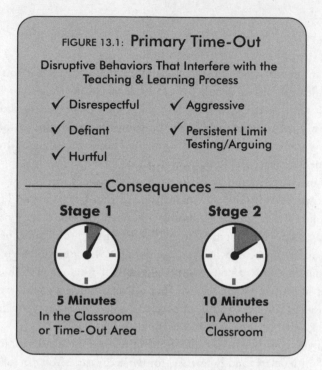

FIGURE 13.1: **Primary Time-Out**

Disruptive Behaviors That Interfere with the
Teaching & Learning Process

✓ Disrespectful   ✓ Aggressive

✓ Defiant   ✓ Persistent Limit
                    Testing/Arguing
✓ Hurtful

———— **Consequences** ————

Stage 1   **Stage 2**

5 Minutes   **10 Minutes**
In the Classroom   In Another
or Time-Out Area   Classroom

available through educational supply catalogues. A kitchen timer with an inoffensive chime also works fine. We don't recommend relying on wristwatches, wall clocks, or other imprecise measures or permitting your students to set the timer or control the time. Teachers who use this practice discover that time-outs in their classroom are very brief. Once you set the timer, you effectively take yourself out of the picture. The remaining part is between the child and the timer.

How long should time-outs be? One minute per each year of age is a good rule of thumb for preschoolers (for example, four minutes for a four-year-old). For kindergartners and primary-level (grades one through three) students, Stage One Time-Outs should be five minutes and Stage Two Time-Outs should be ten minutes. For intermediate students (grades four through six), Stage One Time-Outs should be ten minutes and Stage Two Time-Outs should be twenty minutes. Stage Two Time-Outs should be twice as long as Stage One Time-Outs for each

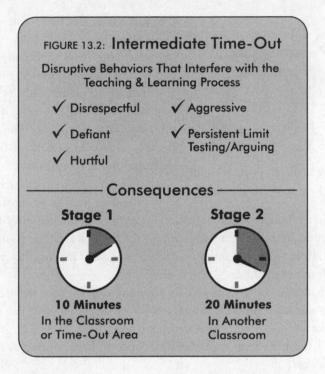

FIGURE 13.2: **Intermediate Time-Out**

Disruptive Behaviors That Interfere with the
Teaching & Learning Process

✓ Disrespectful ✓ Aggressive

✓ Defiant ✓ Persistent Limit
Testing/Arguing
✓ Hurtful

———— **Consequences** ————

Stage 1

10 Minutes
In the Classroom
or Time-Out Area

Stage 2

20 Minutes
In Another
Classroom

respective group. The Setting Limits time-out posters are a good reference guide.

Keep one additional factor in mind. Stage Two Time-Outs should be long enough for the child to restore self-control. For example, if a five-year-old continues to tantrum for twenty minutes before he regains self-control, then that's how long he needs to spend in a Stage Two Time-Out. Don't release him from time-out until the tantrum is over.

FOR LIMIT TESTING, SET UP TIME-OUT
WITH LIMITED CHOICES.

Lindsey, a second grader, knows she's supposed to keep her hands to herself in the classroom but decides to tickle her neighbor. Her teacher notices and gives Lindsey some choices.

"Lindsey, you can keep your hands to yourself, or you can take

five minutes at the back table to get yourself under control. What would you like to do?" Her choices are clear. Lindsey decides to cooperate.

Brad, a fifth grader, whistles while he's supposed to be working quietly on a writing assignment. The noise disturbs others. His teacher asks him to stop, and he does briefly, but he starts up again a short time later.

"Brad, you need to work on your assignment quietly at the back table," says his teacher matter-of-factly. Brad picks up his papers and heads to the back table for a ten-minute time-out, but within a minute he whistles again. This time his teacher gives him some choices.

"Brad, you can work quietly for ten minutes at the back table, or you can go next door to Mr. Jacob's room for twenty minutes. What would you like to do?"

"I'll finish up here," replies Brad. He doesn't have any friends in Mr. Jacob's class.

Brad was testing. When he found the wall he was looking for, he made the right choice and cooperated. When you encounter limit testing, you can usually set up a first- or second-stage time-out consequence with limited choices as Brad's teacher did.

WHEN RULES HAVE BEEN VIOLATED, APPLY TIME-OUT DIRECTLY.

Evan, a kindergartner, wants to play with the new Hula-Hoop his teacher brought to class. When the bell rings for morning recess, he races out to find it, but Carly is already playing with it.

"Hey, I was going to play with that!" Evan shouts when he sees Carly with the toy. He tries to wrestle it away from her, but Carly holds on tight. The struggle continues until Evan decides to bite her on the arm. She screams.

"He bit me," sobs Carly when the teacher comes to investigate. Evan looks remorseful.

"She wouldn't give me the Hula-Hoop," Evan replies.

"We don't bite," says the teacher matter-of-factly. "You need to sit down next to the wall for five minutes. We'll talk about other ways to share the Hula-Hoop when the time is over."

When Evan's teacher arrived on the scene, her rule about biting had already been violated. The time for limited choices had passed. Evan needed to experience the consequence associated with his poor choice. Time-out achieved this purpose effectively.

AFTER THE TIME-OUT, PROVIDE A CLEAN SLATE.

When the timer goes off, the consequence should be over, provided the child has stopped misbehaving and is under control. If the child throws a tantrum or is not under control, then he or she is not ready to come out. You can say, "The timer went off. You can leave the time-out area when you're calmed down but not before that time." When the child is ready to come out, invite him or her back in a friendly voice. Try to resist the temptation to add an "I told you so" or a lecture that personalizes the lesson and sabotages the effectiveness of the consequence.

HOLD CHILDREN ACCOUNTABLE FOR
TIME MISSED FROM CLASS.

When children disrupt to the point that they need to be removed from class, their behavior should be seen as a red flag. The student should be held accountable for time missed and parents should be alerted. If the behavior develops into a pattern, you'll need their backup support.

The notification form shown in Figure 13.3 is a simple method to keep parents informed. Send the form home with students on the days that they require a Stage Two Time-Out. Parents are asked to sign the form and return it with their child the next day. Inform your students that you will follow up with a phone call if the signed notice is not returned.

Figure 13.4 is a sample of the slip the student should present to the buddy teacher upon arriving for a Stage Two Time-Out. The slip should be completed by the buddy teacher and returned to class with the student.

USE TIME-OUT AS OFTEN AS YOU NEED IT.

Time-out is a training tool that promotes children's learning when used consistently and appropriately. Don't assume the procedure is ineffective when students persist in their testing or continue to violate your rules. More likely, they need to collect more data to arrive at the conclusions you intend. Consistent repeated exposure to your consequences should lead to the learning you desire.

FIGURE 13.3

Parent Notification Form

Mrs. Deaver   Notice # _____
Room #22   Date: _____

This is to inform you that _____
missed _____ minutes of class time today because
he/she continued to disrupt the class after being
asked to stop. The problem was handled at school
and no further assistance is required at this time.

Please indicate that you received this notice by
signing and returning it with your child tomorrow.
If you have any questions, please call. Thank you.

_____   _____
Parent signature   Date

FIGURE 13.4: **Time-Out Slip**

Stage Two Time-Out

Student: _____

Teacher: _____

Date: _____ Time sent: _____ Room: _____

Time arrived in Buddy Room: _____

Time to return to Homeroom: _____

Student needs to:
_____ read quietly
_____ complete work

Behavior while in Buddy Room:
_____ Acceptable
_____ Unacceptable

Explain: _____

Buddy Teacher Signature: _____

When to Use Time-Out

Time-out can be used in a variety of settings such as the classroom, playground, library, or cafeteria to address a variety of low- and mid-level disruptive behaviors that interfere with classroom procedures or the teaching and learning of others. The following are some of the many behaviors you can address with time-out.

Attention-Seeking Behavior

Alejandro, age four, loves attention—any kind of attention. While his teacher reads a story about farm animals, Alejandro makes the sound for each animal in the story. His teacher asks him to stop, and he does, for a while, until she comes to the part about pigs. Then he lets out a series of grunts and snorts.

"Take a seat at the back table, Alejandro," says his teacher matter-of-factly. "It's not okay to interrupt while I'm reading." She sets the timer for five minutes. Alejandro loses his audience.

Limit-Testing Behavior

Marcelo, a fifth grader, is told he cannot use his skateboard on the playground during school hours, but he tries his best to wear his teacher down and turn a *no* into a *yes*. "Come on, Mr. Fossum," Marcelo pleads. "I'm not going to get hurt. I know how to use it safely."

"You know the rules, Marcelo," replies Mr. Fossum. "No skateboards on the playground during school hours."

"Well, they're stupid rules," says Marcelo, "and I don't see why I have to follow them."

"We're finished talking about it," says Mr. Fossum, realizing the futility of further discussion. "If you bring it up again, you'll have to spend some time by yourself." Marcelo won't let go.

"Why can't we make an exception, just this once?" asks Marcelo, looking for a little bargaining room. "I'll even wear my bike helmet and elbow pads." Mr. Fossum doesn't take the bait. He's done as much as he can with his words. Now it's time for Marcelo to experience stopping.

"Have a seat at the back table, Marcelo. I'll let you know when ten minutes are over."

Disrespectful Behavior

Rita, a sixth grader, is unhappy with her teacher for not granting her a deadline extension on a term paper. "You're so unfair!" complains Rita. "Other teachers help students out when they are in a bind. Why can't you?"

"Sorry, Rita," says Mr. Simmons. "You've had a month. I can't give you any more time. It's not fair to the others."

"You are so not fair!" says Rita with a biting tone to her voice. "What do you care, anyway? You probably get your thrills making life miserable for your students."

"Have a seat at the back table, Rita," says Mr. Simmons matter-of-factly. "I'll let you know when ten minutes are up."

"Oh, that really hurts," says Rita sarcastically. "What happens if I don't go to the back table?" she taunts.

Mr. Simmons gives her some choices. "You can go to the back table for ten minutes, or you can spend the next twenty minutes in Miss Carlson's class. What would you like to do?"

Rita lets out a big huff. Reluctantly, she heads to the back table.

Defiant Behavior

The kids are lined up to go out for recess when Mrs. Lopez notices that one of her second graders has left his art materials all over his desk. "Gregory, you need to put away your art materials before you can go out for recess," says Mrs. Lopez.

"I'll do it when I get back," he says insistently.

"No," she replies. "You can't leave until it's done."

"Well, I'm not going to do it!" says Gregory, crossing his arms. Mrs. Lopez gives him some choices.

"You can pick up the items on your desk, or you can spend the next five minutes at the back table getting ready to do it. What would you like to do?" Gregory glares at her and marches to the back table to sit down. After five minutes, the buzzer rings.

"The time is over," Mrs. Lopez announces. "Are you ready to clean up your desk so you can go outside?"

"I'm still not doing it!" says Gregory as defiantly as before. "That's up to you," says Mrs. Lopez. She gets up to reset the timer, but Gregory has a sudden change of heart.

"Okay," he says, realizing the firmness of her resolve. He picks up quickly and tries to salvage what's left of his recess.

Antagonistic or Hurtful Behavior

Olivia, a fifth grader, goes to the board to write out a solution to a math problem. She seems unsure. When it's time to go over her work, the teacher finds an error. Olivia looks embarrassed. A classmate does his best to make her feel even worse.

"Nice try, Olivia," says Marco sarcastically. "You only missed it by a hundred." The teacher intervenes.

"Have a seat at the back table, Marco," says the teacher matter-of-factly. "It's not okay to treat anybody like that in this classroom." Marco heads to the back table for a ten-minute time-out.

Aggressive Behavior

Logan and George, both sixth graders, get into a heated argument as they head out to the playground. They yell at each other and call each other names. When the yard duty teacher arrives on the scene, the boys are wrestling on the blacktop with a crowd of students cheering them on. Logan's shirt is ripped, and George has a scratch on his forehead. Both are upset.

"Get up, guys," says the teacher.

"He pushed me first," says George.

"But you called me an asshole," counters Logan.

"You both need to spend ten minutes by yourselves," says the teacher, "then we'll talk about other ways to handle the situation." She directs the boys to separate benches at opposite ends of the playground. When the ten minutes are up, she calls them over to discuss other ways to resolve their differences without fighting.

In another classroom, Cassie, age four, is sitting on the floor building a tower with blocks when the boy sitting next to her accidentally bumps her. "Move!" shouts Cassie angrily. "You almost knocked over my tower." When the boy doesn't move, Cassie gets up and kicks him in the back. He screams. The teacher intervenes.

"Cassie, please sit by yourself at the back table," says her teacher matter-of-factly. "I'll set the timer for four minutes." When the time is over, Cassie and her teacher explore other ways to get people to move without kicking.

Tantrums

Samantha, age five, is accustomed to getting her own way at home. When she hears no, Samantha has a proven strategy for turning it into yes. She throws a tantrum. Her parents usually give in. Things are different in Samantha's kindergarten class.

"Recess is over," announces Samantha's teacher. "It's time to come inside." One by one, the kids file back into the classroom—that is, everyone except Samantha. She continues to play on the monkey bars.

"Samantha, you need to come in, too," says the teacher.

"But I'm not ready to come in," says Samantha insistently. "I want to play some more."

"You can play next recess, but now you need to join the class," replies her teacher. Samantha doesn't move. So her teacher takes Samantha's hand, and together they begin to walk back to class.

"What's going on?" Samantha thinks to herself. "This isn't how it's supposed to work." As they near the classroom, she decides to play her trump card. She throws a tantrum. She plops herself down outside the door and begins to cry. "I won't do it!" she sobs.

"That's up to you," says her teacher. "You can join us in five minutes if you're done crying." She sets the timer and asks a parent volunteer to watch Samantha during the time-out.

Samantha is still crying when the buzzer goes off. Fifteen minutes go by, and Samantha is still crying. Finally, twenty minutes after the tantrum began, Samantha walks back into the classroom.

"Hi, Samantha," says the teacher in a friendly voice. "Have a seat." The tantrum didn't work. Next recess, Samantha returns to class with everyone else.

QUESTIONS AND ANSWERS ABOUT TIME-OUT

Q: What should I do when students refuse to go to the time-out area?

A: This is probably further limit testing to determine whether you will really follow through on an extreme act of defiance. In any event, you should set up the next consequence by giving the student some limited choices. For example, you might say, "You can go to the time-out area as you were asked, or you can go to the office and work it out with the principal or your parents. What would you like to do?" Give the child twenty to thirty seconds to think it over, and then follow through based on his or her decision. If this is an extreme act of defiance, you will probably need assistance from others.

Q: What should I do when students leave the time-out area before their time-out is over?

A: Again, this is probably further limit testing. State firmly that they must stay in the time-out area until the full time elapses. If they leave before the time-out is over, ask them to return to the time-out area and start the time over again.

Q: What should I do when students yell and scream while in time-out?

A: This sounds like a tantrum, or it may be a discharge of pent-up anger and frustration. Do not reward the tantrum by giving in to it or by resorting to threats, lectures, or other forms of coercion. It's time to move on to a Stage Two Time-Out in another setting or possibly the office.

Q: What should I do when students knock over chairs or other items while in time-out?

A: When you introduce the time-out procedure to your class at the beginning of the year, inform them that if they make a mess while in time-out, they will have to clean it up before they leave. A little prevention goes a long way. Remove breakable items from your time-out area.

Q: When I ask some students to go to the time-out area, they mumble, grumble, or talk back disrespectfully as they go there. Should I add five minutes each time they do this?

A: No. That's probably what they want you to do, and if you play it out to the fullest extent, your time-outs will become jail. These students are doing their best to incite a power struggle and get you back out on the dance floor. As tempting as the bait might be, don't bite. If they go to the time-out area and stay there the full time without further disruption, then your time-out procedure is working. If they use obscenities or disrupt during stage one, then calmly move on to stage two. Your students will realize there are no advantages to escalation.

Q: What are students supposed to do while in time-out?

A: The purpose of time-out is to stop the immediate misbehavior and help children restore self-control. Children can do a number of things in the time-out area to achieve this purpose. You may want to present these options as choices. For example, you might say, "You can bring your book and assignment and follow along with the lesson, or you can just sit there quietly." Some teachers set out *Weekly Readers* or other reading material in the time-out area to help disruptive children settle down and restore self-control. If you provide nothing for an angry or upset child to do while in time-out, you increase the likelihood of further disruption.

Q: What should I do when I ask a student to go to my buddy teacher's classroom for a Stage Two Time-Out and I suspect he or she may not go there directly, if at all?

A: Select a responsible student in your classroom to be an escort. Escorts are an effective way to ensure that children arrive at their destination. Or, if they don't, the escort can inform you quickly so you can notify the office or take other steps to intervene.

Q: If I strongly suspect a student will continue to disrupt during Stage One Time-Out, should I skip stage one and move directly to stage two?

A: No. The goal of the two-stage procedure is to keep students in instruction as much as they possibly can be and out of instruction only when they absolutely have to be. Don't preempt the process.

Q: How much disruption is too much? When is it time to use more than time-out as a consequence?

A: Tolerance for disruption varies from teacher to teacher. Some teachers consider two or three disruptive incidents a week to be excessive for any student. Others can tolerate ten or more incidents a week if they see a general pattern of improvement. If you use the Two-Stage Time-Out procedure consistently for four to six weeks and experience only minimal reduction in disruptive behavior, then it's time to investigate the underlying causes for the behavior and consider the next level of disciplinary interventions. In chapters 14, 15, and 16, we'll examine guidance strategies for your most disruptive students.

Chapter Summary

The Two-Stage Time-Out procedure is a stop signal that disruptive children really understand. It stops their misbehavior. It removes them from their audience and payoffs for misbehavior, and it helps them restore self-control quickly so they can rejoin instruction. Best of all, the procedure allows teachers to manage disruptive behavior at the classroom level without involving administrators or support staff. The Two-Stage Time-Out is an inexpensive solution for costly behavior problems.

The Two-Stage Time-Out procedure is also a versatile classroom management tool. It can be used in a variety of situations with children of nearly all ages. For most students, a one-stage procedure is sufficient to stop their disruptive behavior and restore their self-control. Your aggressive researchers may require a two-stage procedure that provides escalating consequences for escalating misbehavior. Each stage further separates the disruptive child from his or her audience and from the payoffs for misbehavior.

Using Parents for Backup Support

Using parents for backup support can be an effective logical consequence when efforts to resolve problems between the student and teacher have broken down. The effectiveness of this procedure, however, depends largely upon the parents' willingness and ability to help. The parents must be "supportive," that is, they must be willing to take responsibility for doing their part to resolve the problem. When parents are supportive, their backup support can have a very positive impact. When parents are not supportive, their involvement can sabotage and undermine our guidance efforts in the classroom. Before asking parents for backup support, your first step should be to determine if they are supportive.

This chapter will show you how to do that and how to get the most value out of this potentially powerful guidance procedure. Let's look at how one teacher does this.

It's the sixth week of school, and Adam, a fifth grader, continues to clown around and disrupt daily. His teacher, Mr. Cory, has exhausted all of the usual steps to resolve this sort of problem. Adam's name is in the Blurt Box on a daily basis. He averages two time-outs a day and has been in the buddy teacher's classroom for Stage Two Time-Outs six times. Adam is a regular at Recess Academy. The work he was supposed to complete when he was out of the class was never turned in.

Mr. Cory suspects Adam's parents will be supportive. "They sure act that way so far," he says to himself. They signed and returned the orientation packet he sent home the first week. They attended back-to-school night on week two, and they signed and returned each of the six notices they received each time Adam was sent out of the classroom. They even provided daytime and evening phone numbers.

Mr. Cory decides to confirm his theory. He calls Adam's mother at work, shares his concerns, and asks if she would be willing to support his discipline plan for Adam and be available for a conference if needed. She agrees. Now Mr. Cory can confidently set up the next consequence with Adam. He approaches Adam after school the next day.

"Adam, I always try to work out problems in the classroom with my students before I involve their parents," Mr. Cory begins, "but we haven't made much progress during the last six weeks. I'm particularly concerned about all the work you've missed when you've been asked to leave the classroom. You haven't made up any of it, and it's affecting your grades. I'm wondering if we need some help from your parents."

Adam wants to avoid this step if possible. He promises things will improve, but the very next day he picks up where he left off. It's as though their conversation never took place. So Mr. Cory follows

through and schedules a twenty-minute conference for the following morning before school.

He begins the conference by commenting on Adam's strengths and positive qualities. Then, he shares his concerns and the steps he has taken to deal with them.

"How can we help?" asks Adam's father.

"When Adam arrives home with a notice because he spent time outside the classroom for disrupting, please make sure he completes the work he misses. I'll write his missed assignments on the notice."

"We can do more than that," replies Adam's mother. "On the days that Adam has difficulty cooperating, we will set aside an hour after school to practice cooperation. I can think of lots of things I would like some cooperation with." Adam doesn't like the sound of this remedy.

With a solution in place, Mr. Cory thanks Adam's parents and arranges a follow-up conference four weeks later to evaluate Adam's progress. Adam's parents encourage Mr. Cory to contact them anytime if more help is needed.

Adam's behavior improved markedly. The parent conference provided the wake-up call and accountability Adam needed to take Mr. Cory's rules and authority more seriously.

In Adam's case, the conference was effective because his parents were willing to take responsibility for helping to resolve the problem. Their support made the difference. Mr. Cory also helped his own cause by following some general guidelines for screening for parent support and conducting effective parent conferences. You can, too.

Guidelines for Screening for Parent Support

How did Mr. Cory determine that Adam's parents were supportive? He used a simple screening test, then confirmed his theory with a brief phone call. He knows, from past experience, how parents behave when they are supportive. They usually do the following:

- Sign and return the packet you mailed home during the first week.
- Attend back-to-school night meetings.
- Provide daytime and evening phone numbers.

- Respond to phone calls and notes.
- State their willingness to support you.
- Consistently complete and return permission slips.
- Attend regularly scheduled parent conferences.

After the screening, Mr. Cory confirmed his theory with a brief phone call. Two important questions should be asked before arranging a conference:

- Are you willing to support my discipline plan for the classroom?
- Are you willing to attend a conference if requested?

If the answer is "yes" to both of these questions, you probably have a supportive parent. There's a good likelihood you'll receive the type of backup support you desire. If you decide, at some point, to arrange a conference, it should be a productive investment of your time and energy.

If, on the other hand, the answer to either question is "no," and parents don't rate very high on the screening test, you probably can't count on receiving high-quality backup support. A conference may even be counterproductive. There are some red flags to look out for. Unsupportive parents usually do the following:

- Respond defensively to issues regarding their child.
- Make excuses for their child.
- Blame you, the school, or others for the problem.
- Bring up other issues unrelated to the concerns.
- Argue or debate with you about the accuracy of your concerns.
- Question your rules or authority.
- State their unwillingness to support you.
- Treat you with disrespect.

Guidelines for Conducting Parent Conferences

Okay, let's say you have a supportive parent, and you've decided to schedule a conference. How do you get the most value from your parent conference? The following guidelines should help.

- **Be proactive.** Schedule the conference promptly after you've exhausted your options to resolve the problem at a lower level. No parent likes to hear that a problem has been allowed to continue for a long period of time before he or she is notified. Parents will appreciate your responsiveness.
- **Set limits on your time.** Before you meet, be very clear about the amount of time you have to devote to the conference (for example, "I have twenty-five minutes to meet with you"). Otherwise, you risk running out of time and not accomplishing your goals.
- **Include the child in the conference.** The fact that the parents and teacher are working together sends a strong message to the child: "We care, and we will work together to hold you accountable." The message might be lost when the child is excluded from the conference.
- **Stay positive.** You can create the right climate for problem solving by beginning the conference with a positive anecdote or comment about the child, such as "Miguel is a real helper in the classroom" or "I know I can count on Greg's leadership on the playground." A positive start helps both parents and the child to relax and become more receptive to what follows.
- **Keep the conference focused.** Sometimes conferences ramble and lose their focus because the parents and teacher do not share the same agenda. The best way to tackle the problem is to state the purpose and goals for the conference at the outset as well as your time constraints. At the very beginning, ask the parents whether they have any additional issues they would like to discuss, and, if needed, schedule a separate conference or arrange a phone consultation to address the additional issues. When parents realize that their concerns will be addressed, they're less likely to interrupt or steer the conference in other directions.
- **Come prepared to offer solutions.** No parent likes to have a problem dumped in his or her lap or to be put on the spot to come up a quick solution. Come to the conference prepared to offer a solution or a backup plan in the event your solution is not feasible. If the solution to the problem is not clear, be prepared to

direct the parents to the appropriate resources for assistance such as counseling, professional evaluation, helpful books, or parenting classes.

- **Schedule a follow-up conference to evaluate progress.**
  Follow-up conferences demonstrate commitment and build accountability into the process. Don't assume parents will follow through and take all the corrective steps you suggest. Build some accountability into the process by scheduling a follow-up conference to review progress and to discuss any remaining steps that need to be taken. Don't bring closure to the problem-solving process until the problem is solved.

When to Use Parents for Backup Support

Parent conferences are used to address repeated low- and mid-level behavior problems after the usual range of interventions have been exhausted. The following are some of the many possibilities:

- When students repeatedly disrupt class after the first six weeks of school.
- When students show a high incidence of Stage Two Time-Outs after the first six weeks of school.
- When students fail to master skills after participating in Recess Academy.
- When students continue to bully or are bullied by others.
- When students repeatedly misbehave on the playground or in the lunchroom.
- When students fail to turn in homework after the first four to six weeks.
- When students are repeatedly tardy or truant.

Chapter Summary

Using parents for backup support can be an effective logical consequence for addressing repeated low- and mid-level behavior problems that do not improve during the first six weeks or when efforts to resolve problems between the student and teacher have broken down. Before involving parents in a conference, there are some questions we need to consider. Are the parents supportive? That is, are they willing to support us in our classroom discipline efforts? Are they willing to attend the conference? The success or failure of the procedure hangs in the balance. A simple screening and a phone call usually provide the answers.

If you have a supportive parent, then you have the green light you're looking for. You're in a position to set up this logical consequence with the student and, if things don't improve, to arrange a conference with the parents. By following a few guidelines, you can greatly increase the effectiveness of your conference.

Using the Office for Backup Support

The vast majority of discipline problems teachers confront can and should be handled in the classroom. However, there are some situations that exceed what can be handled with classroom management alone. We're talking about intensive discipline problems at the top of the discipline pyramid we discussed earlier, in chapter 11. Intensive-level discipline problems require backup support from the office or school administrator.

Some intensive-level problems that require backup support are readily apparent. Others fall into a gray area and require a judgment call. Some problems just feel bigger than they really are. It's difficult to see problems rationally when kids hook us emotionally.

How do you know when it's time to call for backup support? What steps can you expect your principal to take after he or she receives your request? What are some of the problems involved in using the office as a place for guidance and discipline? This chapter will help you to answer these questions. By the time you're done, you'll know how and when to use the office for backup support.

What Is Administrative Backup Support?

Mr. Stewart, a fifth-grade teacher, prepares to pass out a math quiz when he hears Marcus making bathroom sounds to amuse his peers.

"Please have a seat at the back table, Marcus," says Mr. Stewart, matter-of-factly. "You can return to your seat after you finish the quiz." Marcus gets up from his desk very slowly, rolls his eyes, then stomps on the floor as he heads to the back table.

"He's just trying to get to me," Mr. Stewart says to himself. "I'm not taking the bait." Marcus settles down and appears to be working on his quiz. As Mr. Stewart circulates around the classroom, he notices that Marcus is doodling, not working.

"Where is your quiz?" Mr. Stewart asks.

"You didn't tell me to take it with me," replies Marcus with a mischievous grin. "You just told me I could return to my seat after I finish it." He smirks. This time the taunting works. Mr. Stewart loses his cool. He walks to his desk, takes out a referral to the office, and writes a message to the principal. "I've had it with Marcus and his lousy attitude!" the message reads. "Please don't send him back until it changes." Mr. Stewart hands Marcus the referral and sends him to the office.

Clearly, Marcus tried to provoke Mr. Stewart and succeeded, but does Marcus's annoying behavior warrant a trip to the office? Is this an appropriate request for administrative backup support? Is this the best use of the principal's time? Are there other steps Mr. Stewart might have taken to manage Marcus's behavior in the classroom?

Let's answer these questions by referring back to the three-tiered pyramid diagram we discussed in chapter 11 (see Figure 11.5). The diagram is a starting point for helping you identify the type of problem you confront and the appropriate level of disciplinary intervention. Most important, the diagram helps you see the big picture of what's going on so you can view behavior problems in their proper context. Tier 3 on the pyramid represents intensive-level behavior problems and accounts for less than 5 percent of all school behavior problems.

Where does Marcus's behavior fall on the pyramid? Of course, this is an example of a mid-level behavior problem that appeared bigger and more serious than it really was. Sending Marcus to the office was not an appropriate request for backup support. When the principal receives this referral, Mr. Stewart won't be the only one feeling annoyed.

Backup support is not intended to replace the teacher's authority or to make up for ineffective or incomplete guidance lessons in the classroom. Administrative backup support should do what it's supposed to do—back up the teacher's rules, authority, and effective discipline practices in the classroom. Passing discipline problems to the principal or office too early in the guidance process is one of the biggest and most costly abuses of the school guidance system.

Situations That Require Backup Support

What disciplinary situations really do require administrative backup support? What steps will the administrator take when he or she receives the request? Let's refer to the Setting Limits Companion Guide in appendix 1, which was written to help you answer these questions. The Companion Guide specifies the appropriate logical consequence or disciplinary procedures for a wide variety of low-level, mid-level, and intensive-level discipline problems. Additional logical consequences and procedures are provided for repeat occurrences.

As you can see from the Companion Guide, administrative backup support is seldom required for low- and mid-level behavior problems. The few exceptions listed below require a judgment call from the teacher or administrator. If the administrator considers them to be appropriate,

he or she can exercise the greatest discretion in determining the appropriate consequences and discipline procedures.

Administrative involvement and backup support are almost always required for extreme discipline problems at the intensive level. Violations of state educational code or school discipline policy require an automatic referral. No judgment calls are involved. In many cases, the appropriate disciplinary consequence or procedure is specified by school policy or state educational code. We recommend you familiarize yourself with your school discipline policy and the educational codes pertaining to discipline in your state.

MID-LEVEL PROBLEMS THAT MAY REQUIRE ADMINISTRATIVE BACKUP SUPPORT

- Repeated behavior problems on the playground or in the lunchroom that persist for more than six weeks.
- Repeated angry or emotional outbursts and tantrums.
- Recurring disruptive behavior in the classroom.

INTENSIVE-LEVEL PROBLEMS THAT REQUIRE ADMINISTRATIVE BACKUP SUPPORT

- When students refuse to go to Stage One or Stage Two Time-Outs.
- When students continue to disrupt during Stage Two Time-Outs.
- Extreme defiance.
- Violations of school discipline policy.
- State education code violations: dangerous or unsafe behavior, violent or assaultive behavior, bullying, harassment, theft or vandalism, weapons, illegal substances, inappropriate sexual behavior, sexual harassment, etc.

What Is an Appropriate Referral?

What is an appropriate referral to the office? All discipline problems that are specified by school policy, state educational code, or recommended in the Companion Guide in appendix 1 are included in this category.

Administrators can help their own cause by using a referral form that clearly defines the presenting concerns or problems and documents the appropriate steps teachers should take to resolve problems at the classroom level before requesting help from the office. We encourage administrators and staff to use the following referral form to initiate a request for backup support (see Figure 15.1).

FIGURE 15.1: **Sample Office Referral Form**

Student: _____

Grade: _____

Teacher: _____

Date: _____ Time: _____

Reason For Referral:
( ) Extreme or Repeated Disruption
( ) Extreme Inappropriate Behavior
( ) Disruptive Behavior In Stage Two Time-Out
( ) Destructive Behavior
( ) Hurtful /Aggressive Behavior
( ) Dangerous / Unsafe Behavior
( ) Other

_____

Educational Code Violations:
( ) Assaultive Behavior / Fighting
( ) Extreme Defiance
( ) Profanity
( ) Stealing
( ) Acts Of Violence
( ) Harassment / Bullying
( ) Other Educational Code Violation

_____
_____
_____

Description of the Incident or Problem:
_____
_____
_____
_____
_____

Action Taken by Teacher:
( ) Incentive System
( ) Mentoring
( ) Cross-Age Tutoring
( ) Cooldown Procedure
( ) Moved Student
( ) Stage One Time-Out
( ) Stage Two Time-Out
( ) Student Conference
( ) Behavior Contract
( ) Parent Contact
( ) Parent Conference
( ) Recess Academy
( ) Suspension from Classroom
( ) Other

_____

Administrative Action Taken:
_____
_____

Parent Contact:
Yes_____ No_____ Date _____

Date: _____

Follow-Up with Teacher:
Yes_____ No_____ Date _____
Comments:
_____
_____

Parent / Guardian Follow-Up:
Yes_____ No_____ Date _____
Comments:
_____
_____

The Administrator's Role in the Guidance Process

School site administrators play the most important role in the school's guidance and discipline program. They carry out school policy; provide backup support for classroom teachers; coordinate supervision for the playground, cafeteria, library, and hallways; and arrange in-service training for staff. They face the toughest cases. They make the toughest decisions, and they bear the greatest burden of responsibility. The buck stops at their door.

Site administrators must be experts in effective guidance and discipline. They can't afford not to be. Their leadership role requires it, and their credibility depends on it. Staff confidence and school morale hang in the balance. Everyone in the system looks to them for leadership and effectiveness. Site administrators must be skilled at defusing power struggles, deescalating a crisis, using logical consequences, conducting problem-solving conferences, using incentives and positive forms of motivation, teaching social skills, and sniffing out more serious problems.

School principals must have special insight into children and their behavior. Many of the discipline problems that principals confront are symptoms of deeper underlying issues—extreme frustration, discouragement, social alienation, learning problems, academic failure, or undiagnosed emotional or psychological problems. Someone has to sort out what's going on. Often, this task falls first on the administrator. An important part of their role involves recognizing when students have deeper problems and connecting the students with appropriate services both at school and in the community.

Which Students Need Assistance from the Office?

Who are the students lined up outside the principal's door on any given day? They're not the compliant ones who cooperate for the asking, the ones who are eager to please and permit a wide margin for ineffectiveness. These students rarely end up in the office.

No, the students lined up outside the principal's office are usually a mix of students including the most aggressive researchers on campus, discouraged students with learning problems, students with undiagnosed impulse control problems such as ADHD, students with psychological and emotional problems, students under severe stress, and students with many things going on in their lives at the same time. Some of these students need discipline. Some need support. Some need both. Site administrators work almost exclusively with this group.

How does one person respond to all of these different problems? The role requires special training, special skills, special insight into children and their behavior, and a solid understanding of the resources available to support kids in the school and in the community.

Administrators have to be at the top of their game. What happens when they're not? The office becomes part of the problem, not the solution.

Reinforcement Errors in the Office

Contrary to popular belief, the office is not the best place to send misbehaving students. From a student's point of view, the office is an inherently interesting place. It's staffed with the busiest and most friendly people in the whole school, who are also not available to drop everything and deal with misbehaving kids, much less supervise them. So what happens when misbehaving kids are sent to the office? Most of the time, they sit, and what do they see? They see sick kids, upset kids, late kids, kids who have forgotten lunch money, homework, and permission slips; kids with bumps and scrapes; and kids like themselves who are in trouble. They hear complaints about teachers who are late to report attendance or the lunch count, buses that are late to arrive, and they hear about all the messes the custodian has to clean up. To students, the office is one big soap opera and an exciting source of live entertainment.

Some kids want more than entertainment. They want to be part of the action. What do they do? They do the same things they do in the classroom. They clown around and disrupt the office while the secretaries tell them to settle down, be quiet, stay in their seats, and warn them they'll be in even bigger trouble when the principal arrives.

What happens in the meantime? They get live entertainment, negative attention from the secretaries, power and control over the whole office. This is a pretty good deal for disruptive, attention-seeking students. Can the office be any more rewarding? Unfortunately, it can. In some schools, the next round begins when the principal arrives. The following is a typical example.

Mr. Winters, an elementary principal, arrives at his office pressed for time. He has a meeting in thirty minutes. There's a stack of phone messages on his desk, and three students are waiting outside his door for disrupting class.

He calls the first student into his office. Vincent, a sixth grader, slumps into his chair and gives the principal a surly look while the latter reads a note from the teacher. "Vincent used profanity and called me insulting names when I asked him to stop disrupting class," the note reads. The principal picks up the phone, calls Vincent's mother at work, and informs her that Vincent is suspended from school for the rest of the day for using profanity in the classroom.

"He will be waiting for you to pick him up in the office," says the principal. "He can return to school tomorrow."

"Great!" Vincent says to himself. "Now I have a free day to do anything I want! I can play video games, ride my skateboard, or hang out in the mall." He knows his mom will drop him off at home and return to work.

The principal calls the next student into his office. Celia, a fifth grader, was referred for passing notes and talking during instruction. The principal gives Celia a ten-minute lecture on cooperation and sends her back to class.

"Wow! I really like our principal," Celia thinks. "He's nice. All he does is talk." Do you think this intervention will cause Celia to think carefully next time she decides to pass notes or talk during instruction? Not likely. She'll be back.

The principal checks his watch and then calls the third student into his office. Patrick, a fourth grader, is a regular. This time he was sent for talking back to his teacher.

"I didn't do it," says Patrick. "I tried to explain why I wasn't in my seat, but she wouldn't listen. It's not fair!" The principal assigns Patrick trash detail during lunch recess and gives him one hour of after-school detention. Patrick returns to class angrier and more resentful than when he arrived. He's bent on revenge. Everyone knows Patrick will be back.

For students like Patrick, Celia, and Vincent, the office is a revolving door that reinforces and perpetuates their behavior problems. The reinforcement errors begin the moment they arrive, and sometimes the problem is compounded by ineffective guidance in the office. The combination of an entertaining setting and ineffective guidance keeps everyone stuck on a discipline treadmill.

QUESTIONS AND ANSWERS ABOUT BACKUP SUPPORT

Q: My school administrator is too busy and off campus too often to provide reliable backup support. What should I do?

A: This is a great topic to bring up as a concern at your next staff meeting. Every school needs a plan for assisting teachers with backup support in appropriate situations. If your administrator is unavailable, he or she should designate others for that role and provide them with the necessary training, release time, and communication tools to perform the job.

Q: Our school has used the same old referral form for years that doesn't convey any of the necessary information about the

severity of the problem or steps taken to resolve the problems described in this chapter. What do you recommend?

A: This is another great topic for a staff meeting. Effective backup support from the office begins with an appropriate referral that provides the administrator with all the information he or she needs to respond to the problem. It's time to update your office referral form. The sample referral form in this chapter works great for most schools.

Q: When it is appropriate to send a child to the office, and what's the best way to go about this?

A: In an ideal world, the most effective practice is to have the principal or designee come to the classroom to pick up the child. This simple act is a powerful and dramatic statement about the principal's support for the teachers, rules, authority, and discipline practices. In the real world, however, we have to do the best we can. Often, this means sending the student without an escort.

Q: My principal is great about providing prompt backup support, but often forgets to follow up and share the steps she took to address the problem. It's embarrassing when parents call and ask me what's going on. What do you suggest?

A: This is a common problem in the backup support process. The best solution is the easiest one. The office referral form should be in triplicate with a space on the form to indicate the steps taken to resolve the problem. After the principal deals with the situation, she can put a copy in your box in the staff room.

Q: The section in the chapter titled "Reinforcement Errors in the Office" describes our office perfectly before the principal sees each student. What can we do to improve this?

A: Clerical support staff in the office should be trained to manage students sent to the office for disciplinary reasons. Encourage your administrator to include clerical staff in training workshops for instructional staff or arrange to have them trained separately.

Chapter Summary

Administrative backup support begins with an appropriate referral, and most of the time that's where the process breaks down, because teachers and administrators are not always clear about what constitutes an appropriate referral. This chapter attempted to clear up the confusion by clearly defining which problem behaviors do and do not require backup support. The three-tiered pyramid in chapter 11 and Setting Limits Companion Guide in appendix 1 will help you make this decision when you're uncertain.

Backup support should be used as it was intended, to back up the teacher's rules, authority, and effective discipline practices in the classroom, not to replace teacher authority or to make up for ineffective classroom management practices. Both are major reinforcement errors.

As the leader of the school's guidance system, site administrators play the most important and the most challenging role. They carry out school policy, provide backup support for teachers, and are responsible for coordinating and managing guidance practices throughout the school. Site administrators must be experts in effective guidance and discipline. They can't afford not to be. Their leadership role requires it, and their credibility depends on it. They work with the most challenging students, make the toughest decisions, and bear the greatest responsibility for the successes and failures of their school's guidance system.

Contrary to popular belief, the school office is not the best place to send misbehaving students. In fact, it's one of the worst places. The office is a soap opera that provides live entertainment for misbehaving students and reinforces their unacceptable behavior. The practice of using the office as a dumping ground for behavior problems is one of the most costly and divisive practices in the school. It creates resentment among staff and wastes valuable time and school resources. Ineffective discipline practices in the office only compound the problem.

Managing Crises and Extreme Behavior

Most schools have procedures for handling emergencies such as fires, power failures, and natural disasters, but few schools adequately prepare teachers for the types of emergencies they're most likely to encounter in the classroom. We're talking about extreme acts of defiance or disruption, dangerous or destructive behavior, and violent or assaultive behavior. These are automatic "911 calls" to the office for backup support. You won't have time to complete a referral. In these situations, we cannot afford to fly by the seat of our pants and operate without a plan. The cost to our personal safety, the safety and welfare of our students, and to our careers is too great. We need effective plans and procedures to protect us. This chapter will attempt to fill the gap and provide you with the procedures you need to manage the situation until help arrives.

Legal and Safety Considerations

Imagine yourself in the following situation. You're writing instructions on the board when one of your students suddenly becomes enraged and throws a chair across the classroom, narrowly missing several of his

classmates. Do you have a plan for handling this crisis? What would you do? Would you shout at him to stop? Would you plead with him? Would you run to another classroom or to the office for help? Would you risk injury and use physical force to restrain him from throwing more chairs? Would you send an emergency call to the office? What would you do until help arrived?

Without a carefully thought-out plan, you and your students are vulnerable because each intervention involves an element of risk. If you leave the classroom to summon help, you place your job in jeopardy because you have a legal obligation to keep your students supervised. If you fail to take appropriate action to protect your students, you could be liable for their injuries because you have a legal obligation to protect their safety and welfare. If you attempt to restrain an enraged student and injure him in the process, you could be liable for his injuries. If you become injured, a bad situation just became worse because now the situation is even more out of control.

Legal and safety considerations should be paramount when deciding how to manage extreme situations. Your overriding concerns should be to:

- Keep your students supervised.
- Keep your students safe.
- Minimize risk to your students and to yourself.
- Call the office for backup support.

Every school should have a plan for backup support from your school administrator or some other staff member designated to handle these emergencies. Physical restraint and hands-on procedures should be interventions of last resort and should be carried out by those trained to use them. With these guidelines in mind, let's look at some of the extreme situations you're most likely to confront and effective ways to intervene.

Extreme Defiant Behavior

Ross, a fifth grader, started his day with a chip on his shoulder. He bothered and provoked other students in desk group throughout the morning and was sent to time-out twice before the morning recess. After recess, he starts up where he left off. He hums to himself as he works on an assignment and disturbs his classmates. When they complain, the teacher asks Ross to take his paper and pencil and finish his assignment at the back table.

"Forget it!" he shouts. "I'm not going, and you can't make me. I don't have to follow your stupid rules or do anything you say if I don't want to." He stands next to his desk with his arms folded and continues humming, defiantly.

All eyes are on Ross. The tension is extreme. Teaching and learning have come to a screeching halt. All of his classmates are wondering, "What's she going to do?" The teacher's credibility and authority are on the line.

But this teacher has a plan. She takes a couple of deep breaths and then calmly asks her students to line up at the door, leaving Ross standing alone next to his desk. She joins her class at the door and makes an announcement.

"Ross needs to make a decision about whether or not he wants to be part of our class today. Let's give him three minutes of silence to help him make up his mind." She looks at her watch and turns to Ross.

"Would you like to join us and cooperate, or would you prefer to work it out with our principal, Mrs. Donnelly, in the office? I'd be happy to call her if that's what you prefer. I'll give you a few minutes to think about it." She looks at her watch again and waits in silence with the rest of her class. She's prepared to act when the three minutes are over.

The spotlight is squarely on Ross and so is the hot potato of responsibility. It's up to him to decide what he wants to do. He is responsible for the outcome. Ross looks around the room, hums defiantly for about thirty seconds, and then begins to feel self-conscious and stops. He realizes there is no way out but doesn't want to lose face with his peers. He slumps in his desk with his arms folded the full three minutes. His teacher repeats the question.

"What would you like to do?" she asks.

"Forget it," says Ross defiantly. "I'm not budging." She picks up the phone and calls the office for backup support, then she asks the rest of the class to wait in line until Mrs. Donnelly arrives to escort Ross out of the classroom. When she does, the teacher thanks her students for cooperating and asks them to return to their desks and continue with their writing assignment.

This teacher is effective because she's prepared and operates with a plan. She fulfills all of her basic responsibilities. She keeps all of her students supervised. She keeps them safe, and she minimizes risk. She remains in control of the situation the whole time.

Her first step is to separate the parties involved. Since Ross is defiant, the easiest thing to do is to separate others from him. She asks her class to line up at the door and joins them. Everyone is supervised. Everyone is safe. She minimizes the risk by creating a safe distance between Ross and others.

Her next step is to give Ross some time to cool down and a way out of the situation he put himself in. She offers him some choices. He can cooperate and rejoin the class, or she will call the office, where he can resolve the matter with the principal. The choice is his and so is the responsibility for the outcome. She's prepared to follow through with the consequence based on his choice. When Ross chooses defiance, she follows through. She calls the office, and Ross is escorted out of the class. The teacher's rules, authority, and discipline are supported. The students observe their teacher and principal working as a team.

Dangerous or Destructive Behavior

Brent, a sixth grader, disrupts class by throwing pencils and wads of paper at his classmates. He gets caught, and his teacher, Mr. Jeffries, asks him to go to the back table for a five-minute time-out. Things are quiet for a few minutes, and then someone shouts, "Watch out!" When Mr. Jeffries turns around, he sees a chair flying across the room, narrowly missing several students. Brent is standing at the back table with a second chair in his hands. Mr. Jeffries asks his students to put their heads on their desks and cover them with their arms, and then he turns to Brent.

"Put the chair down, please," says Mr. Jeffries, but Brent lets it fly. This one bounces off a counter and shatters a large window. As Brent reaches for another chair, Mr. Jeffries orders his students to quickly exit the classroom and line up outside the door. He joins them at the door and calls the office for help. His kids are safe, but Brent continues his rampage.

"Put the chair down, Brent," Mr. Jeffries says again. His words have little effect.

"You're all a bunch of shitheads!" Brent shouts as he lets the third chair fly; it crashes into a desk. Moments later, the vice principal arrives and escorts Brent from the classroom.

This scene sounds like an educator's nightmare, but Mr. Jeffries had a plan. He knew his first duty was to protect his students from danger, so he mobilized the biggest part of his classroom that was still under his control—his cooperative students. He moved them outside the classroom as quickly as possible; then he called for backup support from the office. A simple two-step plan was enough to fulfill all of his obligations. He kept his students supervised. He kept them safe, and he took the appropriate steps to minimize risk. He didn't put himself or his students in needless danger by attempting to restrain Brent physically.

Violent or Assaultive Behavior

Mr. Tamori, a fourth-grade teacher, prepares for his students to return from recess when he hears a commotion in the hallway outside his classroom. He looks out his door and sees two students wrestling on the ground and punching each other while a group of students shouts and encourages them on.

Mr. Tamori approaches the boys and asks them to stop, but there's so much shouting, the boys can't hear him. "Time to get rid of the crowd," Mr. Tamori says to himself. He asks all but one student to leave and

sends that student to the office for help. Then Mr. Tamori asks the boys to stop a second time.

This time they hear him. The fight is over, but the boys are still very upset.

"He started it!" shouts one of the boys as he gets up off the pavement.

"You're the biggest liar!" shouts the other, pointing an accusing finger.

"Both of you need a few minutes to calm down," says Mr. Tamori matter-of-factly. "This isn't a good time for talking." He understands the futility of problem solving while the boys are upset. His first step is to cool them down. He asks one of them to have a seat in his classroom and the other to sit outside the door in the corridor.

The boys are separated. Now they can cool down. Mr. Tamori stands at the door and waits for backup from the office. Within minutes, the vice principal arrives and escorts the boys to the office, where they can resolve the matter.

Mr. Tamori managed this assaultive incident effectively by following the simple three-step plan:

- Separate the parties.
- Cool them down.
- Call for help.

QUESTIONS AND ANSWERS ABOUT
CRISIS INTERVENTION

Q: I teach in a school where crises and emergencies occur more frequently. I can carry out the three-step crisis management procedure effectively, but after the crisis, I'm too upset to teach and my students are too upset to learn. What should I do?

A: You and your students need a short recovery period or activity to allow emotions to settle down. Some teachers use crises as learning opportunities and hold brief discussions about what happened and how it was handled. Other teachers use short stories as recovery activities. You should decide what works best for you and your class.

Q: My administrator is a very busy person and seldom available to respond to crises or emergencies. What should I do?

A: Every school needs an effective crisis intervention plan. If your administrator is not available, he or she should designate a backup person or persons who are adequately trained to provide the necessary backup support. Operating without a plan is a potential liability issue. Note your concerns and suggest these solutions to your site administrator.

Q: I have one student in my class who requires crisis intervention and backup support from my administrator several times each month. We are four months into the school year. What should I do?

A: The need for this level of intervention calls into question the appropriateness of this child's placement in a regular classroom setting. There is more going on here that should be addressed with an evaluation, additional support services, and, possibly, placement in a more restrictive classroom setting for students with special needs.

Q: I'm a strong fifth-grade teacher in top physical condition. I can easily overpower a violent or out-of-control student in a crisis. Do you recommend hands-on procedures or using physical restraint?

A: We don't recommend using physical restraint unless you've been adequately trained and certified in the management of violent and assaultive behavior and the practice is deemed acceptable by your school discipline policy, state education code, and your site administrator. It's a liability issue.

Chapter Summary

Managing crises and extreme behavior is not something we should undertake without a plan. The cost to our safety, the safety of others, and our careers is too great. We need a set of procedures to protect us. Our overriding consideration should be to fulfill our basic safety and legal obligations to our students—that is, to keep them supervised, to keep them safe, and to take appropriate steps to minimize risk.

Your basic crisis management plan should involve at least the following three steps: (1) Separate the students from the source of danger, (2) provide cooldown time to deescalate the situation and restore control, and (3) summon help. Backup support should always be part of your plan. Physical restraint or other hands-on procedures increases the level of risk and should be used only by staff trained to carry out such procedures. Most teachers report that it's safer and easier to separate an entire class from one defiant or assaultive student than it is to separate that student from the class.

Supporting Students
with ADD/ADHD

Ninety-five percent of classroom behavior problems can be managed in the classroom. There are, however, a small percentage of students on every campus who require more than effective classroom management. We're talking about students with inattention, hyperactivity, and impulse control problems. In this chapter, you're going to meet three of them. Corey, a kindergartner, is in constant motion. He always seems to be out of his seat in the classroom. Colin, a second grader, blurts out constantly in the classroom and has been suspended nine times for disruption. He becomes very upset when corrected. Mikayla, a fifth grader, is easily distracted. She requires constant refocusing to stay on task and seldom completes her assignments within the allotted time.

What do these students have in common? All have, or are suspected of having, a condition called attention deficit disorder (ADD) or attention deficit disorder with hyperactivity (ADHD). Children with ADD/ADHD require special attention. They need a lot of structure, support, and consistent guidance to keep them on track and to help them perform to the best of their abilities. Also, they form part of that 5 percent that pose some of the most challenging behavior management problems teachers and administrators confront.

This chapter will help you understand the special needs of children with ADD/ADHD and learn the behavior management tools you'll need to guide them most effectively. We'll begin by reviewing some basic information about the disorder: what it is, how it is diagnosed, and how it is treated. Then we will follow three cases from referral to intervention so you can see how to develop an effective treatment plan both at home and in the classroom. By the time you're done, you'll know how to provide the structure and behavior management that children with ADD or ADHD need to be successful.

What Is Attention Deficit Disorder?

Imagine that you're nine years old. You're sitting in class. Your teacher just gave you directions for the next assignment, but you missed most of what was said because you were playing with the bead chain of the zipper on your jacket. You look around to figure out what you're supposed to do and notice that others have their science books out. So you pull yours out, too, but you still don't know what to do. When you ask the boy sitting next to you, he gives you a dirty look and tells you to stop bothering him. You ask someone else, who does the same thing and then tells you to ask the teacher.

"Mrs. Peters," you blurt out. "I don't know what to do." Oops! You disturbed the class. She looks annoyed.

"What are you supposed to do when you need my help?" she asks.

You remember and raise your hand, and she comes over to help. She repeats her original instructions, then prods you a little to get you started. "You only have ten minutes," she says. "If you don't finish on time, you'll have to take it home as homework."

Finally you're focused. You complete the first two items, then become distracted when you hear someone using the pencil sharpener. You look around the room for a while, then refocus and do a few more items. Halfway through the assignment, your teacher announces that it's time to put everything away and get ready for recess. You clear your desk and wait quietly. It pays off. Your teacher excuses your group first, but as soon as she does, you sprint for the door to be first in line. She calls you back.

"We don't run in the classroom," she says. "You need to wait until everyone else has been excused." Reluctantly you return to your seat.

At the end of the day, your teacher hands you a daily behavior report to share with your parents. "Oh no!" you say to yourself. "I'm going to get in trouble when I get home." You're right. When you get home, your mom reads the note, gives you a look of disappointment, and informs you that you can't watch TV or play with video games for the rest of the day.

Can you imagine what life would be like if this were how you spent most of your days? How do you think you would feel toward the classmates who avoided you? Or toward your teacher and parents who constantly corrected you? Most important, how do you think you would feel about yourself? This is only the tip of the iceberg for many children with ADD/ADHD. The problems they face at school usually mirror the problems they experience at home.

Attention deficit disorder is a term commonly used to describe a syndrome known in the clinical literature as attention deficit hyperactivity disorder (ADHD). There are a number of subtypes. The syndrome has both neurological and behavioral features and is characterized by impairment in three specific areas: attention span, impulse control, and activity level. Although most children with the disorder exhibit the combined symptoms of inattentiveness, impulsiveness, and hyperactivity, some show a preponderance of symptoms in one specific area. Hyperactivity is not essential for the diagnosis.

Attention deficit disorder is a very common childhood disorder. Conservative estimates indicate that ADD/ADHD affects 3 to 5 percent of school-age children and more boys than girls. The disorder is represented among all racial, cultural, and socioeconomic groups.

Contrary to earlier beliefs, most children do not outgrow their symptoms until they reach adolescence. Recent research shows that ADD/ADHD is a chronic disorder whose symptoms first appear during the preschool years and extend, in most cases, into adolescence. According to information released by CHADD, a national organization for children and adults with ADD/ADHD, 30 to 70 percent show symptoms into adulthood. Most children with the disorder are not diagnosed until they reach elementary school, when they experience significant school performance problems.

What symptoms are you most likely to observe in the classroom? Symptoms of inattention include a high degree of distractibility, difficulty listening to and following directions, difficulty focusing and staying on task, difficulty keeping track of books and assignments, and a tendency to bounce from one uncompleted task to another. Children who show symptoms of inattention without hyperactivity are often the most difficult to diagnose. They are frequently described as "spacey" and overlooked for ADD.

Symptoms of hyperactivity vary with age and developmental level. For example, preschoolers are more likely to show excessive gross motor activity—more running, climbing, and general roughhousing than their peers. Children at the elementary and secondary grade levels are more likely to display excessive restlessness and fidgeting in class. Symptoms of impulsiveness are similar across age groups. They include difficulty staying seated and taking turns, blurting our comments, excessive talking, interrupting, and a tendency to engage in dangerous activities.

In addition to the three groupings of symptoms, children with ADD/ADHD often display a number of secondary characteristics such as poor fine-motor coordination and handwriting problems, tantrums and temper outbursts, and a tendency to become oppositional and defiant when corrected. Few childhood disorders beat up on a child's self-concept, self-esteem, and motivation like ADD/ADHD. Because they have difficulty following directions and rules, their behavior brings them into more frequent conflict with their peers, teachers, and administrators. By necessity, children with ADD require a lot of corrective feedback.

Performance variability is one of the most frustrating and confusing aspects of ADD/ADHD, not only for teachers and parents, but also for the child with the disorder. What is performance variability? This is the erratic, inconsistent, up-and-down performance pattern we see in the learning and achievement of students with ADD/ADHD. One moment they seem to understand how to perform a task, and the next moment they tell you they don't understand, don't know what to do, or can't do the task. If you're a teacher or parent, you're thinking, "Come on, I just saw you do it. What do you mean you can't do it or don't understand what to do?" But most of the time the child means exactly what he or she says. How is this possible?

The majority of academic learning takes place in the left frontal lobe of the brain, the cortex. What part of the brain is most affected by ADD/ADHD? Yes, the cortex. When a child with ADD/ADHD becomes overstimulated or overwhelmed by a task, that's the part of the brain that becomes temporarily impaired. Literally, the child loses full access to the cortex and therefore loses full access to learning. Their capacity to process, conceptualize, and retain learned information is impaired during an arousal state. Dr. Daniel Amen, a pioneering child psychiatrist in the study of ADD/ADHD, has demonstrated this phenomenon with CAT scans and brain imaging. Students with ADD/ADHD are in and out of the cortex throughout the instructional day.

Performance variability helps explain why ADD/ADHD children are easily frustrated and overwhelmed by the quantity or difficulty level of the schoolwork they encounter. To reduce their frustration, they often avoid their work, which sets a self-defeating pattern in motion. The more they avoid, the further behind they become and the more frustration and discouragement they experience. Without intervention, many become stuck in a vicious cycle of frustration and avoidance and end up falling behind in their schoolwork. Remember, skill acquisition is the primary developmental task of early and middle childhood. Students with ADD/ADHD confront significant obstacles as they try to master important academic and social skills and keep pace with their peers. The damaging consequences of ADD/ADHD upon the student's achievement and mental health are often worse than the disorder itself.

As you read about the symptoms of ADD/ADHD, you may notice that several of your students show these symptoms from time to time. Does this mean they have ADD or ADHD? Not necessarily. At times all children show some of the behaviors I've described. This is normal. But children with ADD and ADHD show more of these behaviors more often. Most important, the behaviors they display have an impairing effect on their school performance, peer and adult relationships, and general social-emotional adjustment.

LEVEL OF IMPAIRMENT: THE CRITICAL ISSUE

Do children with ADD/ADHD show their symptoms all the time? No, and the variability in their performance creates a confusing picture. Children with ADD/ADHD have "on days" when they are better focused and controlled and "off days" when they are less focused and poorly controlled, but they have more "off days" than their peers. The pattern of behavior over time is a distinguishing feature of the disorder.

The good news is that ADD/ADHD is treatable. In most cases symptoms can be managed and controlled, and children can be helped to achieve closer to their full potential. The earlier children are identified, the sooner they can be helped to overcome the impairing effects of this disorder.

However, without early intervention and treatment, children run a greater risk for a variety of problems: school failure, poor self-esteem, poor social adjustment, family problems, emotional and behavioral problems, substance abuse, and other mental health problems.

If the profile of ADD symptoms describes a student in your class, we encourage you to point this out to the student's parents. If your school provides assessment services through a multidisciplinary team, a school-based assessment may be the best option. ADD and ADHD are medical problems with behavioral symptoms. Environmental modifications and accommodations are a helpful step in the right direction but not the full treatment. Medical problems require medical interventions.

Evaluating Attention Deficit Disorders

How are children evaluated for ADD/ADHD? There is no single medical or psychological test that provides a definitive diagnosis of ADD/ADHD. Most clinicians rely on a variety of sources to collect their data: a thorough developmental and medical history, behavior ratings scales, a review of school records, observations of the child in the home and classroom, and interviews with the parents, teacher, child, and others.

When learning problems are reported or the child is performing below grade level, some clinicians, including myself, routinely administer a battery of intellectual, perceptual-motor, and academic tests to determine whether learning disabilities are contributing to the child's achievement problems. Around 30 percent of children with ADD/ADHD also have learning disabilities.

Who should conduct the ADD/ADHD assessment? In the past, physicians and psychologists performed evaluations almost exclusively. More recently, schools have become involved in the process in an attempt to comply with section 504 of the Rehabilitation Act of 1973, which recognizes ADD/ADHD as a disability and requires a school-based assessment. School-based assessment is generally carried out by a multidisciplinary team that collects data from many sources and follows diagnostic criteria specified in the *Diagnostic and Statistical Manual* of the American Psychiatric Association (*DSM-IV*).

To qualify for the diagnosis of ADD or ADHD, a child must exhibit a sufficient number of symptoms specified in *DSM-IV*, show onset of the disorder before age seven, and demonstrate impairment in at least two settings (home and classroom). Symptoms must be present for at least six months. Also, the clinician must rule out other medical, emotional, or environmental factors, such as ineffective limit setting or earlier traumatic experiences, that might cause similar symptoms. The level of impairment should be specified as mild, moderate, or severe. Each level has implications for treatment.

Treatment for ADD/ADHD

The most effective treatment for ADD/ADHD is a multimodal approach that combines a number of therapies: medical management, classroom accommodations, behavior modification, and counseling. These therapies are typically carried out in a collaborative effort by a team consisting of the parents, teachers, educational specialists, physicians, and behavioral or mental health professionals.

It helps to think of the complete treatment as a combination of external and internal controls plus support (see Figure 17.1). External controls are provided through increased structure, classroom accommodations, and behavior management. Internal controls are enhanced through medications, supportive guidance from parents and teachers,

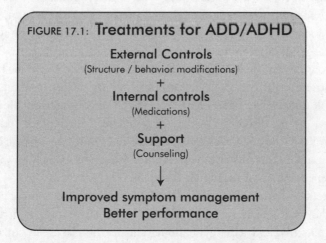

FIGURE 17.1: **Treatments for ADD/ADHD**

External Controls
(Structure / behavior modifications)
+
Internal controls
(Medications)
+
Support
(Counseling)
↓
Improved symptom management
Better performance

and counseling. Once a child is identified with the disorder, the clinician must determine the appropriate combination of therapies needed for effective symptom management and relief.

Not all children with ADD/ADHD require the full combination of therapies. Some with mild symptoms show significant improvement after external controls have been increased at home and in the classroom. Others, especially those with moderate to severe symptoms, require the full combination of internal and external controls to achieve the desired outcome. The need for support varies from case to case. Now that you have a clearer picture of the overall approach to treatment, let's take a closer look at each of the treatment components.

MEDICAL MANAGEMENT

A variety of medications have been used successfully in the treatment of ADD/ADHD. The most widely used medication is Ritalin, a psychostimulant that provides effective symptom relief in many children, with minimal side effects. Concerta and Dexedrine are other psychostimulants used in the treatment of ADD. A variety of antidepressant medications, including Norpramin and imipramine, have also been shown to provide good symptom relief.

How do these medications work? All are believed to act on the body's neurotransmitter chemicals to improve attention span and impulse control, the primary neurological features of the disorder. Medications do not cure the disorder, but they provide effective temporary relief of symptoms so the child has a better opportunity to respond to the external controls in his or her environment. Medications should always be used in combination with other therapies.

Are side effects associated with these medications? Some children may show side effects, including (among others) appetite loss, disrupted sleep patterns, and lethargy at home and in the classroom. In many cases, these side effects can be controlled through dosage adjustments or changes in medications.

CLASSROOM ACCOMMODATIONS

Students with ADD/ADHD require structure, clear signals, and consistent rules to navigate successfully through their day. A well-organized classroom with the necessary modifications in instruction gives ADD/ADHD students the best chance to perform closer to their potential. The following classroom accommodations will prove helpful.

ORGANIZING THE CLASSROOM

- Arrange for children with ADD/ADHD to be seated near the teacher's desk, preferably at the front of a row with his or her back to other students and distractions. Desk grouping often causes problems.
- Position children with ADD/ADHD away from distracting stimuli such as pencil sharpeners, heaters, air-conditioner vents, doors, or high-traffic areas.
- Prepare children with ADD/ADHD with warnings prior to transitions ("It's time to put your books away and get ready to go to the library"). Teachers should develop a plan for handling difficult situations, such as lining up to go outside, getting on the bus, heading out to recess, and school assemblies or field trips.
- Post classroom rules and a daily classroom schedule.
- Teachers should place a tray or basket in a visible area near the front door for children to hand in homework or permission slips. For many students with ADD/ADHD, out of sight is out of mind. Concrete visual cues are very helpful reminders.
- Redirect excess energy by providing classroom jobs, such as erasing the blackboard, passing out papers, collecting lunch tickets, or taking items to the office.
- Provide a quiet area in the classroom for children with ADD/ADHD when they need time to calm down and restore self-control.

MODIFYING INSTRUCTION

Students with ADD/ADHD require greater structure, clarity, and consistency in the way class directions and assignments are presented and carried out. The following instructional modifications should prove useful.

- When possible, present one instruction at a time and keep all instructions clear and concise.
- Present instructions in both oral and written form whenever possible.
- Encourage students with ADHD to ask for help or clarification when they don't understand what to do. Many won't ask, but then will begin their tasks with incomplete information.
- Use the check-in procedure from chapter 10 when students with ADD/ADHD appear tuned out or unaware of what to do.
- Develop a secret signal such as announcing the time remaining for the lesson as a first alert and refocusing device when students with ADD/ADHD become distracted or off task.
- Students with ADD/ADHD are easily overwhelmed by the quantity of work they encounter. Break assignments down into manageable pieces and proceed step by step, offering encouragement for effort enlisted and praise for work completed. Reduce the quantity, not quality, of classroom assignments and homework or extend the time to complete assigned work.
- Provide extra time for completing some assignments or tests, especially those requiring written work. Timed tasks are often difficult for children with short attention spans.
- When written assignments are a problem, allow for different modes of production, such as word processors, tape recorders, scribes, or oral presentations.
- Help students with ADD/ADHD develop organizational strategies for keeping track of assignments, books, and materials.

BEHAVIOR MANAGEMENT

What kind of behavior management works best with students with ADD/ADHD? They do not require different behavior management, just more of it, especially action messages or consequences. They tend to be stronger visual and experiential learners. Often, they have difficulty processing the verbal information that is provided. What does this mean to teachers? It means that teachers will have to rely more heavily on consequences or action signals to get their messages across. The methods we've covered so far in this book will be effective, but you should expect to use consequences much more frequently than you would with other students.

What methods should be avoided? Punitive or permissive methods do not provide the clarity or support that students with ADD need to be successful. These methods are a predictable setup for conflicts and power struggles.

My counseling work with children with ADD/ADHD often involves developing behavior treatment programs both in the home and in the classroom. One of the first steps I take, after reviewing my treatment plan with parents and teachers, is to set up parallel behavior management programs between the home and the classroom and run them simultaneously for eight weeks. The more consistency between home and classroom, the better most children respond. Although the specific parts of the behavior management program vary from child to child, most programs require the following.

- Clear verbal messages (chapter 9)
- Check-in procedure and cooldown technique (chapter 10)
- Regular doses of encouraging messages (chapter 2)
- Role-modeling, "try-it-again," and limited choices (chapter 11)
- Logical consequences and time-out procedure (chapters 11 and 13)

The parallel programs serve a number of purposes. First, they provide parents and teachers with the tools they need to manage the child's behavior. Second, the programs provide children with ADD/ADHD with a clear and consistent set of signals in two settings. Third, the programs accelerate learning and behavior change by increasing treatment effect. Finally, the combined programs provide the clinician with a way to evaluate the impact of increased structure and environmental controls on the child's overall performance.

At the end of the eight-week period, I arrange a follow-up conference with the various people involved in implementing the treatment programs: parents, teachers, administrators, and other educational specialists. We review the child's progress and discuss the need for further interventions. Many children show a marked improvement in response to the increased structure.

SUPPORTIVE COUNSELING

Attention deficit disorder can be stressful not only to the child with the disorder but also to those who attempt to manage the child's behavior. Parents and teachers often feel overwhelmed, frustrated, and worn down. They need a lot of support and understanding to remain positive and stay on course. Counseling can make their difficult job a little easier.

Children with ADD/ADHD often require support and assistance with developing appropriate social skills such as self-control, stress management, and problem solving. The counselor's office provides a safe and accepting atmosphere for learning and practicing new behaviors. Treatment is enhanced when parents and teachers encourage and reinforce the same skills at home and in the classroom.

Three Case Studies

COREY: A KINDERGARTNER WITH ADHD

Corey had been dismissed from three different preschools before he turned four. His parents thought his aggressive and rambunctious behavior would improve as he grew older, so they held him out of preschool until he turned five, then started him in kindergarten. He was referred for evaluation during the first week of school.

When Corey arrived at my office with his parents, I understood the reason for the speedy referral. He was all over the place. He ignored the usual books and puzzles I provide for my younger clients and found other ways to keep himself busy. He yanked on my blinds, grabbed items off my shelf, flicked my light switch off and on, and dumped the contents of my wastebasket all over the floor to see if there was anything interesting.

His parents did their best to restrain him, but each time he wiggled free and got into something new. He was a handful. Finally Corey's father took him outside so Corey's mother and I could get started with the formal parts of the evaluation. We completed the necessary forms, discussed Corey's health and developmental history, and arranged a classroom observation and teacher interview for later that week.

The evaluation was revealing. Corey showed the full symptom picture of ADHD with moderate to severe impairment. He was constantly on the move—roughhousing, bouncing from one uncompleted activity to another, resisting requests for cooperation, and throwing tantrums when he didn't get his way.

Corey's behavior was not caused by ineffective limit setting, but his parents' methods were not helping. His mother was permissive. She did a lot of repeating, reminding, reasoning, and explaining, and usually gave in when Corey threw a tantrum or pushed her to her limit.

Corey's father, on the other hand, compensated for his wife's permissiveness by being very strict. He did a lot of yelling, shaming, blaming, threatening, and spanking. I could understand why Corey did so much hitting.

In the classroom, Corey was fortunate to have such a skilled teacher. Her signals were clear, firm, and consistent. She was highly effective, but she was beginning to wear down because Corey required such frequent correction. He had extreme difficulty staying in his seat, paying attention, and following through on tasks. Morning circle and transition periods were his most difficult times of the day.

Corey's teacher was most concerned about his aggressive behavior. He constantly had his hands on other children—pushing, poking, grabbing, shoving, and hitting. She feared for their safety. Other parents were beginning to complain. The principal intervened on numerous occasions.

Once the evaluation was complete, Corey's parents, teacher, principal, resource teacher, and myself met as a team to discuss the results and develop a comprehensive home/school treatment plan. The evidence was clear. Corey needed the full combination of therapies, but his parents were reluctant to start him on medication until all other steps had been taken to improve his behavior. The team agreed to implement the following plan and meet again in eight weeks to review his progress and discuss the need for further steps.

COREY'S HOME/SCHOOL BEHAVIOR MANAGEMENT PROGRAM

- Clear verbal messages (chapter 9)
- Check-in procedure and cooldown technique (chapter 10)
- Regular doses of encouragement (chapter 2)
- Role-modeling, "try-it-again," and limited choices (chapter 11)
- Logical consequences and time-out procedures (chapters 11 and 13)

COREY'S CLASSROOM ACCOMMODATIONS

- Arrange seating near the teacher's desk.
- Provide a three-foot space between Corey and the nearest child in his table group.
- Use a carpet square to define Corey's space during morning circle and floor activities.
- Develop special procedures to handle transitions, such as lining up for recess or walking to the play area.
- Redirect Corey's excess energy through classroom jobs.
- Provide a designated "quiet area" for cooldowns and time-outs.
- Repeat classroom directions when needed.
- Develop a prearranged secret signal to cue Corey when he needs to stop a disruptive behavior or get back under control.

Corey responded well to treatment, especially at home. His parents were delighted. For the first time, they were able to manage his extreme behavior, even his tantrums, with success. He was beginning to tune in to their words and use acceptable problem-solving skills to get what he wanted.

At school, the results were mixed. Corey was more manageable during morning circle and transition periods. The cooldowns and time-outs also helped him regain lost self-control. But the grabbing, poking, and hitting continued, as did the complaints from other parents. Corey's teacher was beginning to feel resentful.

The principal was also concerned. School policy required a suspension consequence for each hitting incident, but six suspensions in four weeks had little impact on Corey's hitting. The principal had two remaining options: separate Corey from his classmates during recess or reduce the length of his instructional day. When she presented the options to his parents, they realized things had gone too far. They called their pediatrician and started Corey on medication a few days later.

Corey's teacher noticed the change right away. He was more attentive, stayed in his seat longer, and had a much easier time keeping his hands off others. The hitting stopped altogether. His disruptions were less frequent. Medication helped Corey respond to the structure and guidance he received in the classroom. His teacher's job was easier.

At our eight-week follow-up conference, the team agreed that the combination of treatments was on target. Corey's behavior had improved markedly, and everyone was encouraged by his progress. He still required more guidance than his classmates, but his behavior was manageable. The combination of medication and increased structure helped Corey achieve closer to his potential.

COLIN: A DISRUPTIVE SECOND GRADER

If there is such a thing as a typical ADD referral in my clinical work, Colin fits the profile. He didn't appear impulsive in my office, but the behavior-rating scales showed that he frequently interrupted, blurted out, and had difficulty waiting his turn. Often, he was out of his seat. He didn't seem distractible or inattentive, yet he seldom followed directions or completed his assignments. Colin did many of the things ADD children do, but there was a willful quality to the way he did them. When I explored his history and the guidance methods his mother and teacher used, I began to understand why.

At home, Colin ran the show, and he had been running the show since he was three. His mother, a single parent, was extremely permissive. She used a lot of repeating, reminding, warnings, and second chances. When Colin became defiant, she usually gave in to avoid confrontation. Colin was accustomed to getting his own way. He probably expected things to go the same way at school.

In the classroom, Colin's teacher used methods similar to those used at home. She did a lot of repeating and reminding and gave warnings and second chances, but that's where the similarities ended. If Colin tuned her out or continued testing, which he usually did, she wrote his name on the board. If he persisted, she made a check after his name. If he became defiant, she took away his recess, made him call his mother, or sent him to the office. None of these consequences had much impact. After nine suspensions, his teacher was wearing down.

The more information I collected, the clearer Colin's profile became. There were two things going on. He showed many of the symptoms of ADD, but his symptoms were mild, not severe. What made Colin stick out the most was his temperament. He was a very aggressive researcher. His behavior was what you might expect of an impulsive, strong-willed child trained with permissiveness. He pushed hard as long as others were willing to bend. He wasn't finding the firm limits he needed to stay on course at home or at school.

When I shared my diagnostic impression with Colin's teacher, she was relieved and surprised. She never suspected her methods might be contributing to the problem. Colin's mother wasn't surprised. She knew her family's medical history and recognized the likelihood that Colin had inherited the condition from his father.

I introduced the parallel behavior management programs to Colin's teacher and parents, and they were eager to get started, but first we had some cleanup work to do. We needed to eliminate all the steps that weren't working. No more repeating or reminding. No more warnings or second chances. No drama or yelling. No names on the board or calls to Mom. When that was behind us, Colin's mother made a trip to her pediatrician to share the findings. The pediatrician prescribed a trial run of stimulant medication. We put the following program into effect and ran it for eight weeks at home and in the classroom.

COLIN'S BEHAVIOR MANAGEMENT PROGRAM

- Clear verbal signals (chapter 9)
- Check-in procedure and cutoff technique (chapter 10)
- "Try-it-again" and limited choices (chapter 11)
- Logical consequences and time-out procedure (chapters 11 and 13)

The combination of medications and consistency between home and school produced the change we all expected. Colin tested less and cooperated more. The disruptions and blurting diminished markedly, but Colin didn't show a big drop in his limit testing until week four. By week eight, Colin showed marked improvement. The combination of medication and behavioral management helped him control his behavior. Colin was beginning to shine.

MIKAYLA: A STUDENT WITH ADD AND LEARNING DISABILITIES

When Mikayla's parents arrived at my office, they weren't looking for an evaluation. Their fifth-grade daughter had been diagnosed with ADD in the first grade, and she had been taking Ritalin twice a day ever since. Her parents were concerned because they weren't seeing the academic improvement they expected. Each year had been a struggle.

By the time Mikayla reached the fifth grade, she was nearly two years behind in her schoolwork. She complained that her assignments were too difficult, and she spent more time avoiding her work than completing it. When avoidance didn't work, she acted out and disrupted class. She was constantly in trouble.

I explored the various components of her treatment program to see if we could find some answers for her lack of progress. I began with medication. Mikayla's parents reported that she was taking 20 milligrams of Ritalin twice a day, which provided good symptom relief during school hours but none in the late afternoon, when she started homework. Were the classroom accommodations working? I wondered. When I asked her parents this question, they looked puzzled because no steps had been taken to accommodate Mikayla's special needs. She was treated like everyone else. No preferential seating. No modifications in assignment length or time for completion. No adjustments for completing written work. Directions were given once orally, and questions were discouraged. Unfinished assignments were added to her homework. Clearly, this treatment component needed improvement.

Next, I explored the guidance methods used at home and in the classroom. Both Mikayla's parents used a mixed approach. They did a lot of reasoning, lecturing, and explaining. When that didn't work, and it rarely did, they became angry and removed her privileges for long periods of time.

Mikayla's teacher took a punitive approach to classroom discipline. She used a lot of shaming, blaming, and humiliating to keep Mikayla on task. When Mikayla disrupted, which she did almost daily, her teacher made Mikayla write an apology letter to the class, copy the classroom rules, and take a negative behavior report home to her parents. Sometimes the teacher sent Mikayla to the office.

I was beginning to understand some of the reasons for Mikayla's lack of progress. Her treatment program was running on only one of four cylinders, that is, the medication, and the one that worked needed a tune-up in the afternoons. Mikayla required the full combination of therapies, and perhaps she needed more. Her lagging achievement still concerned me.

Her parents and teachers had assumed that Mikayla's academic problems were due to ADD and poor work habits, not to learning problems. Was this an accurate assumption? About 30 percent of children with ADD also have learning disabilities. Mikayla had been complaining for years that the work was too difficult. Maybe it was.

I arranged an evaluation session with Mikayla and administered a battery of psychological and educational tests. The results confirmed what Mikayla had been telling us all along. Some of the work was too difficult. She showed a profile of specific learning disabilities and qualified for special educational assistance. Now we had all the information we needed to request a conference with her school support team and put the full treatment program in place.

Mikayla's parents, teacher, principal, resource specialist, and I met to review the test results and discuss ways to help Mikayla become more successful. We agreed to discontinue all the steps that weren't working. No more shaming or humiliation tactics. No more apology letters, copying class rules, or negative behavior report cards. Mikayla needed to experience success. We implemented the following plan and agreed to review her progress in eight weeks.

Mikayla's Medical Management

Mikayla's parents agreed to consult with their pediatrician regarding an afternoon dose of medication to help Mikayla get through her homework.

MIKAYLA'S CLASSROOM ACCOMMODATIONS

- Arrange seating at the front of a row, near the teacher's desk.
- Select a responsible classmate to be Mikayla's "buddy helper" and assist with questions and directions.
- Present directions in both oral and written forms.
- Use a secret signal to cue Mikayla to the need to refocus when she is off task. Modify length of assignments, especially homework assignments, and provide extra time for completion.
- Provide alternative methods for completing written assignments, such as using a word processor or giving oral reports.
- Provide homework assignments for the week on one sheet of paper to be passed out on Monday.
- Provide special education assistance three times a week at school.

MIKAYLA'S HOME/SCHOOL BEHAVIOR
MANAGEMENT PROGRAM

- Clear verbal messages (chapter 9)
- Check-in procedure (chapter 10)
- Generous helpings of encouragement (chapter 2)
- "Try-it-again" and limited choices (chapter 11)
- Logical consequences and time-out procedure (chapters 11 and 13)

Mikayla's Supportive Counseling

Mikayla's parents arranged individual counseling sessions for their daughter through their health plan.

At the eight-week follow-up conference, Mikayla's parents and teacher reported a noticeable change in her behavior. She completed more work, and she did so with less complaining and avoidance. She looked forward to her sessions with the special education teacher. As she experienced greater success, her acting out decreased. By week five, time-outs were seldom needed, and there were no more trips to the office.

The other components were helping, too. The afternoon dose of medication took much of the battle out of homework, and the counseling provided welcomed support. Mikayla was beginning to feel good about herself. The combined treatment components were working.

Chapter Summary

In this chapter, we examined attention deficit disorder (ADD), a fairly common and treatable childhood disorder that often impairs school performance and interpersonal relationships. Children with ADD and ADHD require special attention. They need a great deal of structure, support, and consistent guidance to navigate successfully through their day. Many also need medication to keep them on track and to help them perform to the best of their potential. Successful treatment usually involves the combined efforts of parents, teachers, physicians, and helping professionals.

Children with ADD and ADHD are action learners. They need frequent and consistent action messages or consequences to learn your rules, and they need you to present this data in a clear, firm, and respectful way. Excessive words, anger, drama, or strong emotion will only pollute the clarity of your message and undermine the teaching-and-learning process. Permissive or punitive guidance methods are a predictable setup for conflicts and power struggles.

Supporting Students
with Special Needs

Who are the other students that make up the 5 percent on each campus that require more than classroom management, the ones who require backup support and other services to be successful? There is no one single profile that describes them all. They are a mixed group. Some have fallen behind academically and start to disrupt. Some are so frustrated and discouraged by their lack of academic success that they avoid their assignments and act out. Some lack social skills, which brings them into frequent conflict with peers and authority figures. Some have unidentified learning or developmental problems. Some are under stress due to factors outside the school, and some have many things going on in their lives simultaneously.

What do these students share in common? They're not enjoying success at school, socially or academically. In most cases, the acting-out behavior is just a symptom of deeper underlying problems. Skill acquisition is the primary developmental task of elementary school age children. Failure registers intensely. These students require a higher level of support. Most of these problems cannot be fixed in the regular classroom, but there are things teachers can do to help. This chapter will address some of the practical and realistic steps teachers can take to support these challenging students in the classroom until they get connected with the appropriate level of support.

The Academically Delayed Child

Nate, a third grader, appears bright and capable, but he's performing nearly two years below grade level in reading, spelling, and written language. He's nearly nine, socially mature, and not a good candidate for grade retention. Nate's school records show that he has attended eight schools in the last four years. He hasn't had any discipline problems until this year, when he began disrupting lessons by clowning around. The pattern is escalating. Nate is becoming a familiar face in the office.

SUPPORT PLAN

Like many academically delayed students, Nate is entering the cycle of frustration, discouragement, avoidance, and acting out. The support goal is to reduce his frustration level and increase opportunities for success. The following tips should help.

- When possible, modify work from frustration level to instructional level.
- Reduce the quantity, not quality, of in-class assignments and homework.
- Use buddy helpers, mentors, and coaches for support.
- Provide generous helpings of encouragement for on-task behavior.
- Emphasize effort, not outcome; process, not product.
- Use the ticket-in/ticket-out procedure for training good homework habits.
- Connect the student with further options for academic support (for example, tutoring, homework club).

The Academically Discouraged Child

Celia, a fifth grader, is a year or more below grade level in all subject areas and has struggled since the first grade. An evaluation, conducted during her third-grade year, revealed that she is bright and capable with no evidence of learning disabilities. Nonetheless, her struggles continue. In the classroom, she behaves as though she has given up. She doesn't listen to directions, doesn't participate in class activities, and sits with her head in her hands when she's supposed to be working on assignments. She requires a great deal of teacher supervision and prodding to complete what little work she accomplishes. Celia hasn't been disruptive or defiant until this year, when her teacher tried to motivate her by taking away recess privileges for incomplete class work. Celia is getting acquainted with the office.

SUPPORT PLAN

Academically discouraged students are more concerned with avoiding failure than achieving success. Often, they're unaware of their successful efforts and need someone else to point them out. The support goal is to reprime the motivational pump by encouraging effort and on-task behavior. The following tips should help.

- Focus on effort, not outcome. Encourage process, not product.
- Try to catch them being on task and acknowledge and reward their efforts.
- Point out their successes, however small.
- Provide generous helpings of encouragement to help them overcome negative self-talk.
- Notes of encouragement are effective (for example, "Good job! I knew you could!").
- Unsolicited phone calls to parents sharing successes is very encouraging.

The Socially Unskilled Child

Deshawn, a second grader, is a frequent visitor to the office. He regularly blurts out, interrupts, and disrupts instruction. When it's his turn to talk, he talks too loud. When he sits at morning circle, he puts his hands and feet on others and grabs things without asking. At lunch, he frequently has to sit by himself at the quiet table. Deshawn's biggest challenges are on the playground. When he gets frustrated or doesn't get his way, he hits.

SUPPORT PLAN

Socially unskilled students need lots of skill training.

- Role-model socially appropriate behavior.
- Catch them behaving appropriately and acknowledge their efforts.
- Try-it-again is an effective skill-training procedure.
- Recess Academy provides opportunities for skill training.
- Encourage parents to role-model and practice appropriate social skills at home.
- Link the student with older, responsible students as mentors and role models.

Students with Unidentified Developmental Problems

Rudy, a fourth grader, has the academic skills to perform successfully but seldom completes classroom assignments on time. He's failing several subjects, but his standardized achievement test scores are strong and show that he's acquiring skills at the appropriate rate. In the classroom, Rudy is not intentionally disruptive, but he's distractible and often asks inappropriate questions. He doesn't have any friends. At recess and lunch, he hangs out alone and doesn't seem bothered by it. Recently, he's become the object of teasing and ridicule on the playground and has responded by making inappropriate violent comments and death threats. His teacher, principal, and some parents are concerned.

SUPPORT PLAN

- The principal should share his or her concerns with Rudy's parents and encourage them to consult with their pediatrician or pursue an evaluation.
- The school should consider initiating an educational evaluation to determine if Rudy is eligible for support services.
- Rudy needs skill training in how to handle interpersonal conflicts. Recess Academy might be a good option.
- Antagonistic students should be counseled to avoid Rudy and should receive the appropriate consequences for further harassment.

Students Under Stress and in Crisis

Kara, age ten, has lived in three different foster homes since age five and has been separated from her two siblings since her initial placement. Child protective services has been involved on at least two occasions. Her mother, a recovering addict, has been in and out of Kara's life during repeated attempts at rehab. Kara's social worker suspects that all three children experienced prenatal exposure to methamphetamines.

Kara's school experience has been very fragmented. Her school records indicate she attended five different schools before third grade and missed the first half of her fourth-grade year between foster placements. Academically, she appears capable, but she is achieving far below basic levels on standardized achievement tests. She hasn't attended any school long enough to complete a full assessment.

In the classroom, Kara antagonizes other students, disrupts instruction, and sometimes responds with defiance when disciplined. She completes very little assigned work.

SUPPORT PLAN

Prioritize the student's needs, then intervene and support in priority order.

- Minimize academic frustration by reducing the quantity, not quality, of assignments.
- Maintain firm limits and enforce limits in a positive, respectful manner. Children under stress tend to act out their conflicts. This requires extra patience on the teacher's part.
- Provide generous helpings of encouragement.
- Acknowledge and encourage acceptable choices, cooperation, and on-task behavior.
- Mentors and coaches can be helpful.
- Older buddy peer helpers can be helpful.
- Assess student to determine eligibility for educational support services.
- Connect family and child with available support services within the school system or in the community.

Chapter Summary

Students with special needs present some of the greatest guidance and discipline challenges in the school. They require a great deal of support, and sometimes they require more than can be provided in a regular classroom setting. There are, however, a variety of things teachers can do to support these students until they're connected with the appropriate support services or classroom setting, where their underlying needs can be addressed. In this chapter, we examined some of those practical and realistic support options that teachers can use until the appropriate help arrives.

Developing a School-Wide Discipline Plan

When discipline practices vary from teacher to teacher, inconsistency and confusion is the rule. Students receive mixed messages and mixed lessons about our rules and expectations. Teachers are unclear about their role and responsibilities in the discipline process, and administrators are unclear about what they are backing up when they receive discipline referrals. Everyone remains stuck on the treadmill of ineffective discipline.

Classroom management and school discipline are too important to be neglected or done ineffectively. The lesson of classroom management and school-wide discipline should be taught with proven, research-based, state-of-the-art methods, consistency across grade levels, consistency between the office and the classrooms, and consistency on the playground, in the cafeteria, and other parts of the campus.

In this chapter, we'll examine the predictable problems that accompany schools with unclear, incomplete, or poorly conceived discipline plans. We'll help you evaluate the effectiveness of your school's discipline plan and show you how to put the parts back together so your program operates in a cohesive, integrated manner. Whether your school's plan requires a minor tune-up or a major overhaul, we'll show you how to implement an effective Setting Limits School-Wide Discipline Plan on your campus.

Ineffective Discipline Policy: Where the Problem Begins

The school's discipline plan or policy, also referred to as "standards for behavior," "code of conduct," "discipline code," or "consequences for misbehavior," describes the procedures that teachers and administrators use for handling school discipline problems. Essentially it's an instructional manual for enforcing school rules and carrying out school disciplinary procedures.

School discipline policies range from permissive to highly punitive and cover all points in between. Some are clear and effective, but most are simplistic, production-line lists of punitive sanctions for dealing with severe or recurring discipline problems. Many use outdated discipline practices that violate learning theory, ignore differences in children's temperaments, and use consequences that are not logically related to the misbehavior. They seem to work with compliant students who give us a wide margin for ineffectiveness, but they fail to address the "aggressive researchers" and students with special needs who cause 90 percent of school discipline problems. The following is a typical list of the types of sanctions or consequences that staff are expected to use at the elementary level.

A TYPICAL INEFFECTIVE DISCIPLINE POLICY

- Warning
- Loss of recess or other school privileges
- Parent notification (a call or note)
- Detention
- Send student to the office
- Parent conference
- Half-day suspension

- Full-day suspension
- Three-day suspension
- Referral to school expulsion committee
- Referral to special program

Not only are these policies ineffective from a teaching-and-learning point of view, they're also ineffective from an organizational point of view because they fail to provide the information that teachers and administrators need to operate as a team. An unclear or incomplete policy is one that fails to adequately define:

- The roles and responsibilities of teachers and administrators in the guidance and discipline process.
- What discipline practices should be used in the classroom.
- What steps should be taken prior to requesting backup support.
- What constitutes an appropriate referral for backup support.
- What discipline practices are used in the office.

Problems That Accompany Ineffective Discipline Policies

When a school's discipline policy is unclear, incomplete, or poorly conceived, a variety of predictable organizational problems are set in motion: confusion over roles and responsibilities, inconsistency among staff, confusion about administrative backup support, inappropriate referrals to the office, and conflict and resentment among staff. The problems are similar to the ones teachers confront when they attempt to teach a lesson without an effective lesson plan or effective instructional practices. Predictably, the lesson will break down. Let's take a closer look at each of these problems.

CONFUSION OVER ROLES AND RESPONSIBILITIES

When a school's discipline policy fails to define the roles and responsibilities of the participants in the guidance process, confusion is the predictable outcome. Teachers aren't clear what steps they should take to resolve discipline problems in the classroom, and administrators aren't clear when they should step in and provide backup support for teachers. It's difficult to function as a team when the team members don't understand their roles or the skills they're expected to perform. The confusion makes the staff appear fragmented and ineffective.

When the school's discipline policy is clear, carefully thought out, and based on effective practices, however, everyone understands their role and the responsibilities they're expected to carry out. Teachers and administrators can work in synchrony as a team. An effective discipline plan should clearly define the roles and responsibilities of all participants in the guidance and discipline process: teachers, administrators, playground supervisors, lunchroom supervisors, and other guidance providers. All participants should be adequately trained to resolve discipline problems in their primary setting. Teachers, in particular, should know when backup support is really needed, how to obtain it, what constitutes an appropriate referral, and what to expect after backup support is delivered.

INCONSISTENCY AMONG STAFF

When schools lack a clear discipline policy and a uniform set of discipline procedures, inconsistency among staff is the rule. The range of disciplinary practices varies from classroom to classroom. Some are permissive. Some are punitive. Some use a mixed approach. Others are democratic and effective.

What lesson do students learn when teachers vary so greatly in the way they define and enforce classroom rules? There is no single, cohesive lesson. Instead they receive a series of mixed messages and mixed lessons that sets everyone up for testing and conflict. When a staff does not operate as a team, the team looks ineffective.

Imagine the chaos that would unfold if a football team tried to operate on this basis. The game is in progress. Each time, the quarterback (principal) calls the team (staff) to the huddle and announces the play, but when the players return to the line of scrimmage, everybody does something different. The play doesn't work, and the whole team looks ineffective.

Inconsistency among staff creates confusion and fragmentation in the disciplinary process and keeps everyone on the discipline treadmill. For students, the experience is like being under the same roof with twenty-five or more governments operating simultaneously. It's confusing. When teachers send students to the office for disciplinary reasons, administrators are unsure what practices they're backing up, which leads us to the next problem.

CONFUSION OVER BACKUP SUPPORT

What is backup support? The answer depends entirely on the school's discipline policy because backup support takes place within the context of the school's discipline plan. The two work hand in hand. You can't discuss one without a clear understanding of the other. In some cases the administrator's backup support role has already been defined by the school's policy. In other cases the administrator's backup support role is not adequately addressed.

As we untangle the issues of discipline policy and backup support, more important questions come into focus: What is the administrator backing up? Are the discipline practices in the classroom effective or ineffective? Is backup support an appropriate use of the administrator's time? Lastly, what practices does the administrator use in the office? Are they effective or ineffective? Let's look at the range of scenarios.

When ineffective practices in the classroom are supported by ineffective practices in the office, we have a worst-case scenario. Reinforcement errors go in all directions. Administrators enable teachers by accepting inappropriate referrals. Teachers enable misbehaving students by sending them to the office. Administrators enable misbehaving students by not resolving the problems. Teachers and administrators become confused about their roles and responsibilities in the discipline process. School morale suffers. Everyone remains stuck on the treadmill.

When ineffective practices in the classroom are supported by effective practices in the office, problems get resolved, but site administrators remain stuck on the treadmill and risk burnout. The office is overwhelmed with misbehaving students.

When effective practices in the classroom are supported by ineffective practices in the office, parents and teachers lose confidence in the administrator, staff morale declines, and the office becomes a revolving door for the same misbehaving students. The office commits the reinforcement error.

The best-case scenario is the only scenario that makes any sense. When effective practices in the classroom are supported by effective practices in the office, teachers and administrators can work in synchrony in a mutually supportive relationship. Teachers handle as much as they can in the classroom, and administrators step in only when needed. Everyone's time is respected.

INAPPROPRIATE REFERRALS TO THE OFFICE

Sending students to the office or involving administrators in the guidance process should be interventions of last resort, reserved for emergencies or when all steps taken to resolve problems at the classroom level have failed. Unfortunately, this is not the practice in most schools with unclear discipline policies. Passing discipline problems to others is one of the biggest and most costly abuses of the school discipline process.

The game is called "passing the hot potato." The object of the game is to shift the discipline problem, and the responsibility for resolving it, from the teacher's lap onto someone else's lap, preferably the site administrator's, as quickly as possible. In busy schools, the same hot potato can be passed back and forth between the classroom and the office many times in the same day, compounding opportunities for reinforcement errors.

In most cases, the cause of the problem can be traced back to one or more of the following factors: an ineffective school discipline policy, inadequate training in classroom management, or confusion about the roles and responsibilities in the discipline process. In some cases administrators invite the problem by accepting inappropriate referrals and involving themselves too early in the discipline process.

Whatever the cause, the destructive consequences of this practice are clear. Hot potato creates division and resentment among staff, wastes valuable administrative time and financial resources, and keeps everyone stuck on the discipline treadmill. Administrators and office staff feel resentful toward teachers who use the office as a dumping ground. Teachers feel resentful and unsupported when administrators and office staff don't respond quickly to their referrals.

Discipline Services from an Organizational Perspective

When we examine traditional delivery of discipline services from an organizational perspective, the issues of inefficiency and cost-ineffectiveness come into focus. Most schools organize and deliver their guidance and discipline services based on a three-tier organizational model. Let's look at an organizational diagram of a typical school discipline program (see Figure 19.1). Notice that the organizational pyramid is divided into three levels.

At the administrative level, the school principal, vice principal, and guidance counselors are responsible for providing guidance and discipline services, that is, if your school is fortunate enough to have a vice principal or guidance counselors. In many schools the principal handles

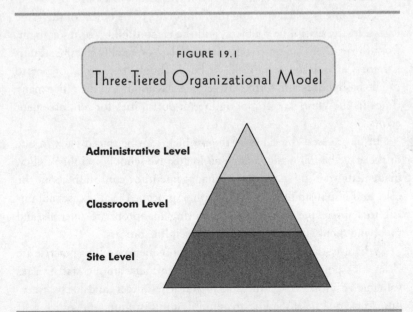

FIGURE 19.1

Three-Tiered Organizational Model

Administrative Level

Classroom Level

Site Level

all discipline services at this level. Teachers are primarily responsible for providing discipline services at the classroom level. The lower level of the pyramid represents guidance and discipline services in settings outside the classroom, such as on the playground and in hallways, bathrooms, cafeteria, library, and bus pickup areas. Once again, the school principal is responsible for managing and coordinating guidance services in these areas.

In the three-tier model, discipline problems are passed up the system but seldom passed down. The higher they go, the more expensive they are to resolve. When you consider the numbers of people at each level of the system, another problem emerges: There are very few people at the top of the pyramid to deal with the problems.

What does this diagram tell you about the way discipline services are distributed throughout the school? Who handles most of the problems and the most difficult problems? It's the administrator. The diagram reveals a fundamental flaw in the way most discipline systems are set up. Too much of the load is concentrated at the highest and most expensive level. The three-tier model might be efficient in small schools with a low incidence of discipline problems, but the model is not efficient in larger schools with a high incidence of discipline problems.

What's the most cost-effective solution? The solution is to train teachers and other guidance providers to resolve problems in the settings in which they occur. Schools need to better distribute the load so problems can be handled at the lowest and least expensive levels. We know that when teachers and other guidance providers have the right discipline tools in their toolbox, 95 percent of school discipline problems can be resolved in the settings where they occur—the classroom, playground, and lunchroom. Doesn't it make the most sense to adequately train staff to resolve what can be resolved in the setting where it occurs?

There's an old saying, "Give a person a fish, and they eat for a day. Train a person to fish, and they eat for a lifetime." Shouldn't schools be training teachers, playground supervisors, and lunchroom supervisors to fish? Effective training and periodic retraining are far less expensive than hiring additional staff to handle problems at the highest and most expensive level.

How Effective Is Your School's Discipline Program?

With an understanding of how most schools organize and carry out their discipline services, let's conduct an informal assessment of your school's discipline practices. Rate your school's effectiveness at each level of your school's discipline system. The more questions you can answer "yes" to, the more effective your school's discipline system is likely to be. We'll begin with the administrative level.

GUIDANCE PRACTICES AT THE ADMINISTRATIVE LEVEL

1. Does your school discipline policy specify the steps teachers are expected to take to resolve discipline problems in the classroom before sending students to the office?
2. Does your school discipline policy specify the steps your site administrator or office support staff is expected to take to resolve discipline problems in the office?
3. Do guidance practices in the office support guidance practices in the classroom?
4. Does your site administrator provide an adequate level of backup support for the classroom?
5. Are guidance practices in the office effective with the 10 percent of students who cause most of the school discipline problems?
6. Does your site administrator discourage the use of lectures, writing sentences, picking up trash, detentions, or off-campus suspensions as regular disciplinary interventions?
7. Does your site administrator encourage classroom teachers to invest time at the beginning of the year to develop effective structure for their classrooms?
8. Does your site administrator discourage using the school's office as a revolving door for the 10 percent of students who cause most of the school's discipline problems?

9. Does your school have procedures for handling crises in the classroom such as extreme disruption, extreme defiance, and violent or destructive behavior?

10. Does your site administrator provide in-service training for staff in effective guidance and discipline?

Based on your answers to the above questions, rate the effectiveness of guidance practices at the administrative level:

Highly effective   Moderately effective   Ineffective   Very effective

GUIDANCE PRACTICES AT THE CLASSROOM LEVEL

1. Are you adequately trained to handle the full range of discipline problems you encounter in your classroom? Are your guidance methods effective with the 10 percent who cause most of your classroom discipline problems? Do you believe most of your colleagues are adequately trained in classroom management?

2. Does your school offer in-service training in effective limit setting, responsibility training, team building, teaching social skills, or using incentive systems?

3. Is in-service training required rather than optional for staff?

4. Do you set aside time at the beginning of each year or semester to create effective structure for your classroom? Do you send a copy of your classroom rules and expectations for student conduct home to parents? Do most of your colleagues follow these practices?

5. Do you notify parents within the first four weeks when their child shows extreme or persistent behavioral problems?

6. Are the guidance and discipline practices at your school consistent from one classroom to another?

7. Is there a prescribed series of steps you're expected to take before sending students to the office? If so, are most of your colleagues aware of these steps?

8. When you send students to the office for disciplinary reasons, do you know what steps your site administrator or office support staff will take to resolve the problem?

9. Do you send students to the office only as a last resort or final step in your guidance and discipline process?

10. Do you believe guidance and discipline should be part of your job description?

Based on your answers to the above questions, rate the effectiveness of your school's guidance practices at the classroom level:

Highly effective   Moderately effective   Ineffective   Very effective

GUIDANCE PRACTICES OUTSIDE THE CLASSROOM (SITE LEVEL)

1. Are the playground and hallway supervisors at your school trained in effective guidance and discipline?

2. Are staff members in the library and cafeteria trained in effective guidance and discipline? Are they adequately trained to handle the types of problems they encounter?

3. Do the playground supervisors at your school handle the majority of behavior problems on the playground before sending students to the office?

4. Does your school discipline policy specify the guidance roles that teachers are expected to play in settings outside the classroom?

5. Does your school discipline policy specify the guidance and discipline methods that staff is expected to use in settings outside the classroom?

6. Does your school have a discipline committee?

7. If so, does your school discipline committee support classroom teachers with challenging discipline problems?

8. Does your school discipline committee regularly communicate with your site administrator regarding school-wide discipline concerns?

9. Does your school site discipline committee assist with in-service training for staff?
10. Do you receive periodic updated training in effective guidance and discipline?

Based on your answers to the above questions, rate the effectiveness of your school's guidance practices outside the classroom:

Highly effective   Moderately effective   Ineffective   Very effective

ASSESSMENT SUMMARY

Enter your ratings here for each of the three levels:

Administrative level: _____
Classroom level: _____
Site level: _____

HOW ARE THESE RATINGS USEFUL?

The ratings help you identify the effectiveness of your school's guidance program at each level of the guidance process and target your repair work. For example, if you rated your school's discipline program as ineffective at either the administrative or classroom levels, then your program likely requires a major overhaul. Fundamental changes are required in the way your school organizes and delivers guidance services. Refer back to the questions that indicate the breakdowns to target your repair work.

If you rated your program as moderately effective at the administrative and classroom levels but ineffective at the site level, then your program can probably get by with a tune-up and some body work. Refer back to the questions that indicate the breakdowns to target your repair efforts. If you rated your program as moderately effective at all three levels, a simple tune-up should put your program back on the road to recovery. You've identified the breakdowns in your guidance program; now let's look at the replacement parts.

Components of an Effective School-Wide Program

In the Setting Limits Program, the parts work together in a cohesive and integrated manner. Each level supports the others, and everyone works from the same guidance plan. All members of the system receive the same effective training, speak the same guidance language, and share a common set of effective guidance methods. Roles and responsibilities are clear and evenly distributed. Everyone understands the steps they're expected to take before passing the problem on to others. Now, let's look at the specific program components at each level of the process.

COMPONENTS AT THE ADMINISTRATIVE LEVEL

- A clear, well-thought-out, and well-developed school discipline policy that specifies roles, responsibilities, and procedures at each level of the guidance process for all staff and parents.

- A school discipline policy based on effective methods that work with the full range of students, not just the compliant ones.
- A discipline policy that defines "an appropriate referral" and specifies the steps that staff are expected to take to resolve discipline problems before sending students to the office or requesting administrative involvement.
- A discipline policy that requires staff to complete an incident report documenting steps taken to resolve problems before sending students to the office.
- In-service training for site administrators in effective limit setting, crisis intervention, relationship building, responsibility training, social skill training, problem solving, positive motivation, and the use of incentive systems.
- Crisis intervention backup support for classroom teachers and site-level staff.
- Backup support for classroom teachers in cases of extreme disruption, extreme defiance, violent behavior, or state educational code violations.
- Assistance with the planning and coordination of in-service training for staff.
- Assistance with the coordination of supervision of areas outside the classroom.

COMPONENTS AT THE CLASSROOM LEVEL

- A discipline policy that clearly specifies guidance and discipline as part of each classroom teacher's job description.
- In-service training on developing effective structure for the classroom.
- In-service training in effective limit setting, problem solving, and using logical consequences.
- In-service training on positive motivation, incentive systems, relationship building, and skill training.
- In-service training on crisis intervention procedures.

- An effective referral form for teachers to complete before sending students to the office or requesting administrative backup support.
- Access to backup support from administrative staff or other designated persons in cases of emergencies or extreme behavior problems.

COMPONENTS AT THE SITE LEVEL

- A school discipline policy that specifies roles, responsibilities, and procedures for staff outside the classroom.
- In-service training in effective guidance and discipline for playground and hallway supervisors, office clerical staff, library staff, and cafeteria staff.
- Incident reports for staff to complete documenting steps taken to resolve problems before sending students to the office.
- A site-level discipline committee composed of staff from each level of the guidance system.
- A site-level discipline committee that provides advisory support for classroom teachers or other staff regarding difficult discipline problems.
- A site-level discipline committee that acts as liaison to teacher and parent groups and provides advisory input to site administrator regarding school discipline concerns.
- A site-level discipline committee that assists site administrator with planning and coordinating in-service training for all staff.
- A site-level discipline committee that assists site administrator with planning and coordinating crisis intervention procedures.

THE ADMINISTRATOR'S ROLE IN THE SCHOOL-WIDE DISCIPLINE PLAN

No discussion about the components of an effective school-wide program is complete without addressing the vital role of the school principal. School principals play the most important role in the school-wide discipline program. They arrange in-service training for all staff, carry out school policy, provide backup support for teachers, and coordinate supervision for the playground, lunchroom, library, and hallways. They face the toughest cases. They make the toughest decisions, and they bear the greatest burden of responsibility.

School principals must be experts in guidance and discipline. They can't afford not to be. Their leadership role requires it, and their credibility depends on it. Staff confidence and school morale hang in the balance. Everyone in the school looks to them for leadership and effectiveness. The principal's leadership is the glue that holds the school-wide program together.

Principles to Guide Your Repair Work

You've identified the breakdowns, and you've examined the replacement parts. The next step is to put the parts back together so your program can operate as a cohesive and integrated unit. As you begin this task, there are some principles you should keep in mind to guide your repair work: Make it efficient; make it effective; make it affordable. Let's look at each of these guidelines.

Make It Efficient

You may have already discovered that some of the replacement parts don't fit within the conventional three-tier organizational model. Why? Because the three-tier model has design flaws that all but guarantee inefficiency and expense. Let's revisit the typical organizational model (see Figure 19.2).

Adding a school site discipline committee to the organizational model improves guidance services at every level. It takes pressure off the administrator, distributes workload, increases support for staff both inside and outside the classroom, and provides an open channel for communication among all levels of the system. Now the levels of the system can support one another at less cost and with more efficiency.

Who should be part of the school site discipline committee? The committee should be composed of staff from each level of the system and preferably staff with the most expertise in guidance and discipline, because they'll likely be called on to provide backup support for their colleagues.

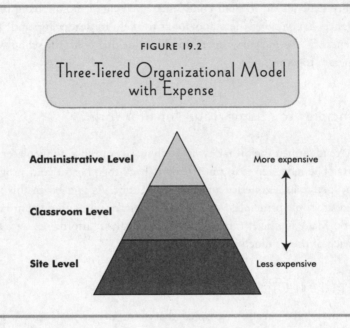

FIGURE 19.2

Three-Tiered Organizational Model with Expense

Administrative Level

Classroom Level

Site Level

More expensive

Less expensive

Make It Effective

The Setting Limits Program is a proven, research-based program that works with all students, not just the compliant ones, and achieves all our guidance goals. It stops misbehavior. It resolves discipline problems at the lowest levels, and it teaches students the skills they need to improve their behavior so teachers, students, and administrators can get off the discipline treadmill. Most important, the program supports the academic program by keeping kids in the classroom and out of the office. Most schools that adopt our program see a 50 percent or more reduction in referrals to the office.

Make It Affordable

We know that the higher the discipline problems pass up the system, the more expensive they become. The Setting Limits Program is designed to resolve problems at the lowest and most cost-effective levels without compromising valuable administrative time or financial resources. To do this, staff must have the necessary training and skills to get the job done. The initial investment in staff training to bring everyone to acceptable skill levels will yield big returns and cost savings to the whole system later on. The program pays for itself year after year. Pay up front or pay as you go, but paying up front is always the cheapest option.

Implementing a School-Wide Discipline Program

You've examined your school's discipline program. You've identified the parts that need repair, and, like most thoughtful consumers, you've considered how to get the most value out of your repair dollars. What's the next step? Should your school attempt the repair work alone? Do you need some help? Does your school need a lot of help? Also, you should consider the extent of the repair job, the motivation level of your staff,

time constraints, and the budget you have to work with. You have at least three good options.

If your school's guidance and discipline program is in good shape and just needs a few minor repairs and your staff is motivated to do the repair work, you should consider doing the repair work without outside help. This book is designed to help you do just that. In appendix 4, you'll find an eight-week teacher study guide course for do-it-yourselfers. The study guide introduces the various skill components in the program on a chapter-by-chapter basis and provides questions and hypothetical situations to help you master the material. We encourage study group participants to practice new skill components in their classrooms between each meeting and share experiences in the group to fine-tune and improve. In appendix 3, there is a start-up guide for practicing new skill components at a comfortable level.

If your school's discipline program needs repairs in multiple areas, and you face time constraints, and your staff is not motivated to commit to eight weeks of study group training, then you should consider some outside help. The Setting Limits Program provides a variety of training workshops and consultation for schools in this situation. See our website (www.settinglimits.com) for more information. We can help you tailor the appropriate combinations of workshops and consultative support services to address your school's needs.

If your school's discipline program needs a major overhaul and has become enmeshed in years of ineffective discipline practices, then outside help with the repair work and long-term supportive consultation is your best option. The Setting Limits Program provides a full-implementation package of training and support services to help your staff accomplish this goal at a very affordable price. Here is a brief description of the program.

FULL-IMPLEMENTATION PACKAGE FOR ELEMENTARY SCHOOLS

The Full Implementation Package provides everything your school needs to create a state-of-the-art guidance program at a very affordable price.

Your staff will receive a full year of training, direct observation, confidential feedback, focus workshops on a wide range of topics, and ongoing consultative support to help them develop and refine their new skills. Materials are available in both Spanish and English. Best of all, this package provides you the flexibility to select the combination of workshops, consultative support services, and guidance materials best suited to the needs of your school and staff. Parent workshops can be exchanged for additional consultative support or special focus workshops for staff.

Package Highlights

The core package of fifty hours of service includes: one full-day staff development training seminar, two part-day follow-up workshops, two parent workshops, twenty-four hours of consultative support for staff, one full-day training for trainers workshop, a 30 percent discount on all books purchased for staff or parents, and a full array of forms, posters for the classroom, and handouts for staff and parents. Workshops and consultative support services will be provided at your school site during a one-year time frame and arranged to fit your school's schedule.

There are three phases of implementation.

Teacher-Parent Workshops/Supportive Consultation

Phase 1   An initial training workshop for all staff
Teacher/classroom observations and confidential feedback
Student focus meetings to develop Individual Behavior Plans
A two-hour workshop for parents (Ending Homework Battles)
Training for playground and lunchroom supervisors

Phase 2   Two follow-up workshops and problem-solving sessions
Coaching and role-modeling in the classroom
Grade-level problem-solving groups
A two-hour workshop for parents (Ending Power Struggles with Logical Consequences)

Phase 3   Selected focus workshops for staff
Individual and small-group consultative support
A full-day training for trainers with materials for future training

Professional Consultative Support

Dr. MacKenzie and his staff will provide a minimum of twenty-four hours of consultative support that can be tailored to address the specific needs of your school. You choose the support options you want, and we will do the rest. Support options include: direct observations in the classroom, confidential feedback conferences, role-playing, problem-solving sessions, student focus meetings, training for cafeteria and yard duty supervisors, direct training and support for teachers in the classroom, and focus workshops on a wide variety of topics. Additional time will be billed at an hourly rate.

FOCUS WORKSHOPS TOPICS INCLUDE

- Teaching Students Good Work Habits
- Engagement Strategies for Effective Instruction
- Structuring the Classroom for Students with ADD
- Solving Problems with Homework
- Working with Challenging Parents
- Accommodating Students with Special Needs
- Conducting Effective Parent Conferences
- Bully-Proofing Students
- Managing Aggressive or Defiant Behavior
- Crisis Intervention
- Developing Individualized Behavior Support Plans
- Preferred Activity Time (PAT)
- Supporting Academically Discouraged Students
- Managing Untrustworthy Behavior
- Developing Individual Behavior Support Plans

Guidance Materials

Staff will receive copies of *Setting Limits in the Classroom, Setting Limits,* and *Setting Limits with Your Strong-Willed Child* in English or Spanish at a 30 percent discount, posters for the classroom, sample workshop flyers, sample letters to parents, sample office referrals, handouts for parents on solving problems with homework, materials on organizing the classroom for students with ADD, instructional training materials on Setting Limits in the Classroom, guides for developing Setting Limits parent workshops, and much more.

Sheldon Elementary School: A Case-Study Example

Sheldon Elementary School in Fairfield, California, is a typical example of the many elementary schools that have implemented the Setting Limits Program on a school-wide basis. They adopted our program five years ago and have been enjoying the benefits ever since. Sheldon Elementary is a kindergarten through sixth grade inner-city school with thirty-six credentialed staff members that serves a diverse population of students—Caucasian (15.9 percent), Hispanic (49.9 percent), African-American (18.4 percent), Asian (5.3 percent), Filipino (5.5 percent), and Pacific Islander (3.9 percent). English learners comprise 26 percent of the students; students with learning disabilities, 13 percent; and 69 percent of students are considered socioeconomically disadvantaged. Since implementing the Setting Limits Program, Sheldon Elementary has been well below the district average for school suspensions, expulsions, and office referrals.

When we first met with the principal and staff to introduce our Full Implementation Plan, we were pleased to realize our two essential conditions for a contract had been met: 100 percent commitment from the site administrator and a 70 percent commitment from staff. We knew they were ready for change. We signed a one-year service agreement, then scheduled dates for the initial training workshop, the first round of confidential classroom observations, and feedback sessions with the staff. The principal provided books, referral forms, and a full set of classroom guidance posters for each staff member. We were ready to go.

As at most schools, the Sheldon Elementary staff was a mixed bag of guidance and discipline practices prior to adopting our program. Some used Assertive Discipline. Others used color behavior cards. Some had permissive tendencies. A few were punitive, and some used a mixed approach. Although classroom management practices varied, the quality of instruction and respect toward students was very high. The school principal was very knowledgeable about classroom management and a highly effective leader.

After the initial workshop, we gave the teachers four to five weeks to practice their new skills in their classrooms before we began our confidential classroom observations. Phase 1 of our program was in full swing. During the observations, we are attentive to their skill levels in each of the four areas of classroom management—structure, relationship, engagement, and limit setting. The observations and feedback are not evaluative. Our goal is provide staff members with the feedback they need to recognize what's not working for them and improve their new skills.

Our observations confirmed what we suspected. Most staff members were off to a good start. Some relied too heavily on consequences because their classrooms lacked structure. Some were reluctant to let go of their old familiar discipline practices, such as the color cards and overuse of the office. Some had blind spots and didn't realize their permissive or punitive tendencies until it was pointed out to them. A few required additional role-modeling and individual training. A few dug in their heels and resisted. All of these are normal and expected steps in the change process. Changing old practices and habits takes time. There is no quick fix.

By week eight, the most aggressive researchers on each campus and the students with special behavioral needs really began to stick out. We arranged a series of student focus meetings to provide additional skill training and strategies for the teachers. Then we followed up with the principal regarding the issue of backup support and trained the playground and lunchroom supervisors. The staff as a whole had achieved a good overall level of skill proficiency. We were ready to move into phase 2.

By mid-November the Sheldon staff was ready for a booster shot. We scheduled two informal workshops to review the skill components, ask questions, problem solve, and refine skills. Most of these activities were carried out informally at staff meetings. We scheduled a series of focus workshops for the winter and spring that addressed special staff concerns such as Supporting Students with ADD/ADHD, Bully-Proofing

Students, PAT, and Developing Individual Support Plans. Teachers were adding new tools to their classroom management toolboxes, and they were enjoying more cooperation in their classrooms. The positive trend was infectious. Reluctant staff members started to buy in when they saw their colleagues enjoying success.

Bringing parents on board in support of the school's discipline program is a secondary goal of the Setting Limits Program and an important part of culture change. We offered a series of parent workshops on topics such as Ending Power Struggles, Supporting Rules with Natural and Logical Consequences, and Bully-Proofing Your Child. Parents appreciated the workshops. By April, we were ready to move into phase 3.

Phase 3 of our program is intended to consolidate gains made by all members of the staff, provide continued support for challenging students, and prepare the staff for what's ahead. This is when the leadership skills of the site administrator have their greatest impact. Change is still fragile at this point. Someone needs to provide the vital leadership component, keep the staff focused on its goals, and encourage them to stay on course.

Fortunately, Sheldon Elementary is blessed with effective leadership. The school principal fully supported the program and her staff as they pursued their goal. She participated in all of the workshops, mastered all the skill components, and participated in the training for trainers workshop at the end of the year. She requested a follow-up package of services to consolidate the gains and keep the ball rolling. The following year, she incorporated the Setting Limits Program into her school discipline policy and articulated that policy to teachers in a staff guide to school-wide expectations and to parents in the Sheldon Elementary School Handbook. The school achieved its goal of developing a school-wide discipline plan and it has become a model for other schools in the district.

A SAMPLE SETTING LIMITS DISCIPLINE PLAN

Sheldon Elementary School's Discipline Plan is too extensive to share in its entirety, so we've included some sections for you to peruse if you're looking for an example of an effective plan. Consequences for misbehavior in various settings of the campus are listed in appendix 2. The full plan is available upon request.

Sheldon Elementary School Discipline Policy and Procedures

Students are expected to behave in accordance with the above rules. They should be aware that there are consequences for failure to observe the rules. We intend that these consequences be logical and consistent. We also plan to use our best judgment and to be reasonable when dealing with individual students.

The primary mission of the school's discipline policy is to develop a structure of consistency in discipline using a proactive, preventative approach where students develop a respect for others, themselves, and learning. An important element of this policy is in how well the students understand the rules and consequences. Please use the book *Setting Limits in the Classroom* as your guide.

Classroom Rules and Consequences

Each teacher is responsible for maintaining student behavior through the use of our school-wide classroom management system, *Setting Limits in the Classroom*. All teachers are expected to have classroom rules and consequences posted in classrooms on the first day of school. All teachers will take the necessary time to teach, model, and practice the rules. If a child breaks a school or classroom rule outside of your class, you will be informed about the action of the student and the consequence given by any teacher, administrator, or yard supervisor. Records of written referrals are kept in the office.

Rules Throughout the Campus

The following three rules will be enforced, supported, and modeled by all students and adults on the Sheldon Elementary School campus.

Rule 1- Be Safe: Cooperate with Your Teacher and Classmates
Rule 2- Be Respectful: Respect the Rights and Property of Others
Rule 3- Be Responsible: Carry Out Your Student Responsibilities

- Keep track of books and assignments.
- Start your work on time and allow enough time to finish.
- Ask for help when you need it.
- Do your own work.
- Turn your work in on time.
- Accept responsibility for grades and consequences.

Classroom Behavior Management

Teachers are expected to manage behavior in and out of their classrooms. A classroom management system should be in place and followed consistently. An effective behavior management system is one that reinforces positive behavior and has logical consequences for negative behavior. Children at Sheldon respond quite favorably to positive reinforcement. All teachers are expected to implement Setting Limits in the Classroom. It is our school-wide behavior management plan.

Each teacher is responsible for turning in their written classroom management procedures to the principal during the first week of school. This will help administrators in dealing with children who are sent to the office. The procedures should indicate sequentially, by steps, when parents are contacted and at what point a child is sent out of the room. Students are to be sent to the office if they have committed a suspendable offense. When students are sent to the office for support, we will assume that all steps of your management plan have been followed and that all other efforts have been exhausted.

Tips for Successful Classroom Management

- Review *Setting Limits in the Classroom*.
- Review rules and procedures frequently.
- Make students aware of consequences and rewards for positive behavior.
- Emphasize expected standards of conduct and procedures prior to beginning activities.

- Save yourself stress by delivering negative consequences calmly. Anger begets anger and soon a situation that may have required only a time-out turns into a suspension.
- Parents should be notified at the first sign of trouble.
- Establish a buddy system for time-outs. Students sent to other rooms must be offered a desk and chair or a seat at a table.
- For safety reasons, students should not be sent out of the room to stand outside the door or sit on the bench.
- *Use the office as a last resort.* The situation should warrant a suspension, either on or off campus. The back of the suspension form lists Ed. Code suspendable offenses.
- When writing the office referral, please convey the seriousness of the situation.
- Treat all students with respect. This is especially important when reprimanding or redirecting. Remember to consider the dignity of the child.

Two-stage Time-out Procedure

All teachers are expected to select a "time-out buddy teacher." You and your buddy teacher will exchange students for time-out as needed. Teachers are highly encouraged to select a teacher from another grade level (for example, grades one through three should select a buddy teacher from grades four through six). The referring teacher will provide work or an activity for their student to carry out during time-out. Time-outs should not exceed twenty minutes.

Behaviors Resulting in Lunch Detention or Quiet Table Assignment

- Classroom disruptions
- Lack of respect for others (teasing, name-calling, talking about someone's mother, etc.)
- Eating outside the cafeteria
- Being in the wrong or restricted area of campus (hallway, park, behind portables)
- Running/moving after the freeze bell
- Getting drinks after the bell has rung

Behavior Resulting in Lunch or After-School Detention

- Second Level 1 infraction
- Disrespectful language (verbal or body language)
- Pushing/shoving
- Taking and/or destroying someone else's property
- Not actively participating in detention

Behaviors Resulting in After-School or In-House Suspension

- Second Level 2 infraction
- Leaving school grounds or activities without permission
- Bullying or making threats
- Forgery
- Inciting violence (encouraging or watching student fight)
- Throwing objects that may cause injury
- Not actively participating in detention
- Verbal assault

ADMINISTRATIVE CONSEQUENCES

When a student is referred to the office, the parents will be notified via a phone call and/or a home visit. Students will receive the disciplinary action deemed appropriate, such as in-school suspension or suspension.

Immediate Office Referral
(State Educational Code Violations)

Students exhibiting any of these behaviors must be written up on a discipline referral and sent immediately to the office.

- Caused, attempted to cause, or threatened to cause physical injury to another person
- Caught stealing or trying to steal
- Caught damaging or attempting to damage school property

- Committed an obscene act or habitual profanity
- Willfully and habitually defying school authority
- Possession of a gun, knife, explosive (or replica of a gun, knife, or explosive), or drug
- Sexual harassment

Behaviors Resulting in Off-Campus Suspension
(State Education Code)

- Extortion, coercion, or blackmail
- Misdemeanor robbery or theft
- Engaging in inappropriate sexual or physical contact, sexual harassment, or sexual abuse whether by word or gesture
- Possession of matches, lighter, or tobacco
- Violating school safety rules (such as pulling fire alarm, playing during fire drill, etc.)
- Committing physical assault
- Committing public lewdness
- Engaging in conduct containing the elements of retaliation against any school employee
- Criminal mischief if punishable as a felony, whether committed on or off campus
- Using, possessing, or exhibiting a firearm, club, or other prohibited weapon
- Arson
- Retaliation against a school employee

Enjoying the Rewards

If this book has fulfilled its mission, you and your school should have the tools and information you need to correct your old mistakes and begin setting limits more effectively. You've discovered many of the obstacles to effective teaching and learning: punitive and permissive guidance styles, soft limits, negative motivational approaches, and the classroom dances that wear us out and make our jobs so difficult. You've learned a variety of effective methods to help you achieve your guidance goals. You know how to prevent power struggles by giving clear messages, how to inspire cooperation with encouraging messages, and how to increase on-task time with positive motivation, PAT, and instructional engagement strategies. You know how to teach responsibility and good work habits, and how to support your rules with effective consequences that don't injure feelings or damage relationships. You know how to use parents and the office for backup support, how to manage crises, and provide support for that small percentage of students that require more than classroom management to be successful at school. Your preparation is complete. The next step is to put your skills into practice and begin enjoying the rewards of your efforts.

The immediate rewards will be stopping misbehavior quickly and effectively, getting better cooperation from your students, and eliminating all those stressful dances that wear you down and leave you feeling so frustrated and discouraged. Soon you'll be hassling less and enjoying your students more. You'll also have the satisfaction of knowing that you're teaching your guidance lessons in the clearest and most understandable way.

The long-term rewards of your efforts should be the most satisfying of all because your methods will be laying a foundation for cooperative and satisfying relationships with students for years to come. By your example, you will be teaching a cooperative process of communication and problem solving that your students will need to be successful, not only at school but out in the world. The skills you teach in the classroom are the skills your students will carry forward. Enjoy setting limits.

Setting Limits Companion Guide

BEHAVIOR	LOGICAL CONSEQUENCE	REPEAT OCCURRENCES
Entering/exiting the classroom in an unacceptable manner (loud, raucous, running, pushing)	Try-it-again (reenter correctly)	Assign Recess Academy (3–5 repetitions of practice)
Bringing unacceptable items into the classroom (e.g., food, candy, electronic devices, toys, hats, etc.)	Limited choices to put item away or remove until end of day if it is out again	Remove the item and return it at the end of the instructional day or week
Sitting in a chair or at desk unacceptably	Loss of chair temporarily (5 minutes)	Recess Academy to practice sitting appropriately for 5 minutes
Blurting out or interrupting during instruction	Enter student's name in the Blurt Box first occurrence, 2nd occurrence is a check by student's name and first-stage time-out, 3rd occurrence is another check and first-stage time-out and assign Recess Academy to practice raising a quiet hand	Phone call to parents requesting help at home to practice the skill of not interrupting
Talking during instruction	Separate students temporarily. Move the desk or use a Stage One Time-Out if necessary	Change seating arrangements during recess with students
Not attending to or following directions	Check-in, clarify understanding, ask student to repeat directions, give information if necessary	Recess Academy to practice listening or following directions; consider buddy-helper
Wasting or misuse of instructional time	Recess Academy to make up time	Contact parent to practice at home with student

BEHAVIOR	LOGICAL CONSEQUENCE	REPEAT OCCURRENCES
Failure to complete work in a timely manner	Set timer, make up work during recess or add to homework	Ticket-In/Ticket-Out
Misuse/abuse of privileges	Temporarily remove or modify privilege	Parent/teacher/student conference
When students fail to cooperate during an activity	Temporarily separate student from that activity	Practice necessary skill during Recess Academy
When students make messes	Students clean it up	When done intentionally, student cleans up during their time (recess, lunch, after school)
When students try to hook us in to arguments or debates during instruction	Use cutoff procedure and separate the student from you	Recess Academy to practice the skill of not arguing
When students distract their classmates	Temporarily separate distracting student from peers (possible Stage One Time-Out)	Parent/teacher/student conference
When students arrive to class unprepared	Use classroom rental center for supplies	Notify parents
Disruptions	Separate student from group, Stage One Time-Out	Recess Academy to practice respectful behavior, involve parents if behavior continues
Attention-seeking, clowning around, inappropriate sounds	Stage One Time-Out	Recess Academy to practice appropriate behavior, involve parents if behavior continues
Arguing or disrespectful behavior	Limited choices with cutoff procedure, follow up with time-out if necessary	Recess Academy to practice, involve parents if behavior continues
Hurtful or unacceptable language	Stage One Time-Out, teach appropriate skills/language at Recess Academy	Parent/teacher/student conference, parents practice with student at home
Failure to master basic skills (i.e., lining up, entering/exiting class, quiet hand, passing papers, etc.)	Try-it-again	Recess Academy to practice, involve parents if not mastered after 4–6 weeks
Angry outbursts	Cooldown or Stage One Time-Out depending on circumstances	Parent/teacher/student conference, involve other staff as needed (administrator, school psychologist, etc.)
When students continue to misbehave in Stage One Time-Out	Move on to Stage Two Time-Out	Disruption in stage two, administrator to determine further consequences (OCS, suspension)

BEHAVIOR	LOGICAL CONSEQUENCE	REPEAT OCCURRENCES
Noncompliant or limit-testing behavior (refusal to follow directions or accept consequences)	Give limited choices and follow through with logical consequence (e.g., "You can do what you were asked, or you can owe me the time you waste during your recess or after school. What would you like to do?") Ask student privately, "Can we work this out between ourselves, or do we need some help from your parents?"	Involve parents. Parent/teacher/student conference; involve administrator if necessary
When mid-level behavior problems persist after six weeks of using logical consequences	Use parents in the problem-solving process	Involve administrator in the problem-solving process
When student continues to misbehave in Stage Two Time-Out	Administrator to determine consequences (OCS, suspension)	Parent/teacher/administrator/ student conference; SST (Student Study Team); involve school psychologist
Defiant behavior (refusal to follow directions or accept consequences)	Give limited choices to keep the responsibility on the student: "You can do what you were asked to do or you can spend some quiet time in time-out getting ready to do it. What would you like to do?"	If student continues to defy: "You may not be ready to be in this class right now. You need to make a decision about what the rest of your day is going to look like. Do we need to call the office? I'll give you a minute to think about it." Call for backup support from the office
If student refuses to go to Stage One Time-Out	"You can go to Stage One now or to Stage Two for twice as long: What would you like to do?"	Follow through with Stage Two
If student refuses to leave the class when asked to go to Stage Two Time-Out	"You can go to stage-two now like I've asked you to, or I can call someone to escort you out of my class and you won't be back for the rest of the day. I'll give you a minute to decide what you'd like to do." Then follow through	If student continues to refuse or does not leave, immediately call for backup support from the office
Ed. Code violations, crises, emergencies	Call administrator immediately	Consequences specified by Ed. Code

Sheldon Elementary
Consequences for Misbehavior

AREA	BE SAFE	BE RESPECTFUL	BE RESPONSIBLE	CONSEQUENCE
Cafeteria	• Keep all food on trays and to self. • Remain seated and facing table. • Walk from place to place.	• Allow anyone to sit next to you. • Use quiet voices and appropriate language. • Follow adult directions.	• Stay in your seat until dismissed. • Place cartons and trash in garbage cans. Place recyclables in blue lid cans. • Get adult help for accidents and spills. • Use utensils correctly. • Use hall/bathroom pass for leaving the area. • Stay in your designated area.	• Finish lunch at quiet table.
Playground/Recess	• Run only in designated areas. • Stay within boundaries. • Be aware of activities and games around you. • No rough play or fighting. • Use equipment appropriately. • Freeze at bell. • Walk to line when whistle blows. • Walk with balls & equipment when returning them.	• Play fairly. • Include everyone. • Share equipment. • Use appropriate language. • No walls are to be used for wall ball. • Follow directions the first time.	• Stay in your designated area.	• Loss of recess privilege for part or all of that recess (sit on bench).

AREA	BE SAFE	BE RESPECTFUL	BE RESPONSIBLE	CONSEQUENCE
Passing Areas, Halls, Breezeways, Sidewalk	• Stay to the right. • Allow others to pass. • Use appropriate language. • Keep hands, feet and objects to self.	• Hold the door open for the person behind you. • Respect hallway displays. • Follow adult directions.	• Stay on sidewalks. • Have appropriate pass in your possession.	• Recess Academy: Practice appropriate skills during recess.
Bathrooms	• Keep water in the sink. • Wash hands. • Put towel in garbage can. • Keep feet on floor.	• Knock on stall door. • Give people privacy. • Use quiet voices.	• Use toilets appropriately. • Flush toilet after use. • Return to room promptly. • Use a bathroom pass.	• Temporary loss of unsupervised bathroom privileges. • Review rules and expectations with the teacher.
Arrival/ Dismissal Zones	• Wait in designated areas. • Keep hands, feet, and objects to self.	• Follow adult directions. • Use appropriate language.	• Stand calmly until gates open. • Walk onto/off school grounds.	• Be under direct adult supervision during arrival and dismissals for several days. • Practice appropriate behavior at Recess Academy.
Assemblies/ Special Events	• Sit quietly during presentation. • Wait for dismissal instructions. • Keep hands, feet, and objects to self.	• Focus on presentation. • Listen to and respond politely. • Keep feet still.	• Listen responsibly. • Applaud appropriately. • Stay seated in assigned area. • Enter and leave through assigned doors.	• Sit next to teacher during assemblies/ special events. • Review skills with teacher.
Gym	• Sit properly. • Report all injuries to supervisor immediately. • Appropriate shoes and attire are required. • Bicycles, skateboards, scooters, Rollerblades, and roller skates prohibited. • When a blood-related injury occurs, stop activity and notify supervisor immediately.	• No food or beverages in gym. • Due to safety considerations, only scheduled recreational activities will be permitted. • Smoking, tobacco, and gum are prohibited. • Spirited competition is encouraged; however, abusive language, fighting, and/ or inappropriate behavior will not be tolerated.	• Personal belongings are not permitted in gym. Please utilize stage or perimeter of gym for storage of all items.	• Temporary loss of gym privileges (sit on bench). • Practice appropriate skills during Recess Academy.

AREA	BE SAFE	BE RESPECTFUL	BE RESPONSIBLE	CONSEQUENCE
Classroom	• Keep hands, feet, and objects to self. • Use materials appropriately.	• Don't distract others. • Use quiet voices and appropriate language. • Follow adult directions.	• Have needed materials. • Have homework. • Complete all assigned work. • Leave classroom with pass only.	• Enforce logical consequences specified in classroom posters.
All Common Areas	• Walk facing forward. • Keep hands, feet, and objects to self. • Get adult help for accidents and spills.	• Use kind words and actions. • Wait for your turn. • Clean up after yourself. • Follow adult directions. • Use quiet voices and appropriate language.	• Follow school rules. • Remind others to follow school rules. • Take proper care of all personal belongings and school equipment. • Be honest. • Have a hall pass.	• Recess Academy.

APPENDIX 3

Suggestions for Getting Started

We recommend starting off with the skills listed in the following sections for students of different ages. We've also included a suggested schedule for adding new skills. These suggestions are based on our experiences with teachers in our staff development workshops, but you may prefer to add new skills to your repertoire at a faster or slower rate.

We encourage you to go at a pace that is comfortable for you. For some, this may mean adding one or two new skills each week, but for others it may mean adding one new skill every two or three weeks. There is no one correct way, but we caution you against trying to learn too much too quickly. The important thing is to learn the methods and use them consistently.

You should expect to make mistakes as you begin practicing the methods. That's okay. The more you practice, the more proficient you will become. If you are having particular difficulty with any one method, refer back to the pertinent chapter for assistance. Note the specific language used to carry out each technique in the examples.

Getting Started with Preschool Students

WEEK 1
    Introduce rules to students (Ch. 1)
    Begin establishing procedures and routines (Ch.1)
    Use encouraging messages (Ch. 2)
    Use limited choices (Ch. 9)
    Use clear verbal messages (Ch. 9)
    Use logical consequences (Ch. 11)
    Introduce time-out procedure (Ch. 13)

WEEK 2

> Continue practicing procedures and routines
> Add one or two new procedures and routines
> Practice transitions
> Add check-in, cutoff, cooldown procedures (Ch. 10)
> Add "try-it-again" (Ch. 12)
> Add role-modeling (Ch. 12)

WEEK 3

> Continue adding a few new procedures and routines and practice

WEEKS 4 AND 5

> Schedule conferences with parents for students who continue to require additional support from home

Getting Started with Elementary School Students

1ST DAY

> Introduce rules and student responsibilities
> Teach and practice procedures and transitions
> Describe guidance procedures, time-out, and PAT (Chs. 1, 4, 13)

WEEK ONE

> Send home rules, student responsibilities, accountability procedures, guidance procedures, grading, and homework standards (Ch. 1)
> Practice procedures and transitions (Ch. 1)
> Introduce Stage Two Time-Out (Ch. 13)
> Use clear verbal messages (Ch. 9)
> Use limited choices and logical consequences (Chs. 9, 11)
> Use encouraging messages (Ch. 2)
> Provide many opportunities for students to earn PAT (Ch. 4)
> Introduce Blurt Box and Recess Academy (Chs. 11, 12)

WEEK TWO

> Review rules, student responsibilities, accountability procedures, guidance procedures
> Add more procedures and routines and practice transitions
> Provide many opportunities for students to earn PAT
> Add check-in, cutoff, cooldown procedures (Ch. 10)
> Begin using the Blurt Box and Recess Academy
> Add "try-it-again" and "role-modeling" (Ch. 12)
> Expect testing
> Practice giving limited choices
> Follow through with logical consequences
> Use Two-Stage Time-Out procedure as needed

WEEK THREE

Continue adding and practicing procedures, routines, transitions

Expect testing and follow through with consequences

Use Blurt Box and Recess Academy

Use Two-Stage Time-Out procedure

Provide many opportunities for students to earn PAT

WEEK FOUR

Continue adding and practicing procedures, routines, and transitions

Expect testing and follow through with consequences

Arrange Recess Academy for small group/individual practice for students who test
excessively or fail to master basic skills

Begin specific interventions for students with special needs (Chs. 17, 18)

WEEK FIVE

Expect testing from some students

Arrange parent/teacher/student conferences for students who test excessively or fail to
comply with rules and standards, or for students with insufficient grades

Continue with interventions for students with special needs

WEEKS SIX THROUGH EIGHT

Inform administrator of students who continue to test excessively after interventions have
been used consistently for at least two to four weeks and may require backup support

Consider developing individual behavior intervention plans for students who are not
responding to intervention

Teacher Study Group Guide

This book is designed to be used as a skills-training manual for teacher study groups. Study groups provide a supportive format for practicing and improving your guidance and discipline skills during the critical first eight weeks of your skills-training experience. The following suggestions will help you get started.

Suggested length: The recommended length for the group is eight weeks. Group sessions are usually sixty to ninety minutes long.

Preparation for study groups: We recommend that all participants read the entire book prior to becoming involved in a group. This preparation will lead to a much richer experience.

Study group leaders: Ideally, a teacher study group leader will have a solid working command of the material in the book as well as formal training in child development, education, or child guidance. Teachers, guidance counselors, school psychologists, school administrators, and special education support staff are all good candidates for study group leaders.

Overview of Study Sessions

WEEK 1

Objective: Participants will develop an understanding of the importance of structure and learn specific strategies for improving structure in their classroom and maintaining that structure throughout the year.

Preparation: Read chapter 1.

WEEK 2

Objective: Participants will learn how to build positive relationships and inspire children's cooperation through the power of encouragement and positive motivation. They will learn how to keep students fully engaged throughout the learning process with a variety of strategies.

Preparation: Read chapters 2 and 3.

WEEK 3

Objective: Participants will learn how to inspire cooperation, increase on-task time, and teach responsibility by using Preferred Activity Time (PAT).

Preparation: Read chapter 4.

WEEK 4

Objective: Participants will discover their own guidance approach, how students learn classroom rules based on their temperaments, the importance of effective teaching in the guidance process, and the classroom dance they may use to get cooperation.

Preparation: Review chapters 5, 6, and 7.

WEEK 5

Objective: Participants will identify the type of limits they use in the classroom, how to give clear messages, and how to stop power struggles and classroom dances.

Preparation: Review chapters 8, 9, and 10.

WEEK 6

Objective: Participants will learn how and when to use logical consequences, Recess Academy, and the Two-Stage Time-Out procedure.

Preparation: Review chapters 11, 12, and 13.

WEEK 7

Objective: Participants will learn strategies for managing extreme behavior, and the appropriate use of parents and the office for backup support.

Preparation: Review chapters 14, 15, and 16.

WEEK 8

Objective: Participants will develop an understanding of the small percentage of students with ADD/ADHD and other special needs who require more than effective classroom management and learn strategies and accommodations to support these students.

Preparation: Review chapters 17 and 18.

Study Group Discussion Questions

Study questions that cover themes and methods are provided for each chapter. The questions are intended to get participants involved with the skill-training material and to give them opportunities to discuss their experiences in a supportive setting. All study group participants are encouraged to practice the methods with their students in their classrooms and share their experiences during the study group sessions.

Don't feel limited by the questions we've provided. These are only suggestions for discussion. Feel free to add additional questions that might help participants become better acquainted with the material. We also recommend setting aside the last fifteen to twenty minutes of each session for a question-and-answer period.

CHAPTER 1

1. Discuss the ten mistaken beliefs many teachers hold about structure. Have you neglected structure for any of these reasons? What changes will you make in the way you approach structure in the future?
2. What components of your classroom structure should you plan before your students arrive? Why is it important to do so?
3. Discuss rules in theory versus rules in practice. What type of rules do you teach your students? Which of the three teachers in the examples do you most closely resemble?
4. What are your expectations regarding your students' work habits and organizational skills? How do you teach these skills? How do you communicate your expectations to parents?
5. What accountability procedures should you use to teach your students to be responsible for arriving to class promptly and prepared? What steps should you take when students fail to complete assigned class work or homework? What steps can you take when your students repeatedly fail to follow classroom procedures such as lining up, entering, or exiting the classroom properly?
6. Discuss the three-step model for teaching procedures. Spend some time reviewing the procedures listed in this chapter and prioritize them. Decide how and when you will teach them to your students.
7. What are the goals of an effective seating arrangement? What factors do you take into consideration when developing a seating plan? How will you determine which seating arrangement is best for your class? How will you assign students to their seats on the first day of school?
8. Discuss the importance of classroom jobs. Which classroom jobs will you have and how will they be assigned to students?
9. What steps can you take to enlist parent support and cooperation? Do you clearly articulate to parents your classroom rules, guidance and discipline procedures, homework and grading policy, and expectations for work habits at the beginning of the year? Do you make early contact to discuss behavioral concerns or wait until the first parent-teacher conference or end of the report period? What changes will you make?

CHAPTER 2

1. Discuss the importance of developing positive relationships with your students, both individually and as a class. How can you help foster positive relationships among your students?
2. What is the primary developmental task of early and middle childhood? How does that relate to why some students are fearful in learning situations? How can teachers help students overcome that fear?
3. Can you identify your motivational style? What type of motivational messages do you use in the classroom? Positive messages? Negative messages? Do you spend as much time catching your students cooperating and being respectful as you do catching them being uncooperative and disrespectful? Is your motivational approach effective with all of your students? Compliant, strong-willed, and all other students?
4. What do positive messages inspire? Why? What do negative messages inspire? Why?
5. Why do negative, discouraging messages and practices often backfire as motivational tools? Discuss the limitations of negative motivational messages and practices. Do you intentionally or unintentionally use these messages and/or practices? Share your observations based on your experiences with children.
6. Imagine you're at a staff meeting, and the agenda topic is ineffective guidance practices. Without warning, your supervisor shares an ineffective practice he observed you use in your classroom. How would you respond? Would you feel embarrassed? Ashamed? Singled out? Humiliated? Would this motivate you to try harder to improve? Would you approach your supervisor after the meeting and tell him that you really appreciated his comments and that you'll be a much better teacher because of it? Put yourself in the position of a student, and imagine what it feels like to be singled out and humiliated in front of your peers.
7. Why are positive, encouraging messages more likely to achieve their intended motivational effect? What basic needs do these messages address?
8. Discuss guidelines for using positive, encouraging messages. Where should the focus of our encouraging messages be?
9. How can teachers increase the motivational power of their efforts to encourage? Discuss strategies for involving parents in the encouragement process.

CHAPTER 3

1. Discuss the importance of engaging students in the teaching and learning process. What effect does student engagement have on student achievement? What happens if we fail to engage students in our lessons?
2. Discuss the strategies that hook students in to a lesson. Why are they effective? What benefits do you see in using the KWL chart? How could

you incorporate it into your lesson plans? What importance does a
"Picture Walk" serve? What lessons could you incorporate the use of this
strategy into? Discuss other ways to use the Concept Carousel to engage
students.

3. Why should teachers consider how they call on and respond to students
during instruction? What are some of the effective guidelines for calling
on and responding to students? How could you use the scaffolding
strategy in your daily lessons?

4. How are Think/Pair/Share and Numbered Heads Together useful for
student engagement? List ideas for using each of these strategies in your
classroom.

5. What are the benefits of using the quick-write strategy?

6. What are the benefits of having your students use whiteboards and
response cards during instruction?

7. Discuss the importance of teaching students to mastery. What happens
if we move on too quickly to another student when the first student is
unable to answer the question? What message do we send to the students
when we hold them accountable for their learning and teach to mastery?

8. What are some ways teachers can make learning relevant beyond the
lesson and help students retain the information they've learned?

9. Talk about other games and strategies you use with your students.

CHAPTER 4

1. Discuss the benefits of the PAT group incentive system. What lessons
is it designed to teach? What are some of the built-in components that
contribute to its effectiveness?

2. What are automatic time bonuses? When are they used? Make a list
of possible situations for awarding automatic time bonuses in your
classroom and assign a time amount to each.

3. What is an unexpected time bonus? Discuss possible situations for
awarding unexpected time bonuses in your classroom. How much time
should be awarded?

4. What is a "hurry-up" bonus? Discuss possible situations for awarding
hurry-up bonuses in your classroom.

5. What is the purpose of penalties? How should they be used? How should
they be recorded? Describe typical off-task behaviors in your classroom
that might warrant time penalties. Why is it important to show bonuses
and penalties, rather than just bonuses? Why not just start with thirty
minutes and take time off when students do not cooperate? What
message does that send?

6. How does PAT contribute to developing positive relationships and
student engagement?

7. Discuss ways to use PAT during small-group or differentiated-instruction
time. What are the benefits?

8. When is it appropriate to use the Teacher-Student Game? How often should young children be rewarded with the PAT they've earned? Make a list of some quick, simple things you can do with your students at the end of a lesson if they "win" the Teacher-Student Game.
9. What are the three primary teacher duties in the PAT incentive system? Why is the teacher's role as timekeeper such a critically important aspect of the PAT system? What's the best way to record time and prevent arguments or protests of unfairness? Why is it important that the teacher be part of the game or activity?
10. Generate a list of possible PAT activities your students might enjoy. How should you approach this topic? What types of learning activities are fun for you?
11. Discuss some of the mistakes teachers make that sabotage the effectiveness of the PAT group-incentive system.
12. What should you do if you have students who try to set up your PAT system to fail? When should a student be offered an individual activity rather than being required to participate in large-group activities?

CHAPTER 5

1. Mr. Harris is a substitute teacher in a fifth-grade classroom. After recess, several students enter the classroom in a loud and disruptive manner. Mr. Harris approaches them and announces that he expects students to enter the classroom quietly and ready to learn. Is he teaching his rules concretely? Is his message complete?
2. Is limit testing normal behavior? Why do students do it? What questions are they trying to answer?
3. How does temperament influence limit testing and learning styles? Discuss the different ways that compliant and strong-willed students test limits. Why are strong-willed students referred to as aggressive researchers?
4. How do you respond to the aggressive researchers in your class? Do you react with annoyance and irritation? Do you sometimes personalize their aggressive research? How do you react to their disrespectful attitude?
5. Based on what you know about your guidance approach, are you teaching your rules in the clearest and most understandable way for the strong-willed students in your class?

CHAPTER 6

1. Can you identify your guidance approach? Are you permissive? Punitive or autocratic? Mixed? Or do you tend to be more democratic? Describe the specific things you say and what you do when your students misbehave. Then, diagram the steps. Ask for feedback from others. Does the feedback validate your suspicions?

2. Why are the punitive, permissive, and mixed training models poorly matched to those students who cause most of the classroom discipline problems and need guidance the most: strong-willed students? How do they respond? What lessons do they learn?

3. Is your guidance approach a good match for all of your students, or does it predispose you to certain types of conflicts with certain types of students?

4. How do students respond to permissive guidance practices? What lessons does this approach teach children about rules, authority, power, and control? What type of learning environment do permissive guidance practices promote? What kinds of relationships usually develop?

5. How do students respond to punitive guidance practices? Is shaming, blaming, and humiliation appropriate in the classroom? What type of learning environment do these practices promote? What types of relationships usually develop?

6. Discuss the advantages of democratic guidance practices. Why is the democratic approach best matched to the full range of students? What type of learning environment do these practices promote? What type of relationships do these practices foster?

7. What lessons do children learn about cooperation, respect, power, and authority in democratic learning environments?

8. Describe the range of guidance practices among your staff. How would you rate the level of consistency among staff members at your school? Low? Moderate? High? What effect does the consistency or inconsistency have on students at your school?

CHAPTER 7

1. Have you been stuck in a classroom dance? If so, let's diagram the steps you usually take to handle classroom misbehavior. Write down how you begin your dance. Do you begin with a clear message? Is the focus of your message on the behavior you want to stop or increase, or is the focus on attitude, feelings, or something else? How do you usually feel when you start your dance? Calm and controlled? Irritated and annoyed? Angry or upset? Write this down at the beginning of your diagram.

2. Write down all of the steps in your dance that rely primarily on words. If you can, write them in the order they typically occur. Next, write down the steps in your dance that involve action or consequences. If you become irritated, annoyed, or angry during your dance, indicate that on your diagram.

3. Draw a circle around all the steps in your dance that rely primarily on words. Then, draw a box around all the steps in your dance that involve action.

4. Count the total number of steps you take in a dance. How many involve words? How many invoke action? Let's see what steps are working for you. Are your verbal steps effective in stopping the misbehavior of your strong-willed or difficult-to-manage students? Are your action steps effective in stopping their misbehavior?

5. Let's analyze your dance. Based on what you've read in this chapter, how would you describe your dance? Permissive? Punitive? Mixed? Estimate how many times you perform this dance each day and each week and each month. Multiply the monthly estimate by nine to get an annual figure. Now rate how much stress you feel during your dances. Low? Moderate? High? Are you beginning to get a better picture of the wear and tear you're experiencing? Are you at risk for burnout?

6. Do you think your dance might be entertaining for some students? Discuss the concept of "reinforcement error." Does it apply in your case?

7. What changes do you need to make to help your verbal steps become clearer?

8. How do students usually respond to your action steps? With cooperation? With anger and resentment? Do they sometimes retaliate? What changes do you need to make to help your action steps become more effective?

9. Draw a new diagram reflecting the changes you need to make.

10. Is your new message clear, firm, and respectful? Do you communicate it succinctly without anger, drama, or strong emotion? Congratulations! You're beginning to chart a new course toward effectiveness.

CHAPTER 8

1. Have you been using soft limits in the classroom? If so, what messages are these ineffective signals giving your students about your rules, your authority, and cooperation?

2. What are teachers really saying when they repeat and remind students to cooperate?

3. Why are speeches and lectures not meaningful consequences for many students? What's missing from these messages?

4. What message do we send students when we ignore misbehavior in the classroom? Is the absence of a red light equivalent to a green light?

5. When we argue, bargain, or negotiate with students about our rules, what are we really saying about our rules and our authority?

6. What are the disadvantages of using bribes and special rewards to gain cooperation in the classroom?

7. Miss Roberts, a fifth-grade teacher, teaches her lesson while several of her students carry on conversations and distract others. She intervenes. "I need a little less talking and a little more listening," she says, with an annoyed look on her face. What does "a little less talking" mean? What kind of message is she giving? What kind of response can she anticipate from her disruptive students?

CHAPTER 9

Directions: In each of the following situations, an unacceptable student behavior is followed by an ineffective message from the teacher. Analyze each message. Is it clear and specific? Is the focus on behavior? Is the message communicated in matter-of-fact terms? Does the student have all the information he or she needs to correct the behavior? Replace the ineffective message with a clear message.

1. Mr. Carol's third-grade class lines up for recess, when he notices that one of his students, Jeff, has left books and papers lying all over his desk. Mr. Carol asks Jeff to return to his desk to put the items away. Jeff complies, but when he returns to the line, several students refuse to let him have his old place back. Jeff becomes angry and gives one of them a push. Mr. Carol intervenes: "I'll bet Tim didn't like that, Jeff. I really wish you'd try to be more considerate."

2. Steve, a fourth grader, leans back in his chair to the point of falling over. His concerned teacher intervenes: "I'll bet your parents wouldn't let you sit like that at home," says the teacher. "I'm afraid you might get hurt."

3. James, a sixth grader, is annoyed with the student who sits behind him. James turns around and calls the student a shithead. The teacher intervenes: "James, I wonder what the principal would think if he heard that kind of language. Do you think we can allow students to talk that way in class? Come on. Think for a change."

4. Sharon, a second grader, interrupts her teacher during instruction by blurting out comments without raising her hand. Her teacher responds: "When you interrupt, it makes it difficult for me to teach, and it's not fair to others who raise their hands and wait to be called on."

5. Late reading group is finishing up when several students enter the classroom laughing, talking loudly, and disrupting. The teacher intervenes: "Hey, guys, can't you see there is learning going on in here? I'd appreciate it if you would try to come in a little more quietly."

CHAPTER 10

1. Shawna, a sixth grader, reads a teen magazine during instruction. When her teacher asks Shawna to put it away, Shawna attempts to engage her teacher in an argument about whether reading magazines in class should be allowed. How should Shawna's teacher handle this?

2. When his teacher asks him to turn around and stop talking, Miles, a fourth grader, responds angrily. "Why are you always picking on me?" he shouts. How should his teacher handle this?

3. When the teacher asks the class to clear off their desks and get ready for recess, he notices one student doesn't respond. "Did he hear my instructions?" the teacher wonders. What should the teacher say next?

4. Jake, a third grader, cheats in a game of four square. Several students complain. Jake insists he's innocent. What should the teacher say to Jake?

5. There are ten minutes until recess, and Jana, a second grader, hasn't even started copying her spelling words from the board. Her teacher suspects Jana is trying to avoid the task altogether. How should the teacher handle it?

6. Cheryl, a fifth grader, talks to a classmate during the first fifteen minutes of instruction. The teacher asks Cheryl to take a seat at the back table. Reluctantly Cheryl complies but gives the teacher a look of disgust. How should the teacher handle this?

7. Keenan, a sixth grader, gets caught playing with his pocket-size video game during instruction. When the teacher asks Keenan to hand it over, he apologizes and pleads for a second chance. How should the teacher handle this?

8. Discuss the difference between attitude and misbehavior. How do you respond to displays of poor attitude? Do you get hooked? Where do you draw the line between poor attitude and misbehavior? Do you agree that role-modeling firmness and respect is more effective than reacting to provocative attitude?

9. Do you tend to personalize your students' misbehavior? Do you sometimes lose your composure and say or do more than is needed? Is it liberating for you to step back and view misbehavior as the student's problem, not yours?

CHAPTER 11

1. Why are consequences a necessary element in the teaching-and-learning process?

2. How is punitive thinking different from logical thinking? Discuss your observations about how students respond to punitive consequences in the classroom based on their temperaments. How do compliant students usually respond? How do strong-willed students respond? How do you respond to punitive consequences?

3. Mrs. Huntington uses a color card guidance system in her classroom. The first time students misbehave, she asks them to pull a yellow card and place it under their name on a board. The second time, she asks them to pull a green card. The third time, she asks them to pull a red card, and they lose their next recess. Then, they start over again. Discuss the advantages and disadvantages of this guidance approach.

4. Grant, a sixth grader, receives his third tardy slip in Mr. Garren's class. Grant knows he'll have to spend an hour in detention after school that day. The next day after class, Mr. Garren pulls Grant aside and gives him a lecture on the importance of promptness. Was this effective? If not, why?

5. What problems can you anticipate when the classroom teacher and office administrator operate from very different guidance models? What problems can you anticipate when staff operate from very different guidance models?

6. Sean, a fifth grader, knows it's not okay to bring comic books to class, but he decides to do it anyway and gets caught. If you were Sean's teacher, how would you handle the situation? What would you say? What would you do?

7. Randall, a third grader, pretends to pick his nose and then wipe it on the child who sits next to him in his table group. If you were Randall's teacher, how would you handle this? What would you say? What would you do?

8. There are ten minutes left until recess, and Sherry, a first grader, hasn't started copying the spelling words from the blackboard. If you were Sherry's teacher, how would you handle this? What would you say? What would you do?

9. Taylor, a third grader, is supposed to be working quietly at his desk but decides to clown around and disturb others in his desk group. His teacher sends Taylor to the back table to work by himself. As he heads to the back table, his teacher adds, "If you continue to behave like a brat, you're going to find yourself at the back table a lot." Is this an example of a logical consequence? What would make this consequence more effective?

10. Describe the steps in using the Blurt Box with your students. Practice using the Blurt Box with your group. How will you introduce it to your students?

11. Discuss the importance of using logical consequences with students with ADD/ADHD or other special needs. How can you make accommodations for these students?

CHAPTER 12

1. What is the ultimate goal of Recess Academy? Discuss the benefits of using Recess Academy with students who fail to master basic behavioral skills. Why is it beneficial to practice these skills on the students' time?

2. How is Recess Academy different from the practice of taking away recess?

3. How is Recess Academy used in conjunction with the Blurt Box?

4. What is the teacher's role during Recess Academy?

5. List some possible situations for using Recess Academy.

6. Discuss the three-step procedure for Recess Academy.

7. What does it mean when the same students end up in Recess Academy? At what point do you seek further assistance with these students?

8. Discuss some options for when teachers cannot be in the classroom to run Recess Academy.

9. Do you sometimes become stuck on the discipline treadmill with your students? Make a list of the situations in which you use consequences to manage recurring misbehavior. Can you improve these situations by teaching your students the skills they need to behave acceptably? What steps should you take?

10. Recess ends, and a group of students enters your classroom yelling and fooling around. How should you handle this? What should you say and do?

11. Karen, a fourth grader, is annoyed with the boy sitting behind her because he keeps tapping her chair with his foot. Finally she turns around and shouts, "Would you cut it out?" Then she gives his chair a kick and says, "How do you like it?" What could you say and do to help Karen learn the skills she needs to handle this situation more appropriately?

12. Susan, a second grader, approaches her teacher after class and complains that several students in her desk group tease and bother her while she tries to work. "Just ignore them," says the teacher. Susan walks away in frustration. Is the teacher's suggestion helpful? Does it go far enough? What more could Susan's teacher say or do to help Susan learn some skills to handle this problem?

CHAPTER 13

1. What are the goals of time-out? Is the procedure appropriate for students who quietly refuse to do their work?

2. What target behaviors are appropriate and inappropriate for time-out?

3. What are the disadvantages of using time-out in a punitive manner?

4. What are the disadvantages of using time-out in a permissive manner?

5. What considerations should you keep in mind when selecting a buddy teacher for Stage Two Time-Outs?

6. When should you use stage two in the time-out process? What additional steps should you take to involve parents after a Stage Two Time-Out?

7. Are the office and hallway appropriate areas for time-out? If not, why?

8. What should you say or do when students refuse to go to the time-out area?

9. If you ask a student to go to the time-out area and he complies but rolls his eyes and gives you a look of disgust as he heads there, should you add more time to the time-out?

10. What should you say and do when the time-out is over?

CHAPTER 14

1. Discuss what is required of parents in order for them to be good backup support for teachers. How can you determine if they are willing to support you? What are some guidelines you can use to determine if they are "customers"?

2. What are some indicators that parents may not be willing or able to support you?

3. Discuss the guidelines for conducting parent conferences. In which situations is it important for the child to be included in the conference? Why is it important to be prepared to offer solutions at the conference?

4. When should you use parent conferences for backup support? What types of situations require a conference?

CHAPTER 15

1. Is the office in your school used as a place for handling disciplinary problems? If so, how is it used? Discuss the problem of reinforcement errors. Do you think this might be occurring in your school?

2. Does your school have a clear discipline policy, one that spells out the guidance procedures all staff members are expected to follow? Are roles and responsibilities clear? At what point in the guidance process is the office or site administrator involved? Is the policy based on effective or ineffective practices?

3. What steps are teachers in your school expected to take to resolve disciplinary problems in the classroom before passing them on to the office or to the administrator?

4. When you send a student to the office for disciplinary reasons, does your administrator know what steps you've taken to resolve the problem at the classroom level? When the student returns from the office, do you know what steps your administrator has taken to resolve the problem? Are your disciplinary approaches compatible, or do they send mixed messages to your students?

5. How consistent is your staff with regard to their guidance and discipline practices? If they're not consistent, what problems does this create for your site administrator and other staff members?

6. Does your school require staff to complete an incident form prior to sending students to the office for disciplinary reasons? Discuss this practice. What are the advantages and disadvantages of requiring staff to complete an incident report prior to passing discipline referrals on to the office?

7. Discuss the training you received during your teacher preparation program in the area of guidance and discipline. Was it adequate? Did it prepare you for the range of discipline problems you encounter in the classroom?

8. What provisions does your site administrator make for in-service training in the area of guidance and discipline? Does the in-service training promote uniform or consistent practices among staff? Are these practices effective?

9. Does the game of hot potato take place at your school? If so, what are the causes of this destructive practice? What is the remedy?

10. Do you believe guidance and discipline should be part of your job description? Before you became a teacher, did you have any idea that guidance and discipline would require so much of your time and energy? How do you feel about that now? What advice would you give someone considering a career as a teacher?

CHAPTER 16

1. Mrs. DeLusso, a fifth-grade teacher, sees two of her students fighting in the classroom and runs to the class next door to summon help. What is the problem with this step? What steps should she take instead?

2. Mr. Brown, a fourth-grade teacher, stands more than six feet tall and weighs over two hundred pounds. When one of his students refuses to go to the time-out area, Mr. Brown's first thought is to physically force the student to go to the time-out area. What is the problem with this approach? What are the legal and safety implications?

3. From a safety and risk management point of view, why is it better to separate an entire classroom of students from one defiant or assaultive student than to attempt to move the student in crisis?

4. Why are cooldowns such an important step in crisis management? What purpose do they serve? What happens if we neglect this step and move on too quickly to problem solving?

5. What backup support systems are available at your school site? Are they trained to use restraint procedures? Are they available during school hours? If not, are there other persons who can serve in this role? Are they trained to use restraint procedures?

6. Does your classroom have an intercom? If not, how would you notify the office in the event of an emergency?

7. Steve and Thomas, two sixth graders, are caught fighting on the playground. The yard duty supervisor stops the fight and promptly sends both of them to the office. The boys are still hot and start fighting again on their way to the office. One child gets injured. What important step or steps were omitted from this intervention? How could this situation be handled more effectively?

8. Julia, a sixth grader, arrives at class looking very depressed. She has two cuts on her right wrist. Her teacher asks Julia to have a seat in the hallway and calls the office for help. No one is available, but the school secretary promises to find the vice principal as quickly as possible. Julia sits in the hallway while the teacher begins her lesson. Is there a potential problem here? What other steps could the teacher take to ensure Julia's safety?

CHAPTER 17

1. What are the symptoms of ADD? Is hyperactivity necessary for the diagnosis? Who is best qualified to evaluate a child suspected of having ADD? How is the evaluation process carried out?

2. Why is early intervention so important in the treatment of ADD? What complications might arise from late identification?

3. Discuss performance variability. How can a student be able to do the work one day and not the next? What reactions do you have when you observe this in your students with ADD?

4. What happens in the brain of students with ADHD when they become overwhelmed or aroused?
5. What are the treatments for ADD both at home and in the classroom? What role does medication play? Why is consistency between home and school so important in the treatment process?
6. What kind of behavior management works best with children with ADD? Why are frequent consequences needed in the guidance process?
7. What can parents do in order to assist children with ADD with the challenges of homework? What is the teacher's role in this process?
8. Discuss the role of supportive counseling in the treatment of ADD. When should this intervention be used? Why is it helpful?
9. What steps should be taken in the classroom and at home to assist children with ADD with the challenges of completing written assignments?
10. Why are "buddy helpers" useful in the classroom to assist children with ADD? Discuss the advantages of using buddy helpers.

CHAPTER 18

1. Discuss the students in your class who require more than classroom management. What are your concerns about them? Do they meet any of the profiles described in this chapter? What steps can you take to support these students in the classroom?
2. What are some characteristics of the academically delayed child? What are some accommodations you can use to support this child?
3. What are some characteristics of the academically discouraged or failure-avoidant child? What are some accommodations you can use to support this child? What is the most important goal?
4. What are some characteristics of the socially unskilled child? What are some accommodations you can use to support this child?
5. What are some characteristics of the student with unidentified developmental problems? What are some accommodations you can use to support this child?
6. What are some characteristics of the student under stress or in crisis? What are some accommodations you can use to support this child?

Index

ABOUT THE AUTHORS

ROBERT J. MACKENZIE, Ed.D., is an educational psychologist and family therapist who founded the Setting Limits Program. He is the author of *Setting Limits* and *Setting Limits with Your Strong-Willed Child*. For more information please go to www.settinglimits.com.

LISA A. STANZIONE, M.A., is a special education teacher and resource specialist, as well as an educational consultant and parent educator for the Setting Limits Program. She has been a consultant for developing and implementing the Learning Center Delivery Model for Special Education services since 2001.

ABOUT THE ILLUSTRATOR

CORIE LEE BARLOGGI is an elementary school teacher for the Fairfield Suisun Unified School District in California.